"More than just the definitive account of a landmark federal investigation, like few books I've ever read, *No Angel* offers a window into the perilous, paranoid dance that is deep undercover work. . . . *No Angel* is **a super-charged insider's look at the modern Wild West—the gunslingers' Colt six-shooters replaced by trunkloads of Uzis, Mac-10s, and AK-47s—and a book deserving of a place on any short list of best true-crime books of the past decade.**"

—DOUGLAS CENTURY, author of *Street Kingdom: Five Years Inside the Franklin Avenue Posse* and *New York Times* bestselling coauthor of *Takedown: Fall of the Last Mafia Empire*

"*No Angel* **is an absolutely amazing account of one man's willingness to go above and beyond.** Jay Dobyns, his team, and those like them live life on the edge in an environment most can only imagine. This book **provides a rare opportunity to share in the intensity, feel the adrenaline rush, smell the fear, and admire true courage and dedication.**"

—MICHAEL DURANT, author of the *New York Times* bestseller *In the Company of Heroes*

"**An absorbing drama** . . . I couldn't put it down. Much like Dobyns' spirit for adventure and his passion for risk, nothing is off-limits in *No Angel*. I can't wait for the movie."

—GREG HANSEN, *Arizona Daily Star*

"**An intriguing look at an undercover cop as he heads toward self-destruction** and loses sight of all that's dear to him . . . and his redemption."

—*Toronto Sun*

"*No Angel* pushes narrative nonfiction to new limits. . . . If you wondered whether the bravura writing of Truman Capote and Hunter S. Thompson has a legacy, look no further. Dobyns leads us into the wacky, white world of the Hell's Angels, and with empathy and precision forces us to admit that bikers are all too human."

—SUDHIR VENKATESH, author of *Gang Leader for a Day: A Rogue Sociologist Takes to the Streets*

"**Unprecedented and unputdownable** . . . Even as a former U.S. Army Special Forces operator and Police SWAT team leader, **I found myself in awe of his death-defying exploits.**"

—DR. RICHARD CARMONA, seventeenth surgeon general of the United States

"**Brutally honest** . . . From the medieval desert clan gatherings to breakneck-paced highway odysseys and high-noon showdowns, this is the real deal from an agent whose knack for the job and ability to transform it into elucidating reading **recalls the story of Joe Pistone, aka Donnie Brasco.**"

—*Publishers Weekly*

"If you want to understand the harrowing emotional realities of long-term undercover work, the balls-out courage and insanity of a multi-year infiltration, or just plain read a great story with an original American voice, then **buy this book, read it, and wonder at every page if you'd have the stuff to pull it off yourself.**"

—STEVE GAGHAN, director of *Syriana* and screenwriter for *Traffic*

"**A wild ride to the dark side.** Jay Dobyns roars through the gritty underworld of organized crime that you never see in TV cop shows or read in the newspaper. He **reveals the true, violent face of outlaw bikers**—but also the tortured souls of the undercover cops who dare to infiltrate them."

—JULIAN SHER, coauthor of *Angels of Death: Inside the Biker Gangs' Crime Empire*

"Ask yourself this question: Would you put your life on the line for a cause? Jay Dobyns did. This book lets you experience some of the most dangerous activities of the best-known biker gang in the world. **Jay Dobyns brought honor to the ATF and is a true American hero.**"

—T. J. LEYDEN, author of *Skinhead Confessions*

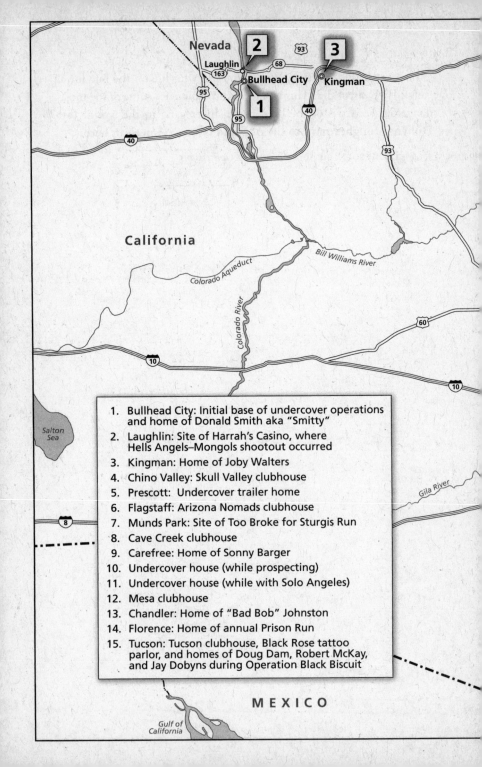

Nevada

2

3

Laughlin

93

68

163

Bullhead City

Kingman

95

1

40

95

40

93

California

Bill Williams River

Colorado Aqueduct

Colorado River

60

10

10

Salton Sea

Gila River

8

1. Bullhead City: Initial base of undercover operations and home of Donald Smith aka "Smitty"
2. Laughlin: Site of Harrah's Casino, where Hells Angels–Mongols shootout occurred
3. Kingman: Home of Joby Walters
4. Chino Valley: Skull Valley clubhouse
5. Prescott: Undercover trailer home
6. Flagstaff: Arizona Nomads clubhouse
7. Munds Park: Site of Too Broke for Sturgis Run
8. Cave Creek clubhouse
9. Carefree: Home of Sonny Barger
10. Undercover house (while prospecting)
11. Undercover house (while with Solo Angeles)
12. Mesa clubhouse
13. Chandler: Home of "Bad Bob" Johnston
14. Florence: Home of annual Prison Run
15. Tucson: Tucson clubhouse, Black Rose tattoo parlor, and homes of Doug Dam, Robert McKay, and Jay Dobyns during Operation Black Biscuit

MEXICO

Gulf of California

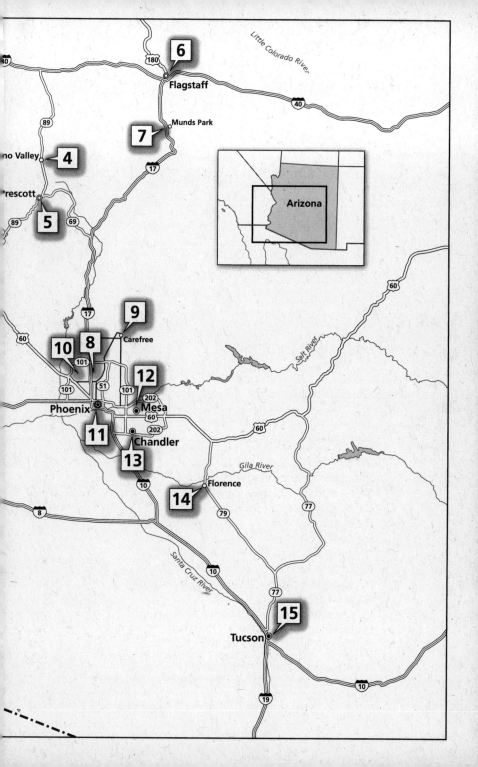

NO ANGEL

My Harrowing Undercover Journey to the
Inner Circle of the Hells Angels

 THREE RIVERS PRESS · NEW YORK

NO ANGEL

JAY DOBYNS AND NILS JOHNSON-SHELTON

Three Rivers Press and the Tugboat design are registered trademarks of Random House, Inc.

Originally published in hardcover in the United States by Crown Publishers, an imprint of
the Crown Publishing Group, a division of Random House, Inc., in New York, in 2009.

Grateful acknowledgment is made to the following for permission to reprint previously
published material:

Hal Leonard Corporation: Excerpt from "Easy," words and music by Lionel Richie,
copyright © 1977, renewed 2005 by Jobete Music Co., Inc. and Libren Music. All rights
controlled and administered by EMI April Music Inc. All rights reserved. International
copyright secured. Reprinted by permission of Hal Leonard Corporation.

Universal Music Publishing Group: Excerpt from "Be Like That" by Brad Arnold and
Christopher Henderson, copyright © 2000 by Songs of Universal, Inc. and Escatawpa
Songs. All rights administered by Songs of Universal, Inc./BMI. All rights reserved.
Reprinted by permission of Universal Music Publishing Group.

Library of Congress Cataloging-in-Publication Data

Dobyns, Jay.
    No angel: My harrowing undercover journey to the inner circle of the Hells Angels /
Jay Dobyns and Nils Johnson-Shelton.
        p. cm.
    1. Dobyns, Jay.   2. Undercover operations—Arizona.   3. Organized crime—Arizona.
4. Motorcycle gangs—Arizona.   5. Hells Angels.   I. Johnson-Shelton, Nils.   II. Title.
    HV8080.U5D63 2009
    364.106'60979—dc22   2008029836

ISBN: 978-0-307-40586-9

Printed in the United States of America

Design by Debbie Glasserman

10 9 8 7 6 5 4 3 2

First Paperback Edition

For Mom, Dad, Gwen, Dale, and Jack—you are my heroes.
And for Jaime, without whom this book would not have been possible.

Contents

PART IV. THE END, AGAIN

Bikers, Cops, and Motorcycle Clubs Involved in Operations Riverside and Black Biscuit

Black Biscuit Task Force Members and Associates by Agency (alphabetical by last name)

Note: The men and women listed below are the principal players found in the text. The Acknowledgments section at the end of the book contains a comprehensive list of officers involved with Black Biscuit.

ATF
Chris Bayless, special agent, aka "Chrisser"
Carlos Canino, special agent, aka "Los"
Vince Cefalu, special agent, aka "Vinnie"
John Ciccone, special agent
Greg Cowan, special agent, aka "Sugarbear"
Jay Dobyns, special agent, aka "Bird"
Alan Futvoye, special agent, aka "Footy"
Steve Gunderson, special agent, aka "Gundo"
Daniel Machonis, group supervisor, aka "Mach One"
Jenna Maguire, special agent, aka "JJ"
Tom Mangan, special agent, aka "Teabag"
Joe Slatalla, special agent, aka "Slats"
Jesse Summers, special agent, aka "Summer Breeze"

OTHER LAW ENFORCEMENT
Gayland Hammack, sergeant, Las Vegas Metropolitan
  Police Department
William Long, detective, Phoenix Police Department, aka "Timmy"
Shawn Wood, sergeant, Arizona Department of Public Safety,
  aka "Woody"

ATF INFORMANTS

Pops (given name not provided)

Michael Kramer, Hells Angels member at Mesa, Arizona,
  and San Fernando Valley, California, charters, aka "Mesa Mike"

Rudolph Kramer, Solo Angeles member, aka "Rudy"
  (no relation to Michael Kramer)

Hells Angels by Charter (alphabetical by last name)

*Note: As above, the men listed below are only the significant players found
in the text. Many more Hells Angels are mentioned in the pages that follow.*

ARIZONA NOMADS, FLAGSTAFF, ARIZONA

Dennis Denbesten, member, aka "Chef Boy-Ar-Dee"

Donald Smith, member, aka "Smitty"

CAVE CREEK, ARIZONA

Ralph Barger, member, aka "Sonny," "Chief"

Daniel Danza, member, aka "Dirty Dan"

Daniel Seybert, president, aka "Hoover"

MESA, ARIZONA, AKA "MESA MOB"

Kevin Augustiniak, member

Gary Dunham, secretary, aka "Ghost"

Paul Eischeid, member

Robert Johnston, president, aka "Bad Bob," "Mesa Bob"

Mike Kramer, member, aka "Mesa Mike" (transferred to San Fernando
  Valley, California, charter during the case)

Calvin Schaefer, member, aka "Casino Cal"

PHOENIX, ARIZONA, AKA "HOTHEDZ"

Robert Mora, member, aka "Chico"

SAN DIEGO, CALIFORNIA

Pete Eunice, member, aka "Dago Pete," "Ramona Pete"

SKULL VALLEY, ARIZONA, AKA "GRAVEYARD CREW"

Rudy Jaime, member

Robert Reinstra, vice president, aka "Bobby"
Joseph Richardson, member, aka "Joey," "Egghead"
Theodore Toth, president, aka "Teddy"
George Walters, sergeant at arms, aka "Joby"

TUCSON, ARIZONA
Douglas Dam, member, aka "Doug"
Craig Kelly, president, aka "Fang"
Robert McKay, member, aka "Mac"
Henry Watkins, prospect, aka "Hank"

Hells Angels' Old Ladies

Dolly Denbesten (wife of Dennis Denbesten)
Staci Laird (girlfriend of Bobby Reinstra)
Lydia Smith (wife of Donald Smith)

Other Suspects of Note

Alberto (last name unknown), vice president, Mexican Solo Angeles,
  Tijuana, Mexico
Robert Abraham, gun dealer, Bullhead City, Arizona
Tony Cruze, member, Red Devils, Tucson, Arizona
Tim Holt, machinist, Mohave, Arizona
Dave "Teacher" Rodarte, president, U.S. Solo Angeles,
  Los Angeles, California
Scott Varvil, school nurse, mechanic, Kingman, Arizona

Arizona Motorcycle Clubs and Charter Locations
(alphabetical after Hells Angels and Solo Angeles)
HELLS ANGELS*
aka "Big Red Machine," "Red and White," "81"
Arizona Nomads (Flagstaff), Cave Creek, Mesa, Phoenix,
  Skull Valley, Tucson

*Note: the charters listed are **only** for Arizona. As noted in the text, the Hells Angels have charters in approximately twenty states and twenty-six countries.

xii   Bikers, Cops, and Motorcycle Clubs

SOLO ANGELES
aka "Orange Crush"
Arizona Nomads (Bullhead City, Phoenix, Prescott)

AMERICANS
Page

DESERT ROAD RIDERS
Bullhead City, Lake Havasu City

DEVILS' DISCIPLES
Tucson

DIRTY DOZEN (DEFUNCT)
Phoenix

HUNS
Tucson

LIMEYS
Charter location unknown

LONERS
Globe

MONGOLS
Phoenix

RED DEVILS
Tucson, Phoenix

SPARTANS
Phoenix
Vietnam Vets Statewide

Major Motorcycle Clubs Traditionally Adversarial to the Hells Angels

BANDITOS
Texas, western states, international; aka "the Red and Gold," "Bandits"

MONGOLS
California, western states; aka "the Black," "the Black and White"

OUTLAWS
Midwest and Southern states; aka "OLs"

PAGANS
Eastern states

ROCK MACHINE
Canada (absorbed by Banditos)

VAGOS
California; aka "the Green," "Greenies"

NOTE TO THE READER:

The worlds of undercover cops and outlaw bikers are colorful and unique, and each possesses its own language. If at any time you're unclear about the terms found on the following pages, please consult the glossary found at the back of this book.

If I must choose between righteousness and peace, I choose righteousness.

—THEODORE ROOSEVELT

If you're not making mistakes, then you're not doing anything. I'm positive a doer makes mistakes.

—JOHN WOODEN

UCLA MEN'S BASKETBALL COACH, 1948–1975

PART I

THE END

1 BIRDCALLS

TIMMY LEANED CASUALLY against the rear fender of my black Mercury Cougar, a cell phone on his ear and a smile on his face. The bastard was typically calm. Twelve months I'd been his partner, in and out of harm's way, both together and alone, and the guy never looked stressed. He was as self-possessed as a rooster in a hen house—my polar opposite.

I paced in front of him, rehearsing what I was going to tell our Hells Angels brothers. I shook the last smoke out of a pack of Newports. "Shit." I lit the cigarette, crumpled the pack, and threw it to the ground. It was 10:00 a.m. and I'd already emptied the first pack of the carton I'd bought that morning.

Timmy said into his phone, "I love you too honey cake. I should be home soon." He'd been saying things like that going on five minutes.

I stared at him and said, "The fuck, stud? Come on."

Timmy put a finger in the air and continued on the phone. "OK. Gotta run. Love you guys. OK. See you tonight." He snapped his phone closed. "What's the drama, Bird? We got this."

"Oh, you know. Nothing really." I pointed at the guy lying facedown at our feet. "Just that if they don't buy it, then we'll end up like this asshole."

There, in a shallow desert ditch, was a gray-haired Caucasian male, his head split to the white meat. A pile of brains had oozed to the ground where Timmy had put Joby's .380. Blood droplets, sprayed into the sand and dirt, made small, dark constellations. His blue jeans were splattered with purple, quarter-sized splotches. His wrists and ankles were bound with duct tape, his hands were limp. It was already over 100 degrees and the promise of coagulated blood and exposed matter had begun to attract flies.

He wore a black leather jacket whose top rocker, that curved cloth patch that spanned the shoulder blades, read MONGOLS.

I asked, "You think he's dead?"

Timmy said, "Dude looks deader'n disco. Shit, those look like his brains in the dirt." Timmy leaned in closer. "Yeah, I'd say he's pretty dead." He spat a stream of phlegm into the brush beyond the grave.

"Dude, no fucking around here. We go home and show the boys we killed a Mongol, then we better be dead-nuts sure it doesn't look like he's coming back."

Timmy smiled. "Relax, Bird, we got this. Like Lionel Richie said, we're easy like Sunday mornin'." And then he started to sing. Badly:

> Why in the world
> would anybody put chains on me?
> I've paid my dues to make it.
> Everybody wants me to be
> what they want me to be.
> I'm not happy when I try to fake it!
> Ooh,
> That's why I'm easy. Yeah.
> I'm easy like Sunday mornin'.

I smiled and said, "You're right, you're right. And even if you aren't, I don't see how it matters. We've come too far."

He thought about that for a second. "Yeah, we have."

We threw a couple shovels of dirt on our corpse and took some pictures. We relieved him of his Mongol jacket, stuffing it in a FedEx box. We got in the car and headed home, to Phoenix.

.   .   .

TIMMY DROVE. I made some phone calls.

I lit a cigarette and waited for someone to pick up at the clubhouse. Inhale. Hold it in. Click.

The voice said, "Skull Valley."

I said, "Bobby, it's Bird."

"Bird. What the fuck?"

"Teddy there?"

"Not now, no." Bobby Reinstra's voice was humorless and empty.

"We're on our way back."

"'We' who?"

Inhale. Hold it in.

I said, "Me and Timmy."

"No Pops?"

"No Pops. He stayed down in Mexico."

"So Pops is gone." I heard him light a cigarette—he'd only started smoking again since he'd met me.

"Yeah, dude."

"Wow." Bobby smoked. Inhaled. Held it in.

I said, "We should probably talk about this later, don't you think?"

He snapped out of it. "Yeah. Yeah, of course. When'll you be back?"

"Soon. I'll call when we're back in the valley."

"OK. Get home safe."

"We will. Don't worry. I'll see you tomorrow."

"OK. Later."

"Later."

I flipped my cell shut and turned to Timmy. I said, "He bit it. Pops's death should work to our advantage."

Timmy barely nodded. He was probably thinking about his wife and kids. Above all else, Timmy was decent. I looked past him. The asphalt and brown California pines, the late-afternoon grid of Phoenix, Arizona, moved beyond him like a sunset movie backdrop.

THE NEXT AFTERNOON, JJ, Timmy, and I chowed at a Pizza Hut. We hadn't seen Bobby or any of the other boys yet. We wanted their tension to build.

JJ's phone rang. She looked at the ID, then at me. I shrugged, stuffed a pepperoni slice in my mouth, and nodded.

She flipped open. "Hello?" She grinned. "Hi, Bobby. No, I haven't heard from him. You have? When? What'd he say? He said *what*?! Bobby, what the fuck do you mean? Pops is—*Pops is dead?*" She lowered her voice and choked out the words with a frightened stutter. "Bobby, you're scaring me! I don't *know* what the fuck's going on. All I know is a FedEx box came to the house this morning. It was sent from Nogales, Mexico." She pulled the phone away from her ear and placed a slice of roasted green pepper in her mouth. She sipped more iced tea. "No way, Bobby! I'm not opening shit. No. Forget it. Not until Bird gets back."

JJ's fear was convincing and effective. Our plan seemed to be working.

I leaned into the leather banquette. We weren't your average-looking cops—we weren't even your average-looking undercover cops—and we painted quite a picture. Timmy and I were bald, muscular, and covered in tattoos. JJ was cute, buxom, and focused. My eyes were blue and always lit up, Timmy's brown and wise, JJ's green and eager. Each of my long, bony fingers was armored with silver rings depicting things like skulls and talons and lightning bolts. My long, straggly goatee was haphazardly twisted into a ragged braid. JJ and I wore white wife-beater tank tops and Timmy wore a black, sleeveless T-shirt that said SKULL VALLEY—GRAVEYARD CREW over the heart. I wore green camo cargo pants and flip-flops, and they wore jeans and riding boots. We each openly carried at least one firearm. Arizona's open-carry, so there you go.

JJ continued. "No way, Bobby. I'm not coming over there with the box. I'm waiting till Bird gets home. All right. All right. Bye."

She hung up. She turned back to us and asked sarcastically, "So, honey, when can I expect you?"

I grinned and said, "Any time, now. Any time."

"OK! Can't wait!"

We laughed and finished our lunch. We'd been running ragged for months and were in the homestretch. With any luck, Timmy and I were about to become full-patch Hells Angels, and JJ was about to become a real-life HA old lady.

With any luck.

PART II

THE BEGINNING

2 MY SUCKING CHEST WOUND

I DIDN'T COME from a line of cops. I wasn't raised in the projects, and an alcoholic father didn't beat me. I grew up in white, middle-class America with a bike and a baseball glove and family vacations. I played football and played it well. I went to college as a wide receiver for the Arizona Wildcats. In that first year, 1982, I showed up at fall camp for two-a-days in a 100-degree hellhole in Douglas, Arizona. The practice field was smack in the middle of the desert. Turf, sidelines, one or two feet of desert scrabble, and then cactus.

Most wide outs want to outrun the defense for game-winning passes, catch the ball over their shoulder, and screw the prom queen. I wouldn't have minded the prom queen, but I wasn't that kind of receiver. The coaches knew this, and they'd put me at number six on the depth chart. That had to change.

I jumped in the play rotation whenever a slant over the middle was called or a crack on a linebacker was needed. I got the dog snot beat out of me, down after down. One play I got an out-route and the ball was overthrown. I ran out of bounds, into the desert, and dove, grabbing the ball but landing in a patch of cholla cactus, which are the nastiest of all cacti. I spent the rest of practice with the trainers pulling needles out of my face and arms with pliers. The other players laughed at me because what fool chases an overthrow into a cholla?

I checked the depth chart the next day. I'd taken the first spot, and for the rest of my college career, I wouldn't give it up to anyone, no matter how fast he was.

By the time I graduated, I was All Pac-10. I was lightly scouted and I went to the NFL Combine, but from the minute I walked onto the field I realized that my chances were slim to none. One scout put it perfectly. He said, "I can coach these guys to catch like you, but I can't teach you how to run faster." Next to the guys coming up that year, I looked like molasses poured into cement. Guys like Vance Johnson, Al Toon, Andre Reed, Eddie Brown, and Jerry Rice. Maybe you've heard of some of them.

I knew I could cobble together a career of two or three years, but every year I'd have to re-prove myself in camp, and at best I'd be a third- or fourth-string option. My dreams were crushed and I didn't know what to do. I'd gotten too used to crowds screaming for me, too addicted to adrenaline, to just let it go.

Eventually I turned to law enforcement. I was young and I bought into the Hollywood vision of being a cop. I considered the FBI and the Secret Service, but ultimately I ended up at the Bureau of Alcohol, Tobacco, and Firearms—ATF. This was where I'd transform from star college athlete to hardened undercover cop.

It happened on one of my first training missions, and it went down like this:

We'd gotten a warrant for one Brent Provestgaard, who'd just gotten out of prison and was rumored to be in possession of a used .38 Rossi. We were going to bust him on ATF's bread-and-butter violation: felon in possession of a firearm, 18 USC section 922(g)(1).

I was assigned outside perimeter cover with my training officer, Lee Mellor. We rode in a crappy 1983 Monte Carlo. We interviewed Provestgaard's mom at her house south of the Tucson airport, at the intersection of Creeger Road and Old Nogales Highway. She said he wasn't in and he'd be back sooner or later. We left and staked out the place.

What Mrs. Provestgaard declined to tell us was that her son had sworn he'd never go back to prison, and that he was out in the Tucson scrub shooting his .38.

He came home on his motorcycle. We swarmed and he bolted on foot. I took off, passing everyone and disobeying orders to stay back. While a 4.6 in the NFL is nothing special, it's sick speed for a cop. It was a full-blown foot chase, but he knew the area and I lost him. I reassembled with my team and they ribbed me about how I was supposed to be some sort of star athlete, but I couldn't catch a 150-pound junkie in motorcycle boots? No wonder I was in ATF and not the NFL, that kind of thing.

As we restaged, a neighbor yelled from her window that she'd just seen Provestgaard. We took off.

First rookie mistake: no matter how out of breath you are from chasing a perp, never, ever take off your ballistics vest when there's a lull in the action.

Which is exactly what I'd done.

The team split up. I walked behind our much-loved boss, Larry Thomason, through an overgrown tract between a development and the road. Tall grass and low trees were everywhere. We crept past the hidden Provestgaard. I caught movement out of the corner of my eye but before I could react he was up with his gun on me.

"Drop it, motherfucker!"

I knew better. I held my gun, a .357 Smith & Wesson revolver, at the ready position: pointed to the ground at a 45-degree angle. He cocked the Rossi's hammer, yelling, "Motherfucker, I will kill you where you stand! Drop the fucking gun!"

I holstered my revolver and put my hands in the air. Thomason cocked his hammer. He had Provestgaard in his sights, but he was toting a two-inch-barrel revolver and he was thirty feet away. Thomason knew that if he fired there was a good chance he'd hit me. He held. It was the right decision, but one that gravely altered his psyche: He was a committed leader in charge of showing a young man the ropes of a dangerous profession, and he never forgave himself for not taking that shot. I've always told him that the blame was mine, but he never accepted that.

The others, searching an adjacent area, responded. When Provestgaard saw the empty Monte Carlo, his eyes—intense, bottomless specks—lit up. He was going to get out of there.

Provestgaard's gun was thrust out in front of him. When he got close enough, I planned on pulling his arm and using it as leverage to disarm him. That plan died when he tucked the gun to his side. Before I knew it he had me in front of him, his arm around my neck, the cold barrel of the Rossi at my temple.

I didn't like that. I suddenly realized that it had rained earlier and the desert brush smelled like a clean backyard, which is what I imagine heaven must smell like. I hoped I wasn't about to find out if my imagining was correct.

We moved to the car. Provestgaard shoved me into the driver's seat and squeezed into the back, keeping the gun on my head. ATF agents surrounded us, their weapons drawn and their mouths running.

Provestgaard said, "Close the door and drive, motherfucker!"

I didn't. The car wasn't running. The keys were in the ignition. He shoved the barrel into the hollow of my neck. I wondered: Should I drive, put the seat belt on, and run into a telephone pole? Or get shot here and let my partners waste him? Or hope one of them gets a clean line on him *right this second*? Or lie down and try to stay out of the way of everyone's bullets that were sure to puncture the Monte Carlo any second? Or, or, or . . . drop the keys? Yes, drop the keys. If I was going to die, then he was going to die too. I pulled the keys out of the ignition and let them fall into the footwell.

I said, "I dropped the keys."

"Motherfucker—"

I leaned forward and Provestgaard did too. Mellor, who was closest to the passenger's side of the car, stuck his revolver in the rear window gap and emptied it. Others fired. Provestgaard, his body shocked from the bullets cleaning out his heart and lungs, reflexively squeezed the Rossi's trigger. The bullet went in between my shoulder blades, just missed my spine, punctured the top of my left lung, and exited under my collarbone.

Provestgaard had the death rattle.

I had a hole in my chest.

They call it a sucking chest wound because when you inhale, air is sucked through the wound directly into the void of a collapsing lung. Blood gushed out of the hole like water from a garden spigot.

We were dragged out of the car. Provestgaard was cuffed (you have to love police procedure in times like this), and laid in the dirt faceup. I was shoved into the backseat, in pools of Provestgaard's blood and bile and tears, and Thomason jumped into the front seat and took off. I was in and out of consciousness as Thomason channeled Dale Earnhardt Jr. through the Tucson dusk.

I said the Lord's Prayer and apologized to my parents for not being a good enough cop to make them proud. Then I took a little nap.

I came to at the hospital. I was on a gurney, the ceiling rushed by in blue and white streaks, the soft but anxious pitter-patter of nurses' and orderlies' feet on linoleum filled my ears. There were two black nostrils above me, and above them a tuft of brown hair, and around that a half-moon of white paper. A hat. My nurse. Her gaze was locked on the horizon.

I asked, "I'm—I—am I going to die?"

She looked down. She was pretty. Her left hand pushed into my chest. "You're hurt bad. We're not sure yet."

I passed back out.

I woke back up to a screaming pain in my chest. A boyish resident was inserting a clear tube into a hole he'd scalpeled through my rib cage to prevent me from drowning in my own blood. The tube would also be used to clear blood clots before I went into the operating room. I'd never felt such pain and discomfort. Having an inch-wide tube inserted into a raw hole of flesh was like, well, it was just like that. I was not anesthetized—there hadn't been time. I was dying. I looked at the tube, which was attached to a pump. Stewed tomatoes—aka my blood and guts—pulsed through it. When he was done with that, the resident directed me to a video screen. He said proudly that they'd put a shunt in my femoral artery that helped guide a medical camera through my torso. He said they were looking for heart and arterial damage caused by bullet frag. I thought, Far out.

I passed back out.

I woke back up naked and freezing. A nurse leaned over my midsection, holding a thin tube, giggling. I asked her what was so funny? I knew she was laughing at a shriveled dick whose size would have embarrassed a twelve-year-old boy. I gathered all my strength and said, "You could have a little respect for a guy who should be dead, and what exactly is your name?" She straightened up and stuck the catheter in. She covered me up and put her hand on my forehead. I passed back out.

I woke back up. I was in a bed. The bed was in a recovery room. There were all the usual machines going beep-beep. There were IV bags

and fresh flowers and foil balloons. There was an oversized teddy bear.
My feet were elevated. And there was the tube, inserted cleanly into
my chest, surrounded by white gauze and tape. A beep-beep went off,
unlike the beep-beeps monitoring my heart and respiratory rates. A
sound like a small servo followed. Not ten seconds later I was as high
and happy as I could be. I passed back out.

I woke up, I passed out, I woke up. Nurses changed my bedpan and
sponged me down. I recovered some strength, I got up and walked
around, dragging my setup—the IV, the morphine drip, the chest tube
detached from its pump—around with me. After a few days I could
walk up and down the hall once. After a week I could walk around the
recovery unit. Being so weakened was a new experience and a definite
low point. It's truly humbling to be reminded that ultimately we're just
a body. The mind gets a lot of attention, but it is housed, for better or
worse, in such a fragile thing. The body goes and, well, who knows?
This is why I believe in God.

I prayed. I've always been an imperfect Christian. I prayed for my
family and for myself. I prayed I'd get to go back to the streets, to go
back to work.

As I improved, I began to spend equal amounts of time awake and
asleep. I befriended Dr. Richard Carmona, the surgeon who'd operated
on me. He was a high-school dropout who'd enlisted in the Army,
joined the Special Forces, became a decorated Vietnam vet, and then
returned to civilian life, where he took up a career in medicine. He was
the head of trauma services in Tucson and moonlighted as a SWAT
operator with the Pima County sheriff's office. Not ten days after I
came in, he was shot himself while executing a warrant. He made a full
recovery and eventually went on to become the seventeenth U.S. surgeon general. Gaining Dr. Carmona as a friend was one of the best
things that came from my getting shot.

People visited, they stayed too long, my mother cried. My dad,
shocked and pale, said he was proud of me, even though I pointed out
that I'd been a fool. We agreed that I'd been lucky. Other people came:
college buddies, cops, my first wife, whom I'd married out of college.
The pump attached to my chest tube ran nonstop. It cleared my wound
of clots and errant blood, emptying the stuff into an otherwise white
bucket by my bedside. When people stayed too long, I wiggled until
the suction caught something, expelling it into the bucket like a tiny
abortion. That usually sent them packing.

I got deathly bored. You can watch only so much TV, and the flowers die if they're not watered. I didn't do a good job of watering them. The balloons deflated. It's as if these things are brought to give their meager life-forces to your recovery, dying along the way. I was being reanimated by withering roses and expiring helium. Hell, morphine makes you think funny things. I'd developed quite a taste. No doubt, I was in excruciating pain, especially the first week, but after that it was more recreational than essential. My morphine bump was self-administered but limited by a timer—I couldn't hit myself more than once over a three-hour period. So I secured the switch with some medical tape from my IV and I'd get a narc bump whenever the timer went off, awake or asleep. I had some wild dreams. It was heaven.

The director of ATF called. He called me his golden boy. I didn't like being called a boy, I was twenty-six. He said he'd heard good things about me, and that if I played my cards right I could have his job one day. He told me to get well soon and get back on the job, that they needed more guys like me in ATF. I thanked him and hung up.

At night I'd wake up from time to time. I had a funny feeling. The lights were low, the machines beep-beeped. As I got better, there were fewer and fewer of them in the room. A good sign. The feeling I got was a new one. It was a rush I'd never known. On the football field, I'd been hit a thousand times by hundreds of guys my size or bigger. I'd taken some real kill shots and always tried to get back up right away. It was a pride thing. When they dragged me out of the car, my chest spurting and gurgling, I actually pulled myself into a sitting position. It was the best I could do. The new feeling was this: I couldn't be stopped. After being shot, I began to feel the first pangs of invincibility. The rush of near-death did something dangerous to me, though I couldn't see it at the time. I didn't want to get shot ever again, but I wanted to get as close to that flying bullet as I possibly could. Getting cheered by eighty thousand football fans was an incredible feeling, but it didn't even register when compared with the rush of walking the line between life and death when no one was watching.

I'd taken the prescribed amount of painkillers, but that didn't change the fact that when I left the hospital I felt like a full-blown junkie. I had black circles under my eyes and puked brown tar for a week. No appetite for anything but the smack I couldn't have. I cleaned up: shakes, sweats, tears, the whole thing.

My wife at the time wanted to know if that was it for me. She wanted me to get out. I couldn't blame her. I said this was why I was in it. She asked, "To get shot?" I said, "No, to go toe-to-toe with these guys. I lost this time, but I won't lose again." Not long after that, we got divorced.

The director's words rang in my ears: *I could have his job.* His job involved a large slab of wood and an executive-style telephone with lots of buttons and lights. Shoot, in that year, 1987, he probably even had his own computer. It didn't appeal to me. The bullet put the rush of the streets in me and through me. It guaranteed I'd never direct anything but myself, and convinced me that large desks were for castrated dummies. I thought, Fuck that, I'm gonna be an undercover.

3 "YOU'RE LOOKING AT THE LOVES OF MY LIFE IS WHAT YOU'RE LOOKING AT."

AUGUST 2001-JANUARY 2002

IF ANYTHING, THE shooting proved that my job, and therefore my life, was not glamorous in any way. Pathetically, I'd imagined that undercover life would be like *Miami Vice*—full of cigarette boats, fast cars, expensive clothes, and perfect tens in bikinis sitting in my lap while I negotiated with drug kingpins. Instead, I confronted toothless strippers and disgruntled Vietnam vets, and did deals with jonesing tweakers in trailer parks while getting shot by a broke-dick ex-con who lived with his mom.

Still, I loved the job. After the shooting, I went back to the academy to complete my training. Upon graduation, they sent me to Chicago, where I learned my new job with another young agent, Chris Bayless, a dynamic and intelligent undercover operative who remains one of my best friends.

And what a job! In the years between the shooting and the summer of 2001, I'd done and seen things that citizens simply don't do or see. I'd been in another shoot-out, I'd had an inhuman number of guns shoved in my face, I'd bought and sold tons of drugs, and I'd made hundreds of solid collars. I'd worked African-American gangbangers and

Italian mobsters with Chris; the Aryan Brotherhood with Special Agent
Louis Quiñonez; and bikers from Georgia to Colorado with a bunch of
different partners, including one of my ATF mentors, Vincent Cefalu.
By 2001, I thought I'd seen it all.

Yet, after nearly fifteen years on the job, I still had something to prove.
I still had more to see.

IN THE SUMMER of that year a young, ambitious case agent named Greg
"Sugarbear" Cowan called about running some game up in Bullhead
City, Arizona.

Sugarbear said that Bullhead was ripe for the picking, and that getting evidence up there would be like shooting fish in a barrel. He said
we could take a lot of guns off the street. I agreed to have a look. One
morning I got up, ate breakfast, rustled the hair of my son, Jack, kissed
my daughter, Dale, grabbed a plate of cookies that my wife, Gwen, had
baked, and hit the road.

Bullhead City is near the southern tip of Nevada, ten hours from
where I lived in Tucson. It's a broken-down town full of semi-employed
mechanics who've shacked up with women who are—or were—
"dancers." It's a meth capital teeming with high-school dropouts, and
it's all set down in a brown and tan valley that looks more like Mars
than Earth. Across the brown Colorado River is Laughlin, Nevada,
Bullhead's dusty twin sister, with her twinkling strip and brand-name
outfits: Flamingo, Golden Nugget, Harrah's.

I met Sugarbear at the Black Bear Diner on Route 95. We sat in a
window booth in the refrigerated air while the desert sweltered outside
at 115 degrees. He slurped coffee and nibbled at dry toast while I
crammed a bacon double cheeseburger into my mouth.

He talked about a local gun shop called Mohave Firearms. The
owner, Robert Abraham, dealt with a band of regulars who were all gun
strokes. Most of the deals were off the books and there were significant
numbers of modified machine guns going in and out of the shop. A guy
named Scott Varvil, a former Marine sniper and ace bike mechanic, did
the machine-gun mods in his garage.

We drove around town after lunch. I watched the dusty roads and
subdivisions skim by from the comfort of our car's air-conditioning.
Sugarbear said I'd go undercover as a biker. I said fine, in spite of the

heat and the fact that I wasn't a biker expert. He said he knew I'd be fine, that I looked the part and that bikers were respected in Bullhead. I said I imagined they were. He said that all the guys, especially Abraham and Varvil, were Hells Angels groupies. He said the Angels were around but not everywhere. I didn't think much of it either way. I agreed to come on board.

We got started in late August. Cowan continued to run an informant while I staged-up in Tucson. I got my bike tuned and checked out an ATF car—a black Mercury Cougar. I took target practice at the field office. I helped Gwen get the kids off to another year at school, making trips to the mall. Jack, a good athlete, got cleats and gym socks and a book bag. With saved allowance he bought a box of Fleer football cards. He was on the hunt for Drew Brees rookies. He got three from that batch. I bought Dale a used guitar, with the promise that if she applied herself I would get her a brand-new one down the road.

In the early morning of September 11, I was at home getting ready to leave when Chris Bayless called. He said turn on the TV.

The ride to Bullhead was off. Gwen and the kids and I sat mesmerized in front of the TV, like everyone else. Jack, who was seven at the time, is a fun-loving kid who's always smiling. Dale, then eleven, is a little moodier, endearingly righteous, and occasionally indignant. Gwen and I sensed fear and confusion in them. We sensed fear and confusion in each other. We watched the gray explosions over and over and over. I told my kids, "Be brave. That's what this is, a chance for you to be brave. Set a good example for other kids who might be scared. And be proud that you're an American because we're about to kick some ass."

I spoke with Sugarbear later that day. We were pretty sure the Bullhead case would be deep-sixed or at least put on hold, but to our relief this didn't happen. I looked forward to work. I didn't want to sit around and think about how America had just been attacked.

By the end of the following week I was holed up in Bullhead at Gretchen's Inn, a contemptible riverside hideaway off Route 95. From the outside it looked harmless, but from the inside it was something else. A fleabag meth flophouse, busted locks on the doors and windows that wouldn't close, people screwing all day and night. I slept with my arms folded over my chest and one of my beloved Glock 19s in my hand.

On the night of October 22, 2001, as I listened to methed-out tweakers bang away above and below my room, I lay down for the last time as 100 percent Jay Dobyns. The next day our case, code-named Operation Riverside, would go into full swing. Sugarbear's informant, Chuck, would take me to Mohave Firearms for some introductions. Chuck would say, "This is Jay Davis. Good guy to know. Good guy to be known by."

HERE'S WHAT I SAID:

What's up? This's a nice place you got here, looks like you know your business. Yeah, Jay's my name, but everyone calls me Bird. Here's my card. *Imperial Financial.* I do collection work. Yeah, that kind. You know, a John Doe fucks up at the Bellagio and goes back to Omaha with a line of unpaid credit, they can't send a security detail to beat the gold out of him on his front lawn. Bad publicity. That's where I come in. Yeah, I guess it's pretty cool, if I stop to think about it, which I don't. Pays the bills, keeps the lawn green, and doesn't take up too much of my time. Yeah, I ride. You see a patch on my back? Well, then I'm not a One Percenter, so quit asking. Yep, that's my bike, the one with the baseball bat strapped to the sissy bars. What's it for? I'm a huge D-Backs fan, Luis Gonzalez is my boy. Naw, man. Whaddaya think? That's right, dude, the collections. Baseball bat can come in handy in my line. But, listen, I got another business, maybe you can help me out? I need guns. Small ones, big ones, fast ones, slow ones. No papers. Hit-and-run deals I can throw in the river, you know what I'm saying? I appreciate your discretion, dude, you're a class businessman. Yeah, so what if I already got a couple pieces? My Glocks are my babies and they're for me and me alone. Right now I'm looking for .45s. Also, know anyone who can work on my bike? You do? Thanks, dude, I owe you one. Anytime you wanna go down to the Inferno for beers, you let me know. Next night out is on the Birdman.

Bob Abraham, the owner of the gun shop, filled in the blanks. He was forty-seven, short, portly, strong, and knowledgeable about every gun under the sun. The intro went well—Abraham ate every scrap and crumb.

The next day he sold me two .45s, no papers, no forms. All cash. It was too easy.

Through the years I was often amused by how quickly suspects decided to trust me. Criminality is a brutal, sometimes comical, game of one-upmanship. Bad guys are constantly trying to prove to one another—and themselves—that they're badder and harder than the next guy. This is one reason Abraham wanted to know if I was a "One Percenter."

This phrase originated when rogue bikers ran roughshod over a 1947 motorcycle rally in Hollister, California. These troublemakers were described as "the one percent of the American motorcycle riding public that is criminal" by the American Motorcyclist Association. The name stuck, and was proudly worn by those riders who considered themselves to be "outlaws." Since law-abiding bike enthusiasts— "Ninety-nine Percenters"—had ostracized these outlaw riders, and since they were usually societal outcasts to begin with, they formed clubs. These riders were easily identified by their motorcycle vests— leather or denim jackets, usually with the sleeves cut off and therefore known as "cuts"—which were adorned with the "three-piece patch" of the outlaw biker. This patch was really three separate patches found on the back of the vest; it consisted of a large center patch depicting the club's logo (the infamous laughing winged skull, or "Death Head," in the case of the Hells Angels); a curved, rocker-shaped "top rocker" containing the club's name; and a "bottom rocker" containing the vest-wearer's charter affiliation, usually the name of a city, state, or, in the case of international clubs, country. The four major American outlaw clubs are the Pagans in the east, the Outlaws in the Midwest, the Banditos in Texas, and the Hells Angels, who are found throughout the country in at least twenty states. The other three clubs may beg to differ, but the Hells Angels are the *premier* outlaw club in the United States—and the world.

Abraham wanted to know if I was a One Percenter because if I was, I would've had instant credibility. It didn't matter that I wasn't a One Percenter, though, because for small-time guys like Abraham, credibility was cheap.

After a couple more sales, Abraham intro'd me to Scott Varvil, John Core, and Sean McManama, who intro'd me to Tim Holt, a machinist who ended up making me a bunch of silencers. Each of these men had four things in common: They loved guns, they were white, they were not rich, and they all told me they knew Smitty, the local Hells Angels brass.

Smitty belonged to the Arizona Nomad charter of the Hells Angels. Most large One Percenter clubs have Nomad charters. They're divisions within the club that belong to a state but don't have a fixed location. At the time, the Arizona Hells Angels had fixed charters in Tucson, Mesa, Phoenix, Cave Creek, and Skull Valley, while their Nomad charter kept a small clubhouse in Flagstaff. They had the state covered.

I'd seen Smitty around. He looked like a hippie granddad—a swirling black and white beard, big old-man eyeglasses, a bald crown that topped a curtain of long, stiff hair. When he smiled, which I'd learn was often for a Hells Angel, he looked like a lovable goofball.

Varvil loved Smitty the most. Varvil maintained that the Angels wanted to recruit him, but that they couldn't because of his job, which he refused to give up. He was a school nurse, which was simply not badass enough.

Varvil was the most interesting of the Mohave Firearms bunch. I first got with him on November 7, three short weeks after having met Abraham, when along with Abraham and the informant, Chuck, we paid Varvil a visit. I wanted to drop off my '63 Panhead to see if Varvil could fix it. He said he could. We admired his Harley Road King for a while, and as Varvil gloated over it, Chuck said, "Well, we've seen your scooter, now where's the guns?" Varvil asked Abraham if he trusted us, and Abraham said, "They know about my toys, so if we're going down, I guess we're all going down together—yeah, I trust them. I trust them with my life."

Varvil proceeded to let us into his gun vault, a fifteen-by-twenty-foot room off the cluttered garage. Every wall of the room was lined with guns of every kind from damn near every decade of the twentieth century and probably two dozen countries. Varvil handed me an AR-15 with a three-position switch and said, "Yep. Fully auto. Did the work myself." He stuck a thumb in the direction of a hulking machine mill. "Man, I can trick out these ARs all day."

Good for him. After a while, we left.

Weeks passed and we worked. The guys were flush. I did a ruse deal with John Core. I told him I was selling guns to some Mexican gangsters at a body shop, and I asked him to come along as backup. Before we went to the shop, we stopped at a 7-Eleven for gas and Big Gulps. After the Cougar filled up, I dumped my soda on the pavement and filled the Big Gulp cup with gasoline. I said, "Look, these are bad fuckers. We're gonna go in there and take care of business, but if shit goes bad, I'm gonna throw this on the main dude and flick my cigarette at him, send him up in flames, got it? Then we run like hell." The guys we were "dealing" with were all cops, and this was never going to happen, but Core thought it was as real as daylight. He was so nervous during the deal that he ashed his cigarettes into the tops of his shoes so as not to offend the buyers by littering on their floor.

After that I set up some deals with Core and Sean McManama, and, with McManama's help, had Tim Holt custom-manufacture the silencers. McManama also asked me to kill his wife's ex-husband and gave me the gun to do it.

This "murder-for-hire" scenario was one I was familiar with. My MO in these situations was to slow-play the request, demanding that if I were to undertake such a serious crime, it had to be on my own terms. Often, in the interim, suspects would come to their senses and I'd be called off. Murders-for-hire were usually beneficial—I could gain credibility for being willing to kill for money, and the prosecutors would have a good conspiracy charge to level against a suspect when his or her day came in court.

I accepted McManama's request according to my guidelines, and sure enough, a few weeks down the line, he called me off, while I cultivated the reputation of being a hit man.

I stayed on Varvil, but he only danced around deals. I went to pick up my bike and found him fiddling at his workbench, wearing baby-blue nurse's scrubs. When he saw me he got up and took a Sig Sauer pistol from the table, stuffing it into his waistband, the grip hanging over the lip of his drawstring pants. We shook hands and he walked me over to my bike. He straddled it, started it up, and rode the throttle in neutral.

He yelled over the engine, "That Spectre pistol Core's selling you? How much he want?"

I yelled back, "A grand."

"Mommy. That's too much for a pistol, Bird. It was me I'd charge you three hundy."

"That's cool of you, dude, but he ain't budging. All the same to me,

just have to work extra hard"—he turned off the engine and in the sudden silence I was still yelling—"on the next collection."

He shrugged, said, "Hey, it's your money."

I stuck my chin at the bike. "Sounds good."

"Like a motherfucker." He cut the engine and swung his leg over the
seat in a fluid motion, the pistol still in his waist. It defied gravity, with
so little baggy cotton medical nonsense holding it in place. "Hey, come
with me. Wanna show you something."

He led me to the gun room. It was the same as before: gun after gun
after gun. Varvil opened a large drawer and started rummaging through
it, pulling out rags and rifle butts and holsters and bulletproof vests,
throwing everything in a heap. He spoke in a stream of words. He
sounded like he was tweaking on meth: "Abraham and those guys want
me to trick out everything they got. Fuck that. I don't need more auto-
matic shit sitting around to incriminate my ass. These guys don't
understand the risk I take doing all their fucking mods. Shit, I already
got a PVC garden out back that would make Ted Nugent cream his
pants." I assumed this referred to his backyard, where he'd buried his
excess firearms in sealed PVC piping. He stopped going through the
drawers and put his hands on his hips. "There you are."

Varvil removed an MP-40 from the drawer. "This's a German
Schmeisser. The Nazis used it during the invasion of Poland. It's an
open-bolt, blowback, slow-cycle machine gun. And this"—he pulled
out another gun—"is British. Sten gun. Come by these once in a while."

"Cool. Can you get me any of those?"

"Sure. I'll keep my ear to the ground. This! This is an STG-44, Rus-
sian, precursor to the AK-47. You can switch this shit on the fly. Better
have your clips handy. And this. This is a snowplow. A flat-top AR-15,
but the sighting mechanism is for clearing brush."

He lined the machine guns along the blank wall next to the door-
jamb. He handed me the Sten. I placed it alongside the MP-40 and we
stepped back. Varvil looked down on his collection, his arms folded. He
gave his head a slow, prideful, almost disbelieving shake. He took a
deep breath through his nose, filling his lungs, and made a little stab
with a short exhale from the back of his throat. He was in awe.

"Bird? You're looking at the loves of my life is what you're looking at."

. . .

WE RAN AND ran and ran, and I cracked the whip. Sugarbear had trouble keeping up. Within twelve weeks I'd purchased a grab-bag of guns: a Czechoslovakian .32-caliber semiauto pistol; a Rohm .22-caliber revolver; an FIE model A27 .25-caliber pistol; an Intratec Tec-22, 9 mm pistol with compatible silencer; a Sites Spectre HC 9 mm semiauto pistol; a Ruger .22-caliber model 1022 rifle with a sawed-off thirteen-inch barrel; and a Colt AR-15 .223-caliber machine gun. I bought forty-odd silencers from Holt, with McManama acting as a middleman. The silencers, the machine gun, the sawed-off, and the Tec-22 with the silencer were all banned weapons. I was never asked to fill out any paperwork, as I'd always implied to them that I was using them for kills or that I was running them south to Mexico to sell at a markup. The guys didn't ask questions. They made quick tabulations with the criminal calculus and nodded to me like I was their dear old brother. I danced around four murder solicitations, delaying or bluffing, never actually killing anyone for money. They all kept me very busy.

During that fall and winter my son, Jack, kept me busy too.

I made sure to drive down to Tucson twice a week to coach a rabid gang of seven- and eight-year-olds in a T-ball league. During the whole Riverside case I never missed a single game, even if I had to drive through the night, showing up as the boys took the field. I did this because I felt guilty for not being there, but I also did it because it was a pleasure. For a couple of hours a week I was around innocence. I could encourage kids to succeed and hug them after they did something fun. It was the highlight of my week.

One Saturday in mid-January, Jack reminded me that we didn't have a T-ball game on Tuesday.

I asked, "Why not?"

"I dunno. Martin Luther King Day's on Monday, so for some reason they canceled the game on Tuesday."

"Right, then next Saturday it is."

On Sunday I went back to Bullhead with a trunkful of food made by Gwen. As I left the house, my family stood in the front yard, waving. I thought, Jay, you're a lucky man.

That night I hung out at the Inferno Lounge with Abraham and Varvil. The Inferno was the place to be and be seen in Bullhead City. It was a dark, bland bar in an unremarkable two-story concrete building, with bikini-clad bartenders keeping the customers coming back.

Regular citizens and small-time crooks were the main clientele, but it also attracted a fair number of outlaw bikers. Smitty came through two or three times a week.

Varvil and I sat at the bar, talking about the Florence Prison Run. Everyone knew about the Florence Run. All the Arizona clubs saddled up and rode out to the Florence prisons to pay tribute to their incarcerated brothers. I said I'd never been, and Varvil said it was a sight to behold. I told him I thought I'd go, even if I had to go alone. It sounded too damn cool.

Abraham emerged from the john, walked over to us, and climbed onto his stool. He wrapped his hands around his beer and stared at the TV, which showed a Colin Powell interview intercut with images of the Taliban in Afghanistan. Abraham said longingly, "Man, talk about a fucking market." Neither Varvil nor I said anything. We weren't sure what he meant. Abraham said, "Man, if I could, I'd build a fucking bridge from Afghanistan to the front door of my store . . ."

Varvil was shocked. "Bob, what are you talking about?"

"I'd sell those Arab boys some guns, is what I'm talking about!" He pointed the glistening top of his beer bottle at a group of bearded Taliban.

Varvil nearly choked. "So they could kill Americans with them?!"

"Hell, yeah! I don't give a shit. Money is money, and if a mother-fucker needs a gun, I want to be his guy."

I said, "Dude, you're fucked up."

Varvil, the ex-Marine, looked at Abraham like he was a leper and went back to drinking.

Abraham changed the subject. "Say, Bird, you doing anything tomorrow?"

"Not that I know of."

"I'm going shooting, out in the desert. Wanna come?"

"What's the occasion?"

He took a long swig of beer and said, "It's Nigger Monday. I know those lazy feds always take their holidays to drink beer and sit around, therefore I know I won't get caught with any of my really fun toys out in the bush." He tapped his temple, indicating his brains, which, had it been acceptable, I would have enjoyed bashing.

I said I didn't think I'd make it, finished my drink, and left.

I didn't take Martin Luther King Day off. I did paperwork, concentrating on Abraham, and visited Holt at the machine shop to pick up another batch of silencers. The whole time I thought, Abraham, you fat fuck, here is one fed who's working the long weekend, and one day you are going to go to jail for just a little bit longer because I decided to work on "Nigger Monday," 2002.

4 HOEDOWN AT HARRAH'S

JANUARY-APRIL 2002

I WENT ON the Prison Run in late January.

Florence, Arizona, is a small desert town whose main distinction is that it's home to the state's—and the nation's—largest correctional facilities. Thousands of bikers stage up and slowly ride out to the prison complex in a massive pack of chrome, steel, leather, and denim to pay their respects to those unfortunate enough to be doing hard time. As the ragged column crawls past the yard, orange-jumpsuited inmates caged behind thousands of feet of curlicued razor wire stand at parade rest while the bikers file past, saluting, hooting and hollering. To establish some semblance of order, the law comes out in a show of force. Helicopters, antipersonnel vehicles, cruisers, motorcycles, SUVs, paddy wagons—the whole fleet.

Varvil, who didn't go, was right: It *was* a sight to behold.

I rode with a confidential informant from another case out of Los Angeles. The CI's name was Mike Kramer, aka Mesa Mike. He was one of the few Angels we ever got to flip, but at that time his case agent, ATF special agent John Ciccone, didn't know exactly *why* he'd flipped. At the run, Mesa Mike intro'd me to some of his closest friends—Mesa

Angels Cal Schaefer, Kevin Augustiniak, and Paul Eischeid. He pointed out others from a distance: the Mesa president, Bad Bob, and his vice president, Whale; Smitty from Bullhead, who I easily recognized; and a huge guy named Chico out of the Phoenix charter. Mesa Mike warned me never to tangle with Chico, that he'd kill anyone—cop, woman, child, dog, bunny rabbit, even a Hells Angels brother if he deserved it—without losing a wink of sleep.

After the run I returned to the Bullhead UC house. It was in a cul-de-sac named Verano Circle. The house was decorated like a bomb shelter for motorheads. I'd boarded the windows with plywood. Every door but the front was barricaded with a two-by-four. The living room was a gym: full power rack, dumbbells, free weights, heavy bag, speed bag. There was a red pipe wrench hanging next to the front door, and a bulletproof vest hanging on the living room wall. I kept a machete and a shotgun in the closet. One corner of the house was stacked with sandbags. There was a pantry full of canned food, bottled water, three cases of Coors Light, and a large bottle of Jack Daniel's. The purpose of all of this was to suggest that if the police came I was going to hunker down and shoot it out, Butch Cassidy style.

I continued to go to Tucson twice a week to coach Jack's games. I took a couple of days in late March to sit around the pool in my backyard and live the good life. In the evenings I played flashlight tag on the golf course with Jack, and then came inside and listened to my daughter, Dale, practice guitar. She was pretty good for a beginner. Gwen, stylish and forgiving, fawned over me in ways I didn't deserve.

April rolled around. I went back to Bullhead. Another motorcycle rally, the River Run in Laughlin, was gearing up. Since it was on my turf, I resolved to meet some of the local Hells Angels when it took place.

At the time, ATF had some real interest in the Angels. In addition to Agent Ciccone's investigation, a well-known rock star of a case agent named Joseph "Slats" Slatalla was conducting a historical case based in Phoenix. This kind of case is built around existing police reports, warrants, affidavits, arrests, convictions, financial documents, and public records. Slats sought to prove that the Angels were a criminal organization, indictable under RICO, the Racketeer Influenced and Corrupt Organizations Act.

Slats knew the Angels had been in Arizona for a little under five years. He'd learned that before them the state's top One Percenters were the Dirty Dozen. The Dozen had been violent and well established. They'd extorted money and committed violent acts. They'd trafficked in weapons and drugs. Their members had included Chico and Bad Bob.

The Angels came onto their turf when Ralph "Sonny" Barger, the iconic godfather of the Hells Angels, "retired" his forty-year presidency in Oakland, California. He'd served a prison term in the Phoenix area and had fallen in love with the climate and the state. Leaving Oakland, he relocated to Cave Creek, Arizona, a suburb north of Phoenix. With him came the Hells Angels, and with them came the intolerance for any club claiming to be their equal. The Dirty Dozen were in a hard spot. They were tough, but they lacked the resources—to say nothing of the international reputation—of the Hells Angels. The Dozen's members were given a choice: Disappear or patch over to the Angels. Most enthusiastically chose the latter. Others hung up their cuts for good. Others sought Angels membership but were denied.

These facts were significant. For a club to go from nonexistent to the main show in town in under five years proved to Slats that the Angels were wielding their influence ably and willfully. These are the types of bricks that RICO cases are built with.

Historically, two main barriers have prevented law enforcement from wholeheartedly investigating the outlaw motorcycle gangs, or OMGs. On the high end, the bosses don't give them much credit as criminals. It's much more fashionable to go after volume dealers of drugs, arms, or explosives. If the bosses are more concerned with making a lot of cases, then it's easier to move against small-timers like the Varvils and Abrahams of the world. Going after groups like the Hells Angels takes time, commitment, trust, risk, and money—a lethal recipe for a bureaucracy like ATF.

On the low end is the fact that some biker investigators assimilate and sympathize with their adversaries. Some even form their own clubs. This has always been a mystery to me. Cops don't mimic mafia dons or dress as Crips and Bloods and form up neighborhood sets, so why would some choose to create their own motorcycle clubs patterned after criminal syndicates? Maybe it's because they're bound by the bikes themselves—one thing that cuts across all of them is the "live to ride, ride to live" credo—but I wouldn't know since I don't really love bikes. Go figure.

Regardless of the reasons, these forces—a disregard for their legitimacy from above, a wary respect and kinship from below—combined to give the bikers some semblance of a safe haven. Here's what I thought. Yes, guns and drugs ruin people's lives, but what truly ruins people's lives is violence, and violence was and is the source of the Hells Angels' power. In the coming months, as we'd meet to discuss the Angels, Slats expanded on this notion. He understood that outlaw bikers were easy to misconstrue as white, overweight, middle-aged illiterates who wore dirty bowling vests, drank beer, and sat around telling war stories about toothless hags they picked up on the side of the road. Not all of these guys were killers, rapists, or dopers. Slats knew that the majority of these guys had something in life—a job, a family—that restrained them. But he also knew that every outlaw who wore a three-piece patch had the potential for some serious ugliness. A small percentage of One Percenters was crazy, violent, and wired enough that all they did was dope, booze, and commit crimes. He also knew that, being brothers, this smaller group had a lot of influence over the larger, less volatile group. When you mixed these guys with alcohol, drugs, guns, hammers, knives, and honor, and added a violent leader, then violence became the probable—even the preferred—outcome of any conflict. They were like a Greek fraternity with guns. We all knew that when these guys felt comfortable they were capable of horrible things: rat-pack beatings, assaults, stabbings, shootings, rapes. When it got bad, outlaw bikers fed off each other for each other, because, in their minds, all they had was each other.

My thinking as a street cop has always been that I don't care who you are or what club you belong to, if you are being a violent asshole and engaging in illegal activity, then it's my job to try to arrest you. My feeling is that the OMGs are tailor-made for ATF: guns, explosives, drugs, and violence—these are the cornerstones of our mandate.

I also believe that OMGs are America's only truly indigenous form of international organized crime. Mafias come from places like Italy, Russia, and Japan. Drug cartels issue from South America and Southeast Asia. Street gangs are local and not unique to this or any other country. But the bike gangs started *here* in the forties and fifties, with the Hells Angels at the forefront, and now they can be found on every continent in nearly half of the world's countries. The Hells Angels themselves have charters in twenty-six countries on five continents—Germany alone

has more members than the United States—and it all started with
the visionary guidance of one Ralph "Sonny" Barger in Oakland,
California.

For those reasons, I've always believed that investigating biker gangs
was a worthwhile endeavor.

And on April 27, 2002, my less-than-convinced colleagues would
come to believe this too.

THE RIVER RUN didn't commemorate anything like incarcerated felons. It
was merely a large bike rally in a Nevada casino town. It had been going
on since 1983. It attracted corporate sponsors and big-time music
acts. It featured custom bike contests, Miss Laughlin contests, lots of
strippers, shaving-cream-and-baby-oil fights between said strippers,
gambling, and general partying. The vast majority of the attendees were
law-abiding citizens. But no run would be complete without the
presence of the OMGs. They were idolized and highly respected, and
since everyone loves being idolized and respected, they showed up in
force.

The Hells Angels were the stars of these events. But there were other
gangs there too. Not to be at the same event as your rivals was the most
cowardly of retreats, and no club willingly got shown up in this way.

So it was that a Hells Angels rival, Southern California's Mongols,
were in town too. These clubs had been in a violent feud for thirty
years, but it had yet to explode into a full-blown war.

In addition to the bikers, Laughlin was flush with cops. State and
local guys were supplemented by feds like Ciccone and Slats. In support of them were Sugarbear and me, plus some of my oldest undercover friends and colleagues, guys like John "Babyface" Carr, Sean
"Spiderman" Hoover, and Darren "Koz" Kozlowski. The support staff
also included a young female recruit named Jenna "JJ" Maguire.

Koz teamed up with me on the night of April 27. Koz was a crazy,
improvisational UC who *always* looked scary. He was famous for joking, "If I die on this job, I sure as fuck don't want it to be in a traffic
accident or because I had a heart attack at my desk. I don't want to get
hit by a bus on my motorcycle. I want to be duct-taped to a chair and
shotgunned in the face. I want those motherfuckers to cut my head off.
I want the boys to say, 'Did you hear? They cut Koz's head off!'"

We went to the Flamingo, which was where all of the Angels were staying. We went to a centrally located bar and took a couple of stools. Everyone eye-fucked us. There were Hells Angels coming and going all around. JJ, in an observational role, sat at the end of the bar and watched while fighting off offers for free drinks and motorcycle rides.

The situation in the casino was palpably tense. The Angels knew the Mongols were around. They expected a fight, but they didn't know when or where it would start. The Angels had sent spies to the Mongols' hotel and were convinced that the Mongols had returned the favor. No one seemed approachable, and I hadn't yet seen Smitty, the main guy I wanted to meet. After an hour of nursing beers, Koz and I concluded that maybe it wasn't our night.

That's when Smitty stopped at the bar a few stools down. He was by himself. He ordered a Crown Royal and Coke.

I knew I had to mind my p's and q's. If I screwed up the intro, then Koz and I would be at the bottom of a pile before we knew it, and any hope of establishing a rapport with the Angels would be nixed. I wasn't exactly scared—we had a cover team and there were cops everywhere—but I still had to look tough while being respectful. As for Koz, he didn't care. He'd shoot it out like in an old western—and love every minute of it.

Koz and I approached Smitty. Before we got close enough to make him uncomfortable, I said, "Excuse me. You're Smitty, right?" He turned to us.

Something registered. He nodded owlishly and grinned. It was as though the line of his smile had been drawn on his face by a cartoonist. He said, "That's right."

"My name's Bird. This is my buddy Koz."

He nodded at Koz but talked to me. "Yeah, I know who you are."

"Really? That's flattering."

He said, "Well, the BHC's a small town," referring to Bullhead City.

"Maybe, but the way I see it, you're like the mayor over there and I'm barely a citizen." He didn't say anything, but it was obvious by the way he turned up the corner of his mouth that he was flattered too. I continued, "Anyway, I just wanted to introduce myself and say that I think you're doing a hell of a job hosting the party."

Smitty smiled some more and finished his drink. I got the feeling he thought I wasn't much more than a groupie.

He said, "Thanks. Nice to meet you too, Bird. Hope to see you around." And then he walked back into the casino throng, civilians and Angels parting for his passing.

Not long after he left, another Hells Angel with a Dago (San Diego) cut sat on the same stool, accompanied by some other Dago Angels. They all ordered beers. The guy who'd taken Smitty's seat was stocky and looked like a young Kris Kringle—wavy hair, a long, wavy, fanned-out beard, beady eyes, and rosy cheeks. I thrust my hand toward him and said, "Hey, I'm Bird from Bullhead City. Can I buy you a shot?"

He shook my hand. "Hey, I'm Ramona Pete. No shot tonight, Bird, but thanks." He was very congenial and we talked about the Run for a few minutes while he drank his beer. As he finished, he flashed us a toothy smile and said, "Whenever you're in Dago come see me at Dumont's Bar. Can't miss it. S'right down the street from our clubhouse."

"Cool, I'll do that."

He left.

We stayed at the bar well into the night. Smitty crossed the floor a couple more times, usually with other Angels. One stood out in my memory, not only because of the way he looked, but because he whispered with Smitty on two occasions.

This man was thin and twitchy. His flash—the small cloth patches stitched onto his front of his cut—identified him as a Skull Valley member and as one of the "Filthy Few." This meant he'd committed extreme violence on behalf of the club, most likely a murder. He had a mullet of swept-back, battleship-gray hair. He wore sunglasses and had buckteeth. He reminded me of the Nestlé's Quik Rabbit.

Smitty and the Rabbit disappeared from our radar for a while, but eventually they rejoined us next to a blackjack table not far from where we sat. Smitty looked nervous, and the Rabbit sweated visibly. His hands were shoved into his pants pockets, and his elbows were locked. They spoke intently for about five minutes and then broke, the Rabbit briskly walking away. Smitty didn't look happy. He rejoined some Angels at another blackjack table and nodded to the dealer, who stopped slinging cards. Smitty spoke to them quietly but purposefully.

We turned our attention back to our drinks, playing it cool, pretending the Angels weren't there and didn't matter to us.

When we looked back to the blackjack table, the Angels were gone.

We looked around. *All* of the Angels were gone. Koz said, "What the fuck?" I shrugged. Something was up, we just didn't know what it was.

We finished our drinks, paid the tab, and went outside. It was almost 2:00 a.m.

As we walked to our bikes, police cruiser after police cruiser screamed down the Laughlin strip. Some people ran in the direction of the squad cars, but most ran against them. I could almost smell the craziness, as if trouble came with a hint of sulfur.

Koz said, "Well, guess we know where the Angels went."

THERE'S A LONG bar at the Harrah's Laughlin Casino and Resort called Rosie's Cantina. It's rectangular, with purple columns at the corners. People huddle around it to play Keno and smoke long white cigarettes. It's surrounded by the usual American casino scene: ecstatic slot machines and dozens of video poker and blackjack consoles that play a dinging soundtrack dedicated to elusive cash.

Mongols watered themselves around the bar. They were everywhere. They sat on stools and stood in their boots. They were decked in leather and denim. Their chests puffed like those of rare birds. Their backs twitched like those of horses. They acted as they always do: paranoid and defensive and conscious of their ability to intimidate.

At the northern end of the bar a small group of San Francisco Hells Angels tried to drink. Bay Area Angels are as prideful as they come, since their ancestral line is shot directly into the golden days, their inheritance being Sonny Barger himself, the famed Bass Lake runs, Angel Dust, and Altamont.

The Mongols did not want the Angels there—Harrah's was their home turf. The Frisco Angels knew this, so they'd put out a surreptitious distress call, and Smitty answered it. He went to Harrah's as an Angel undercover agent—no HA cut, no flash—just another dude surveying the lay of the land, seeing which table was bathed with the aura of Lady Luck. He stepped to the bar for a drink. A group of Mongols stood next to him. He overheard strands of their conversation. I can only imagine the bullshit insults that wafted from their lips—but it's not hard to do that. The Mongols would have called the Angels "Pinks," "faggots," "losers," "cocksuckers." I'm sure Smitty heard it all, and I'm sure he didn't like it. He forced a broad smile and sipped his

beer, wiping the suds from his mustache. He watched the far end of the
bar, where his Frisco brothers huddled. A group of Mongols orbited
them. Something had to give.

He walked away from the bar slowly and then, once out of sight,
raced back to the Flamingo. He grabbed John "Cowboy" Ward and
Rodney Cox and enlisted the Rabbit to help him muster the troops. He
put his cut back on. Angels disappeared and reemerged a little more
flushed, a little redder with rage, a little more armed. Ten minutes
passed. The group fired up in the parking lot.

The rumble.

They rode down the strip, some doubled-up "bitch style." They rode
down the hill to Harrah's main entrance. They kicked their stands and
fired down. Few talked. There were about thirty of them.

They ran into the lobby and turned right. Keys and metal clanked
on their waistbands. As they passed the restaurant, they broke off and
fanned into the machines. A group of ten moved toward the bar,
toward their stranded San Francisco brothers.

The Mongols started to act like rats in a flood. Movements became
jerky. Adrenaline was so abundant it could have been put on sale. Hank
and Mary Citizen were among the fated bikers, playing their games.
Some noticed. Some thought, What the—? Some left quickly. Several
Hells Angels sat on stools in front of a bank of slots and slipped items
out of their vests and boots. Shiny things, dull things, wooden things,
metal things. Some of these things made clicking sounds, some of them
were silent.

Words were spoken. Pete Eunice from Dago, the one who'd been so
nice and charming to us, tried to broker a truce. He didn't try too hard.

The Hells Angels instinctively understand things other clubs don't.
They know that action is character. You can stitch all the patches you
want and paste your chest high and low with them—telling the world
you've killed for your club, you've eaten menstruating pussy, you're a
rapist and a gangbanger, you're a sergeant, a president, someone who's
taken a bullet or a beating for the club, someone who's been given the
opportunity to rat and hasn't, someone who's kicked the shit out of a
cop—but those little pieces of rectangular flash don't mean a thing if
you don't know how—or when—to kick, shoot, stab, or swing.

The first guy to make a move, an Angel named Ray Ray Foakes,
kicked a Mongol in the chest. A large group of people clung to these

two as they fell away from the bar. People moved toward or away from the melee based on their allegiance: to themselves, away; to their brothers, toward. The fanned-out Angels converged. Mongols got blindsided by hammers and Mag-Lites. The hammers took cheeks and ears. The lights took necks and knees.

Knives were pulled and re-sheathed through the ragged layers of bikers' sides and legs, only to be pulled back out into the recycled casino air, dripping with blood. Repeat. Repeat. Repeat.

Guns were drawn and fired.

The place danced. Concerned faces looked in every direction. Some Mongols got truly scared. They inched to the periphery, trying to avoid an Angel-in-waiting, and hunkered by a twinkling slot. Most avoided contact. Once a safe distance was reached, some Mongols turned and ran. Others, fearing a larger assault, stripped their cuts and stuffed them into garbage cans and the spaces in between the game machines.

The Angels stood their ground.

More shots were fired.

The gunplay created random spaces around the shooters. Pete Eunice was no longer trying to make truces. He was firing away. Smitty didn't have a gun, but he covered Pete. Another shooter was the Angel named Cal Schaefer. No one covered him. When firing, he stabbed the gun into the air, as if his target was within arm's reach. The flare lit up the muzzle and the slug let fly. He twirled around, looking for another target, then twirled around again. The barrel sang.

No Angel removed his cut. Not one. Especially not those killed. The Nestlé's Quik Rabbit tried to revive one of his fallen brothers and gave him mouth-to-mouth on the casino floor. It didn't work. He hid his gun under the body of his fallen brother.

The riot took less than two minutes, and it was there for all to see on video surveillance. Watching it later, I was struck by the hapless choreography of it. People moved together as if attached with invisible strings. Hands moved up at the same time, faces turned to the same spot, shoulders inched in the same direction. There was no sound on the tapes, which made the reactions all the more surreal. Everyone moved like a dumb organism, like a cell drifting through a teeming medium of life and liquid. It was very strange and even beautiful.

But it was not beautiful. Three were killed—two Angels and one Mongol—and dozens were hospitalized. Later that night, another

Angel was gunned down on a dark desert highway outside town. Average tourists and workers were traumatized but miraculously uninjured. The Laughlin riot remains the worst case of casino violence in Nevada history, a brazen act completely disrespectful of authority or the threat of death or imprisonment; a challenge to us, the people who are supposed to protect the public; a challenge to me, who felt even more compelled to use Bird against some truly violent sons of bitches.

5 BLACK BISCUIT BBQ

AT THE END of April, I went to Tucson to be with my family for a few days. Jack's T-ball team was doing well and having fun, Gwen was running the house like an easygoing quartermaster, and Dale played her used guitar. She wanted a new one. I told her to keep at it a little longer. I said that when Gwen and I thought she was dedicated, we'd get it for her—a Gibson or whatever was best. She said OK. Daisy, our lazy hound dog, alternated between sleeping on a pad under the veranda and barking into the desert bush, warning rattlers, gila monsters, and roadrunners to keep their distance. I did yard work, cleaned the pool, and patched a spot on the roof. It was warm enough to be outside at night, and we ate dinner on the back porch.

A week later I headed back to Phoenix to meet with Joseph "Slats" Slatalla. He'd called to ask if I'd be interested in joining him on his Hells Angels case. We'd never worked together, but our wives were friends, so we knew each other socially. Where I was regarded as an accomplished undercover, Slats was renowned as a major-case guru. He'd worked in Detroit in the eighties and nineties—the Vietnam of federal law enforcement—and Phoenix and Miami after that. He'd recently returned to Phoenix and had been looking for a challenge commensurate with his drive and skills.

We met at the Waffle House at Baseline and I-10. We both had pecan waffles with fried eggs and sausage and hot coffee. The place smelled like a tar pit brimming with bacon drippings, syrup, and industrial-strength cleaners.

He said he'd been keeping tabs on Operation Riverside, that Sugarbear and I were doing good work. I said his case in Phoenix sounded promising.

He bit into a juicy sausage. Grease dripped down his fork and chin. "Just got a hell of a lot more promising. Those fucks fucked up at Laughlin." I sopped up egg yolks with a wedge of waffle. He drank his coffee and continued, saying the Hells Angels had played their hand and played it wrong, that they'd practically forced us to step up to the plate and take a swing at the world's baddest, most infamous OMG.

I put down my coffee mug. I knew he was right. I said, "So?"

"So."

"So what are we talking about here?"

"You're in a unique position." He took a forkful of hash browns and swirled them in a pile of ketchup and Tabasco sauce. "Riverside is on autopilot. You're gonna make a good case there. I'd love to have both of you come on. You'd be the lead UC for the whole thing, and Sugarbear could run the northern end of the op."

"I can only speak for myself, but that sounds damn tempting."

He stuffed the hash browns into his mouth. He spoke before swallowing. "So you'll do it? You'll come on board with me?"

"Dude, say the word and I'm there." I could hardly believe I was about to be working with Joseph Slatalla. I wasn't so much starstruck as I was excited. I knew that if we put in the hours, we'd have a legacy-maker of a case.

"Good." He signaled to the waitress, who looked like she'd rather be playing pinochle.

I asked, "What's the plan?"

Before answering, Slats asked the waitress for a Diet Coke with lemon. He watched her walk away. Then he turned to me with a wise smile and said, "Oh. Don't worry. You'll love it."

. . . .

SLATS PUT THE team together and we got under way in late May. Working undercover with me would be ATF special agent Carlos Canino, an old friend and partner we got on loan from the Miami field office, and veteran Phoenix police detective Billy "Timmy" Long. In addition, two very different informants would work with us. The first was Rudy Kramer, a confidential informant Slats had flipped. The second was a man simply known as Pops, a fifty-something paid informant and ex-street hustler who I'd worked with many times.

I'd met Pops in 1996 through investigators working with the Air Force's Office of Special Investigations (OSI). Pops worked as a traditional confidential informant in those days, exchanging legal leniency for information. Pops helped the OSI with a home invasion crew—a band of robbers who targeted residential homes—that included an Air-Force officer. At the time Pops was heavily involved in meth. He was a tweaker whose life could've easily ended in prison or a ditch. The OSI case went well, and after he took care of his legal problems, never having to serve any time, Pops started doing informant-for-hire work for the Arizona Department of Public Safety. His work was good, but he was inconsistent and he had trouble staying clean. He was recommended to me, but before we could work together I had to lay down the law. I told him I wouldn't tolerate drug use and that if I found out he'd lied to me about anything, I'd cut him loose. He agreed to the terms, and it was the start of a unique relationship.

Over the course of several cases, I groomed Pops into a skilled operative. He learned to remember license plates, addresses, gun serial numbers, and names from utility bills. He became an excellent note-taker, emptying his brain of details as soon as the opportunity arose. He was as good at these aspects of the job—if not better—than most agents. He worked entirely for money, and initially money was his sole motivation. But over time he grew to enjoy working for the good guys. He dug the jazz and rush of running a good scam on bad people. Eventually I came to trust him as much as I trusted any of the other men or women I worked with. I introduced him around, and he got hired onto other investigations, always coming away with high praise and improved skills. By the time I'd asked him to join me on Black Biscuit, he was making a living working exclusively as a paid informant.

When I told Slats I wanted Pops, he asked why. I said, "This guy knows the meth game from the street up. He's not a One Percenter, but he *knows* these guys in ways we simply can't. He wouldn't be faking."

"Do you trust him?"

"Enough to let him carry a piece. Yes, I trust him like he's one of us."

"I'll have to meet him, but OK. Go talk to him."

I did. I went to Pops's place in Tucson—he lived there with his wife and two whip-smart girls—and asked him if he wanted to work a big case for me. "Hell yes," he said. I gave him the details. He said he was game to play a big role. I told him I couldn't give him that, that he'd just be an associate. I didn't make any bones about it: "You'll get five hundred a week, no overtime, plus expenses. You're going to make runs to Mexico for us. Agents can't go down there. You'll be traveling with another, less trusted informant—make sure he stays in line. As always, you're our drug guy. You know the shit better than we do, and if there ever comes a time when one of us needs to take a bump or a puff, when we got no dodge or escapes left, then you gotta come to the rescue and be that guy."

"All right."

"Think you can handle that? Without getting hooked again?"

"Jay, I hook that shit again, I'm telling you now to go ahead and arrest me when it happens. That or shoot me. It won't happen."

"Good."

In addition to the undercover crew, Slats put together a stellar task force staff of cops from a broad spectrum of agencies: ATF; the Phoenix, Glendale, and Tempe police departments; the Arizona Department of Public Safety; the Maricopa County sheriff's office; and the Drug Enforcement Agency all contributed. Put together, the task-force members had over two hundred years of law-enforcement or military training and experience. Slats couldn't persuade Sugarbear to come on board. He opted to see the Riverside case to the end. He eventually arrested all of the guys in that case and sent them each away for quite a while.

Every case gets a code name. We wanted something mysterious—"The Sonny Barger Investigation" or "The Arizona Hells Angels" didn't have any pop. We also needed a name that would help keep the case hush-hush. Undercover work cuts both ways—we try to get in on them and, one way or another, they try to get in on us. There are plenty of cops who are buddy-buddy with Angels or Angel associates, and the Angels have plenty of friends, usually wives or girlfriends, who work for state or municipal offices. For those reasons we needed to keep our case on the down-low. Slats was a huge Detroit Red Wings fan, so he decided to call our case Black Biscuit, which is slang for hockey puck.

We were ready to go.

The Saturday before the day-to-day operations were to commence, Slats had a barbecue at his place. His wife cooked up a feast. Everyone was invited, including wives and kids. Making a weekend of it, Gwen and I checked into a hotel and left the kids with the grandparents. At the party we laughed and drank beer and sweated in the Slatallas' backyard. It was a blissful state of communal denial.

At the height of the party, Slats made his way through the crowd, asking people to come inside. Gwen and I were chatting with Carlos, who was there alone, when Slats came up to us. We followed him, and on the way he threw out an empty beer can, grabbed a dripping fresh one out of an ice bucket, and snapped it open.

Once inside, he took his wife by the arm and climbed a few steps leading to the bedrooms upstairs. He turned around.

"Friends. Everyone. Please. You may think otherwise, but I'm not much for speeches. I just wanted to thank you all for coming. This meal we've made for you is a very small token of appreciation for what you are about to undertake. This is gonna be a long haul. It'll take nearly all our time and energy. Make no mistake, no one has done what we're about to do in the way we intend to do it. It's going to take all the brains and balls and heart that each of us has." He paused to take a long swig of beer. "I gotta warn all of you: This is going to be a shit detail." Slats's wife nudged him for cussing with kids around. He continued, "The work will be big and good, but the demand will be high. So I'm here to say now that if you or any of your families have any reservations about being involved, then, please, with my blessing and understanding, say so now and walk away."

He paused. Silence.

I raised my hand. "Fuck it, Joe, I'm out."

Everyone laughed.

Joe said, "All right, then, I'll see you on Monday. Enjoy the last free Sunday of your foreseeable futures."

6 RUDY WANTED TO KNOW WHERE I DID MY TIME

OUR CI, RUDY Kramer, was a longtime biker and repeat offender. His rap sheet revolved around meth, which he had cooked, dealt, and used, thereby violating rule number one of the Successful Drug Dealer's Handbook. He'd been pinched on a felon in possession of a firearm, which was made worse by the fact that the weapon in question was a machine gun. Given the alternative of turning informant versus going away for a very long time, he wisely chose to cooperate.

Rudy was not a Hells Angel, but he could name an impressive number of them from mug shots and claimed to be on speaking terms with at least three prominent Arizona Hells Angels: Mesa charter president Robert "Bad Bob" Johnston, Cave Creek charter president Daniel "Hoover" Seybert, and Sonny Barger himself. He told us Sonny had exchanged alcohol and drugs for the pleasures of Pepsis and ice cream. He also said that Sonny rode with a windshield to protect the tracheostomy hole he'd received as a result of laryngeal cancer.

Rudy also knew a guy named Tony Cruze, a greedy drug user who dealt openly in guns and narcotics. Cruze was the president of the Tucson Red Devils, a Hells Angels support club. Support clubs are distinct from their superiors—they have their own member rolls, clubhouses, and officers—but they operate with the official sanction of their parent clubs and do basically whatever's asked of them. Other Hells Angels support clubs in Arizona at the time included the Spartans and the Lost Dutchmen, but the Red Devils were the largest and most dangerous. They mainly provided muscle to the Angels for enforcement, collection, and extortion jobs.

This was all great, but Rudy had one more box in his checkered past that sealed his importance to us. He was an inactive member of a Mexican OMG called the Solo Angeles, based in Tijuana, Mexico. The Solos had about a hundred total members, with minor representation in the San Diego–Los Angeles area.

We knew the Hells Angels were paranoid, but we also knew they weren't insecure in the ways the smaller clubs were. If we'd run straight at the Hells Angels as average Larry Bad Guys, they would've ignored us or, at the most, handled us with extreme caution. We had to be invited into their house. It was an issue of respect. In biker circles this was universally understood, just like it's understood that the sky is blue.

The plan was to have Rudy ask the HA permission to set up an Arizona Nomads charter of the Solo Angeles, and then we'd tell them we were Rudy's crew. The fact that this club was Mexican dovetailed perfectly with my established claim that I ran guns south of the border. Being Solo Angeles Nomads, we wouldn't need affiliation with an established charter, so existing members wouldn't have an opportunity to get in our way. It also set the stage for RICO charges, since it would establish that the Angels controlled the outlaw clubs in Arizona. It was pluses all around. Rudy would be our president. Carlos would be a full patch. My trusted informant, Pops, would be a prospect, as would Billy "Timmy" Long. And I, Jay "Bird" Dobyns, would be the Solo Nomads' vice president.

BEFORE WE GOT started, I had to meet Rudy. Slats set up a date at the Embassy Suites near the Sky Harbor International Airport in Phoenix.

Rudy knew practically nothing about me. By design, Slats hadn't told him I was a fed. We wanted his first impression of me to be formed with as little prejudice as possible.

I rode my '63 Harley-Davidson Panhead to the hotel. Slats's car was out front. I was dressed in my usual. I wasn't openly armed.

I knocked on the door of room 11. Footsteps came to the door and it opened, streaming sunlight into the otherwise dim room. Slats held the doorknob and waved me in.

Seated at a round table to the right of the door was a thick man with close-cropped brown hair who wore wraparound sunglasses. He kept a tidy mustache he was obviously very proud of, and a triangular tuft of brown hair was tucked below his lower lip. He had a deep, horizontal worry line on his forehead. He wore a black tank top. His entire upper body—arms and neck included—was covered in tattoos.

I turned to him and stuffed an unlit cigarette in my mouth. He pushed his seat back and stood up. A couple of seconds passed while we sized each other up.

"I'm Bird."

"Rudy."

I stuck out my hand and he took it. It was a knuckler of a handshake. He looked at my shoulders and chest, checking out my ink. He didn't let go of my hand. I didn't let go of his.

"Where'd you do your time? What'd they get you for?"

I smiled at Slats and turned back to Rudy. "Man, they didn't get me for shit, and I've never been inside." Neither of our hands buckled, but both must have hurt. Mine sure did.

"Then what the fuck're you doing with this guy?"

"Hey, dude, I don't know what Big Boy over here told you about me," even though I did, "but I'm here because Slats and I have a working relationship." I paused. "I'm a fed."

Rudy let go of my hand and drew his head back in a motion of disbelief. Pleasant sensations returned to my knuckles. I wanted to shake it out but didn't. He said, "Bullshit."

"Nope. God's honest truth. They send me a check every two weeks to dress like this and hang out with guys like yourself."

Rudy laughed, looked at Slats, and pointed at me. "That's not fair. How are we supposed to win against motherfuckers who look like this?"

Slats shrugged.

"You're not, dude." I motioned for us to sit at the table. "That's why there *are* guys who look like me—and there are more of us than you can probably imagine."

He considered this. Maybe he ran through a file of faces and names, picking out candidates. "Fuck it. No point in me worrying about that now."

I sat down and took off my shades and placed them on the table. I put my cigarette behind my ear and laced my fingers together. My rings joined in a tinny little symphony. I projected calm. I said, as kindly as possible, "Look. We got you, it's true. I know Slats has told you this already. You're an old-timer, you know the game as well as we do. This is a good chance for you, dude, a good chance for you to correct past wrongs, if you care to. If not, then you know what's waiting for you."

He said, "Look, man, I'm here to work."

"Good. Then let's talk."

I told him all about Bird and nothing about Jay Dobyns. I told him how I'd managed some token intros to a few of the Angels he claimed to know. We talked about Smitty and Bad Bob. I told Rudy he'd be an essential component of the next phase of the case. Slats reiterated that we needed him. It's always good to talk up an informant, especially one who's separated from you by a flow of ambivalence. You need to build trust, or at least the illusion of trust, in a case like Rudy's. He asked what we wanted from him. Slats outlined the plan. Rudy listened carefully, nodding and smiling from time to time. When Slats was through, Rudy said it was risky, especially for him. But he also said it was so crazy it might just work, and that we'd chosen the right guy. I said we couldn't do it with just anyone, we needed him and only him.

I pulled the cigarette from my ear and lit it. We all lit cigarettes.

He said, "You don't need to flatter me so much."

I said, "Maybe not. But you'll be in charge as far as anyone knows, and you can't forget that you're not. If this works, and we start to roll as a unit with you as our 'leader,' then you have to remember that it's us—and especially me—who's calling the shots on the street. Got it, dude?"

He went, "Mmmmm." I stared at him. He still had his sunglasses on. I knew I wouldn't get to see his eyes that day. Maybe it was the shame of being put in a bad spot, or maybe he was jazzed by the prospect of doing something so ballsy—but whatever the reason, he kept them hidden behind his shades. I couldn't blame him. He was a man with no choices, and you don't want to stare in the face the guy who's taken control of your life, not right after you've met him.

I asked, "Well?"

He didn't say anything for a minute. Then he pointed at my left arm and said, "That tattoo."

"Yeah?"

"What is it?"

"It's Saint Michael."

"Oh."

"You know him?"

"Think so. He's the patron saint of cops, right?"

"That's right. And grocers. I looked it up on the Internet once."

"No shit?"

"No shit."

He didn't think it was cute. Whatever.

He said, "Well, you're gonna have to come up with some other story about that if you wanna run with these guys." He sat back in his chair and twirled his finger at the ink on my torso.

"Shit, dude, you think I got to where I am without a story for my Saint Mike? I'm the guy with the sword, the dragon's my addiction to junk, and I'm killing that motherfucker. I've been around the block, Kramer, don't sweat it."

Satisfied, he grunted and parted the drapes. "What about that?"

"My bike?"

"Yeah."

"What about it?

"It looks OK, but it won't keep up with the guys we'll be seeing."

"I'll keep up."

"Not on a worn-out Panhead, you won't. You might be king-shit undercover, but I'm king-shit biker, so watch and learn."

"I can't argue with you there, dude, I can't argue with you there."

And I didn't.

PART III

THE MIDDLE

7 TOO BROKE FOR STURGIS, WHERE TIMMY LEARNED THE FINE ART OF FETCHING SAUERKRAUT

JUNE-JULY 2002

JUNE AND THE better part of July were spent getting our Solo Angeles story straight.

After Rudy got our Solo charter official—he and Pops had to make a couple of trips to Tijuana to pay dues and sort it out—he set to work in Arizona. He ran a few meth deals with Tony Cruze and reestablished contact with Bad Bob. Rudy had to answer questions of perception and politics: The Angels were curious why, all of a sudden, Rudy had become so hot to set up shop in Arizona. He said it was because of the proximity to Mexico, where his club was based and where his boys— that is, us—had established "some business," alluding to our gun-running ruse. They also wanted to know what we thought of the Mongols. Rudy assured them the Solos didn't have an official position on the Mongols, but that we didn't think much of them at all. He told Bad Bob we'd be happy to watch the Nogales border on behalf of the Angels, letting them know when any Mongols showed up there. Bad Bob thought it over.

On July 13, Bad Bob offered Rudy a deal he guaranteed would be formalized at the next Hells Angels officers' meeting: We'd be allowed to operate freely in Arizona so long as we agreed never to fly an Arizona rocker—this honor was reserved for Hells Angels alone—and so long as we backed up the HA in their struggles with the Mongols. Additionally, we wouldn't be wed to the Angels in the way that the Red Devils or the Spartans were—we'd have their back and pay them their due respect, but we wouldn't be another puppet club.

As Rudy secured our standing, we worked on putting together a bona fide bike gang. We got the bikes up and running and our backstop stories down pat. Christopher "Cricket" Livingstone, an ATF agent and Slats's right-hand man on the task force, used Rudy's jacket as a template and got his mom to make the patches we'd sew onto our brand-new leather vests. Our club's colors were orange on black, so all of our patches were stitched with pumpkin-orange thread. The ones on the front of our jackets—small rectangles and diamonds collectively referred to as "flash"—were mostly abbreviations: SFFS (Solos Forever, Forever Solos), IIWII (It Is What It Is), and FTW (Fuck The World, a biker favorite). On our backs were sewn our three-piece patches: a round center patch depicting an orange motorcycle, a top rocker that said SOLO ANGELES, and a bottom rocker that said TIJUANA. In addition to these we had a side rocker that said NOMADS.

We were ready to roll.

A COMMITTED BIKER'S calendar is filled with rallies and runs, and we Solos wanted to commemorate our coming-out on a large run, which, in addition to being ceremonial, would maximize our exposure. We chose an "all clubs" rally at Mormon Lake called Too Broke for Sturgis.

The afternoon before the run, Slats told me we needed to have a sit-down. We'd been having meeting after meeting, going over details and procedure and backgrounds for weeks, and I felt like we didn't need to have another. Slats's way was methodical, whereas mine was improvisational, a method Slats would later dub "smokin' and jokin'." I was eager to get going, my nerves shook, my adrenaline began to flow. I knew Slats must've been nervous too, and I figured this would be the last pre-op meeting he and I would have, so I agreed to see him. He told me to meet him at Jilly's Sports Bar in Tempe.

I pulled up in role, got off my bike, and walked inside, test-driving the "dick-out" style I wanted to trademark. I figured a yuppie sports bar was as safe a place as any to let it all hang out. I pushed the door open, guns in my waistband, wife-beater on my back, camos on my legs, flip-flops on my feet, and a belt buckle so big Ty Murray would've been proud. My eyes struggled to adjust from the Phoenix sunshine to a dimly lit bar. As they did, I saw before me a smiling Slats, his family, Carlos, and, most important, Gwen, Dale, and Jack. I'd completely forgotten it was my birthday. I let go of my attitude and returned to my old self. We ate cake, opened presents, and talked about everything but work. For three hours I made a point of putting as much loving on the kids as possible. It was one of the best birthday celebrations I ever had. Toward the end, Carlos elbowed my ribs and said, "Nice, huh? Slats wanted you to see Gwen and the kids one more time before we die in the forest tomorrow."

I nodded. It *was* nice.

THE NEXT MORNING the team gathered for breakfast at the Waffle House on I-17 and Bell Road. We finished before Rudy showed up, and waited for him. Eventually he pulled into the parking lot with a piggish piece of trailer trash clutching his sissy bars. He got off the bike and ordered her to stay outside.

As he sauntered in, Carlos asked, "Who's the beauty queen?"

"Can't remember her name. Grabbed her in the parking lot at the Apache Junction Wal-Mart."

"Well, get rid of her," Carlos said.

"Fuck that. We go bitchless, they'll think we're a bunch of homos. Not cool."

"All right, fair enough. But if she becomes a liability, then the gig's off. I think Jay and Timmy will agree." We said we did. Rudy said don't worry about it.

Mormon Lake is about two hundred miles north of central Phoenix, off I-17. Rudy and I rode up front, him on the left, me on the right—the usual positions for the president and vice of an OMG. The members fell in behind us. Behind all of us, keeping their distance, were the two vehicles that carried the cover team: a white rental truck and a passenger van.

About a hundred miles in, we pulled off at Cordes Junction to gas up. We stopped at a Mobil and unassed. My legs and shoulders were killing me.

I felt as old as the road was long.

Rudy slouched on his bike like a vacationer in a hammock. He yelled, "Prospect! Go get me a pack of Reds, and make sure you tell the bitch-ass attendant we're filling up. Pay for all of it." He spoke to Timmy. An absent grin faded from the lips of the nameless woman clutching Rudy's waist. She looked like she'd lived the lives of three women put together. Rudy slapped her on the thigh and she slowly draped her arms over his shoulders, like a bored bitch doing a trick for which she no longer got rewarded.

Timmy shook his head, but did what was asked. He was an experienced cop who'd dealt with perps and CIs like Rudy for years. He knew we were on our way to a real-life run, and we were all playing dramas that would make us more like the genuine article. As a prospect, Timmy had to get used to being ordered around.

I went inside and bought a pack of Marlboro Lights and two packets of Advil. I slammed the pills dry and packed the cigarette box on the heel of my palm. I lit a cigarette as we pulled out.

We rode on for another hour and pulled off at Munds Park. At the bottom of the ramp, Rudy turned to me and said, "That sucked. You better speed the fuck up. My club ain't gonna roll like bitches."

"*Whose* club?"

"Slats told me to kick you up. You're s'posed to be following me. I'm your P." "P" meant president.

"We ain't at the run yet. And I thought we did pretty good."

"Maybe we hit seventy. That's too slow. You gonna work the Angels, then kick it up a notch or twenty."

"All right, President Kramer, next time we'll make you prouder, sir."

"Good." He turned back to the road and gunned it. We followed, but at a distance, just to piss him off.

We rode through flat land toward blue mountains rising up in the east. On either side of the road, broad swaths of green-yellow grazing grass alternated with massive stands of ponderosa pines. It was a nice ride.

Rolling into a biker rally wearing a three-piece patch is like walking into a high school cafeteria naked. It was no different at Too Broke. Before we got there I'd been nervous, but as we rolled in I got scared. This was a feeling I was used to. A huge part of undercover work is hiding your fear and channeling it into things that bolster you. Everyone we passed looked at us. I decided to take the attention as a compliment and not an accusation. My ego was hungry and ate it up. I accepted the fear, and the attention felt good.

Rudy sped up as we approached the entrance gate. We did too. He blew by the attendant, flipped him off, and yelled, "SOLOS DON'T PAY FOR SHIT!"

That felt good too.

We pulled into a parking area and walked around. Rudy led us to a group of Red Devils and intro'd us to Tony Cruze. Cruze looked like Jerry Garcia without a smile. He ordered a prospect to get beers, Rudy ordered Timmy to help him. Rudy yelled at Timmy to bring him two, and to make sure they were both "like ice." Timmy marched off. Carlos and Pops and I stood behind Rudy as he talked to Cruze. Rudy bitched about setting up the new charter, never missing an opportunity to flatter himself and his ability to sway the Angels. Cruze asked if I was the one who did the business down south. I said yes. He said we needed to get together, Rudy said one of us would be in touch. Two women, one short and skinny, one tall and overweight, walked up to Cruze. He grabbed and jiggled the ass of the taller one. She leaned toward him and bit his ear. The smaller one winked at Rudy's gal, who, to her credit, hadn't said anything. The women walked away. The backs of their jackets had single patches that read PROPERTY OF THE RED DEVILS. This referred to both the women and the jackets.

Timmy returned toting a load of Silver Bullets. I took two. I popped one and wedged the other into a back pocket. I was always an amateur drinker, but knew I'd have to get in shape fast on this job. I took a large gulp. The cold beer sliced through the dust kicked up by bikes and wind. Timmy stepped between Cruze and Rudy to hand his president his beers.

"Prospect, I am trying to talk to this guy and you're getting in my way!"

Timmy looked over his shoulder. Cruze stared at him, his long curly hair blowing around his face. Cruze's prospect had delivered the beer without interfering.

Timmy turned to Rudy and said, "Sorry, prez. Won't happen again."

"It better not or you're gonna have the shortest biker career ever."

Timmy turned away, took two steps, and rolled his shoulders. If he had done it facing Rudy, it would've been an obvious challenge. He played it off like he was stretching.

Rudy let it go.

We stood around and bullshitted. The Red Devils mingled with a couple other OMGs, most noticeably the Spartan Riders. Their center patch was a vertically oriented battle ax bisected by a pair of crossed swords on a blood-red background. Looking at that patch, it hit me for a moment that these guys were, for the most part, just as full of it as we were. It's a simple formula: If you look tough, then you are tough. The posturing—by us, but especially by these so-called "outlaws"—was unbelievable.

A big Spartan by the name of Bruno came up to us with a couple of his boys, each carrying a can of beer. Two women came with them. Old, broken-down women. Everyone had been living too hard for too long.

Bruno had an extremely short buzz cut. His head looked like a giant, lumpy summer gourd. All he wore on his upper body was his cut. He had a jiggly beer gut that parted his vest, and his fat had declared war on his belly button, which had all but disappeared.

It was immediately apparent that he didn't like any of us.

At one point he turned to Carlos and said, "Homes, what the fuck with your cuts? They're like brand new."

Carlos, Pops, Timmy, and I all wore squeaky clean vests. Rudy's, the genuine article, had been around the block, but ours were fakes and it showed. Carlos thought fast.

"Fucking cunt. This bitch we had trim our shit—you know, we came here for Rudy from other charters—this cunt was like a three-year-old with a pair of garden shears. She cut our old shit up taking the rockers off, so we had to freshen up."

Bruno didn't buy it. Cruze did. He said, "Damn, man. A man's cut is like his skin. What'd you do?"

Carlos ignored Bruno. "What can you do? It is what it is." He pointed at the IIWII tab on his chest.

Bruno rubbed his belly like it contained his brain. He suggested, "You could've fucked her up."

Carlos said sadly, "Yeah, well we would have. 'Cept it was one of our brothers' moms." He gunned the rest of his beer and threw the empty into the dirt.

Cruze put up his hand and said, "It is what it fucking is, I guess."

Carlos belched. I said, "Yep. It is what it is."

I asked Rudy if we were going to head over to the Angels' tent. He said, "Oh, yeah," like it wasn't a big deal. He asked Cruze to join us. Bruno said he'd hang back.

We left and drifted down the fairway. It was something. The crowd stared and parted for us like we were royalty.

Fear tickled over the nape of my neck and down my forearms. This was not like the Flamingo in Laughlin. That had been a venue full of non-bikers and cops. This was a crowded event exclusive to bikers and seriously underrepresented by law enforcement. I was scared and I was excited.

We were going to meet the Hells Angels.

Their area was a series of large open-air tents shading them from the sun. There were two large Angel prospects standing guard at the entrance. Cruze walked up and exchanged words with them. Rudy greeted them. They invited us in.

The Allman Brothers crooned from some far-off speaker. On the left was a T-shirt booth. Two young, large-breasted women worked it. Stretched across their tight shirts was the phrase SUPPORT YOUR LOCAL RED AND WHITE. The Angels' colors were red and white, and this was one of their more common nicknames. The women wore high-cut jean shorts. Neither of them smiled, and both smoked cigarettes.

I pulled out a smoke and lit up.

We passed loitering Angels and their stares. They knew Cruze and the Red Devils, but had never heard of the Solos. They asked out loud, "Who the fuck are these orange motherfuckers?" We didn't say anything. I tried to look casual, but my insides were knotted up.

We approached the two ranking members at the rear of the last tent. Cruze said, "Boss."

The larger one, who weighed upwards of 250 pounds and had a rosy complexion and white hair, bellowed, "Cruze. What's up?"

"Got some guys want to meet you."

The smaller one stepped forward. He had a squeaky, impatient voice. His eyes were hollow and distracted. He whined quickly, "Hey. You're Rudy, right?"

Rudy stepped forward and extended his hand. "Yeah. You must be Dennis."

"Yep," answered Dennis. He jerked his head to the larger one. "This is Turtle."

"Good to meet you." Rudy waved at us. "These are my Solo Angeles." He pronounced our name *Ahn-HELL-ess.*

Dennis's head was almost completely encased in a swarm of ratty off-blond hair. His beard went to his chest, his ears were covered. His quick voice and worn eyes said it all: meth-head tweaker.

I placed them both from the files we had on convicted Angels. Dennis's last name was Denbesten, and he was a drug felon recently out of prison. Turtle's name was Warren Kuntz, and he was a convicted sex offender. Dennis was an Arizona Nomad and close to Smitty.

Dennis squeaked, "Turtle and I are glad to have you. Bad Bob told us you might drop in." His weary eyes paused on each of us.

Turtle offered hot dogs and beer. Dennis insisted the Angels feed us. "You're here as guests of Bad Bob," he said, waving to a prospect standing nearby. He said this in a kinder, gentler tone. I liked Dennis from the start. It was as if, after we'd walked into the cafeteria naked, Dennis had walked up and put his varsity jacket around our shoulders.

A prospect appeared at Turtle's side, awaiting orders.

Rudy said, "This is my VP, Bird, my sergeant at arms, Carlos, and this is Timmy and that's Pops, our prospects."

"We know," said Dennis. "We've heard of all of you." He smiled.

Rudy barked at Timmy, "I'll take that hot dog, prospect. Mustard and kraut. You got kraut?"

Turtle smiled. "Yep."

"Good. Kraut. Don't forget."

Turtle told his prospect to go get beers for everyone. He left.

Timmy turned to follow, and I grabbed his arm. "I'll take mine with equal amounts of mustard and ketchup. Mustard down one side, ketchup down the other. Get it right."

"Right," answered Timmy.

Carlos said, "Onions if they got 'em. Otherwise, plain."

Timmy said, "Right," and turned again.

Pops didn't say anything. As a prospect he didn't have the clout to place an order.

Timmy stalked away angrily. I asked where the john was, and they pointed to some Porta Pottis beyond the blackened, halved oil drum that served as a grill. I caught up with Timmy before he got to the grill, grabbed him, and turned him around. No one else was in earshot.

"What the fuck, dude?" I jabbed my finger at the ground.

"Fuck that guy."

"Shut up and suck it up. What are you, a rookie? You're a fucking fighter ace. We all know you can kick Rudy's ass, but if you do it now,

the show's over before it started. Choke this bullshit down and wear
your big-boy pants today. Dude, you're Serpico and Baretta in one.
You're a fucking master. Come on. Play your role."

He straightened up. "All right, all right. But fuck you, for the record.
I ain't a step-and-fetch for you, Rudy, or anyone else."

I raised my eyebrows and we parted. I knew it took a lot to piss off
Timmy, and if we pushed him far enough he'd have no problem whip-
ping any of our asses.

Back at the tent, Dennis asked me what that was about, and I said I
was standing up for my P and for my club, that a prospect couldn't act
angry when he was ordered to do something he didn't want to do.

Dennis said, "That's good. Shows your head's not fucked."

The Hells Angels prospect came back with an armload of opened
beer cans. He passed them out, Turtle nodded to him, and he stepped
back into a ready position.

Then Timmy came back with four hot dogs. He handed one to Carlos, who dug in. He handed me mine and Rudy his, this time careful
not to step between him and Dennis or Turtle. I took a bite. It was juicy
and crunchy. There was mustard on one side and ketchup on the other.

"What the fuck is this?!" Rudy barked. He threw the hot dog on
the ground and mashed it with his boot. "Motherfuck. You got grease
for brains? I said sauerkraut. I *repeated* sauerkraut, fucknut. Get me
another. If you can get this one right, then I'll bump you up to burgers."

Timmy spun around and headed back to the grill. I yelled over my
shoulder, "You got mine right!"

"Mine too!" added Carlos.

When Timmy gave him his second frank, Rudy held it up and
inspected it like it was a model airplane. He nodded. He took one bite
and said, "Good job. You and Pops can go get some food now if you
want." Timmy and Pops walked toward the grill.

We ate our lunch and drank our beer and talked about Bad Bob and
how happy we were to have received the blessing of the Hells Angels. I
said it was an honor I'd never thought I'd know. Dennis said he'd heard
good things about me. Rudy said Bad Bob was a good man. Pops and
Carlos and Timmy stood back, eating hot dogs and drinking beer.
Cruze excused himself. Dennis said Bob wanted to meet us. We spoke
generally about Laughlin and the brawl. Then we said we had to get
going and thanks for the food and letting us pay our respects. Catching
a little break, Turtle asked me to sign a guest banner they had strung

across the back of the tent. It read HELLS ANGELS NOMADS and had a
five-foot-wide Death Head in the center. The request made me smile
and relax. Would an Angel vet like Turtle ask someone he didn't like or
respect to autograph club property? No, he wouldn't. I signed it "Love
and Respect, Bird, Solo Angeles Nomads."

I felt pretty good as I rejoined the group. That's when Turtle asked,
"Hey, guys, what the fuck with your cuts?"

And that's when Carlos—with some embellishments from Pops—
told them our bullshit story about Cricket's mom again.

We owed her a roomful of roses.

THE RIDE BACK to Phoenix was a joke. Rudy's bike took a dump and we
paid some guy to haul him, his gal, and his bike home; mine coughed
and wheezed and wouldn't go faster than fifty since, bike genius that I
am, I'd only opened the fuel petcock halfway; and Timmy, exhausted
and dehydrated, continually wretched the day's food and drink over his
shoulder onto the road. He fought through it, never complaining, but
by the time we got back, his right side was covered in dried-up chunks
of hot dog.

We regrouped at task force headquarters, a place we called the
Pumpkin Patch, or just the Patch, on account of the Solo Angeles
pumpkin-orange colors. It was a one-story warehouse in a metro
Phoenix industrial park. The surrounding businesses included furniture companies and small software firms. We had an office up front that
never had a secretary in it, and behind that, through a nondescript
door, was operations. A dozen desks, twice as many computer termi-
nals, a couple offices, a conference room, and a loading bay where we'd
end up spending a lot of time tinkering with our lame-ass ATF bikes. An
overused kitchenette and bathroom. Posters of pinup girls and a whole
wall devoted to my college football career, which the other agents made
endless fun of. We had space for a suspect matrix—basically a wall of
photos and names—and stations for evidence processing and a safe.
Over the course of the following year, the Patch would become the closest thing to home many of us had.

Timmy cleaned up, Slats made coffee, and then we debriefed. Two
main things came up. First, we had to put some mileage on our cuts.
We took them to the loading area, poured water and beer and handfuls

of dirt on them, and ran the van over them. We held them up and they looked fantastic. Mine was a little too dirty for my liking—I like clean, orderly things—but I knew the now worn-looking cut wouldn't draw any undue attention.

Second was Timmy. He took Slats aside and demanded to be made a full patch Solo on the spot. Slats, chewing a wad of Copenhagen, said no dice. He said in order to come off real, we needed to run him and Pops as prospects for a couple of months. Timmy said if that was the case then he'd end up beating Rudy into the hospital. Slats told him to suck it up, just like I had. Slats said he'd tell Rudy to chill out, that he'd remind him this was a big game. Timmy said that wasn't good enough. Slats spat on the ground and said too bad.

We broke and went home. Our Phoenix undercover house wasn't set up yet, so Carlos and I crashed at hotels. Slats, Timmy, and Pops went home—to wives, kids, dogs, and everything. Before he left, Timmy secretly grabbed a center patch, a top rocker, and a Nomads side rocker from the "flash stash." He didn't tell anyone. He got home at 3:00 a.m., snuck up to his bedroom, and nudged his wife awake.

Timmy would not be a prospect. He'd paid his dues through years of undercover work on gangbangers, sex offenders, and street dealers. He had more property-crime experience—robberies, larcenies, home invasions—than all of us put together. He knew that the Angels prospected their guys for no less than a full year, and that, to keep up appearances, he was probably expected to prospect for Rudy for at least three months, the lesser standard that most other clubs demanded. As far as he was concerned, this was unacceptable. He knew he could serve Black Biscuit better and faster as a "full patch," an official member.

His wife sat up in bed. He showed her the patches and his vest and begged her to sew them on. She said OK. He made a pot of coffee and they sat together over the sewing machine in the room off the garage.

The next day Timmy showed up at the Patch decked out in all his flash. We laughed it off. Rudy fumed. Slats shrugged, said, "All right, let's get to work." I slapped Timmy on the back, glad to have him as a full partner, and said, "I guess that's how us Solos roll."

Timmy said, "Damn right. Fast and right at you."

8 JESUS HATES A PUSSY

AUGUST 1, 2002

FIVE DAYS AFTER Too Broke, we got an invitation to meet Bad Bob at the Mesa clubhouse.

Bob expected us at 9:00 p.m. We decided to meet at a church parking lot in Gilbert, Arizona, a former town that had been engulfed by Phoenix's insatiable sprawl. Pops, Carlos, Timmy, and I were about as close as we could be to shitting our pants. Too Broke felt like it had taken place months ago. Meeting the Angels in a tent outside during the day wasn't the same as riding our bikes into their driveway at 153 South LeBaron, kicking down, unassing, and walking right into their cinderblock stronghold.

At night.

I felt certain we were setting ourselves up. I thought our game might be too tight, and imagined Rudy was a tweaker dickhead cop-hater who wanted to see us smoked. We knew that it didn't take much for a UC to end up as dead as Elvis. If we'd miscalculated or been too brash, we'd be gone before we could finish saying, "Mister Hells Angels, sir, it's an honor to—" Sure, the cover team would storm in a few minutes later, but they'd only be able to even the score, hose our brains off the wall, and snap some tags around our toes.

We sat around a picnic table under a mesquite tree, waiting for Rudy. The sun was down, but the desert twilight lingered. Pops and I smoked like twin furies. It was August in Arizona, and the sweat sealed our Solo cuts to our torsos like second skins.

I had my Glocks, and Carlos and Timmy each carried Beretta .380s. Pops had a Smith & Wesson five-shot revolver. It's basically forbidden to arm an informant, even a paid one like Pops, but I trusted him and was unwilling to put him in harm's way without a means of defending himself.

I flipped, closed, flipped, closed my Zippo. Carlos popped gum. Pops talked to his wife on his cell. Timmy just sat there, calm as a lizard on a rock. Bastard.

Rudy pulled in. He revved his engine, fired down, and jumped off. He didn't have a gun. Pops was a friend; Rudy was a means to an end. He was still a convicted felon with revoked gun rights.

"Sorry I'm late." He didn't sound sorry.

I didn't care. I said, "No worries. We got time."

Timmy said, "It's only seven, prez."

"All right." Rudy unwrapped a new soft pack of Reds, bit off the foil, and shook out a smoke. I lit it for him.

We didn't say anything.

Then Rudy said, "OK, I'm in charge when we're inside, don't forget it. You step on my toes and the show's over. The Angels operate by the book, and they expect us to also. I don't wanna lose the stature I've built up for you snouts. I need to see the pride you got for your colors. Also, we might ride with these guys tonight. Hate to break you off so fast, but you gotta know a couple things. We'll be at the back, keeping up. We gotta keep up. They blow a light, we blow a light. They get traffic-stopped, we get traffic-stopped. Mesa rides like the Blue Angels on Memorial Day. Other charters hate riding with 'em 'cause they're such fucking road Nazis. Stay eighteen inches off the wheel in front of you. And stay back. Never, ever cross the line of a full patch's front wheel. You pass one of these guys and there will be hell to pay."

No one said anything.

Rudy said, "The fuck? You guys ready?" We looked at each other in silence. Even grizzly old Pops, who on most days couldn't have given a shit if someone put a bullet in his head, stayed quiet. Rudy was disgusted. "Listen, if we're gonna do this, then let's roll over as fast and hard as we can. We're gonna get off our motorcycles and walk up to these guys like we're the baddest pricks on earth. We're gonna look 'em in the eye and tell 'em who we are. What comes next, comes next. We'll handle it." Rudy looked directly at me. "If you don't have it in you, if you wanna go home right now and tell your neighbor's wife what a badass you are, then let's call this bullshit off and close the case, because it has to start right here and right now." Our silence continued, born more of shame than of fear.

"Jesus Hates a Pussy." I blurted it out. The guys looked at me with what-the-fuck? looks. I said, "It's my old partner Chris Bayless's mantra for this kind of situation. He were here, he'd say, 'So, your stomach's in knots and you wanna go home. Well, strap your nuts up and go to work. Jesus hates a pussy—you're a fucking undercover, you gotta do what you gotta do!' C'mon, guys, I'm nervous as hell, but Jesus hates a pussy, all right?"

Timmy repeated it quietly. "Jesus Hates a Pussy." Carlos and Pops said it together.

Rudy said, "All right then, Jesus Hates a Pussy. Now let's get the fuck out of here!"

It worked. We rode out. To call what followed white-knuckle would be like calling a severed leg a scratch. Rudy put Pops and Timmy, both fearless, hard riders, at the back and told them to choke it up. Carlos and I held on for dear life. We stayed within two feet of the bike in front of us and rode like a chain through a jumbled crank box. Cars flew past at obscene angles as we banked our massive Harleys over the Phoenix freeways. Twilight gave way to nighttime. The lights coagulated in smears of orange, red, and white. The sound ate into our legs and asses and chests, and before we knew it, the machines clicked like they were breathing. It was my first real ride, there was no question about it.

We pulled into a Circle K south of Mesa proper. Timmy and Pops went in to buy Red Bulls and cigarettes.

Carlos said to no one in particular, "Muh-ther luh-ver! We're gonna die on these fucking things. You know that, right?"

It certainly felt that way. The hogs were exhilarating death traps. Period.

Rudy said, "That was better." He patted my thigh.

Slats called and also said, "That was better."

I told him thanks and that we were getting ready to head over. He said the wire was running and the cover team was already in place. They could be at the clubhouse, Ithaca pump-action shotguns blazing, inside of forty-five seconds. I said cool and hung up.

Civilians looked at us from the corners of their eyes. I smiled at one woman and her ten-year-old. She turned the boy's shoulders away from the group of scary-looking men I was a part of, hustling him toward their car. For the first time in days I thought of my son, Jack.

I'd missed a lot of my kids' milestones. The worst was when I was working a casino bombing case in Vegas and I missed Jack's first steps. Gwen called and left a message as soon as it happened. I couldn't pick up the phone because I was in a piece-of-shit undercover car with our suspect and my partner, Vincent Cefalu, cruising around the Las Vegas fringe looking for a place to have tacos while we talked about a plastic explosives deal. That's the kind of thing I've habitually traded the most precious moments of my life for.

The woman with the little boy put her car in gear and pulled out in a quick, sharp arc, her axle whining. We hung around the parking lot a little while longer and Rudy said let's go. We all said Jesus Hates a Pussy, and we went.

9. FIRST NIGHT IN MESA

THE MESA CLUBHOUSE was in a residential neighborhood. A single-level ranch with a carport on the west side, fronted by a shoulder-high cinderblock wall painted white and topped with red roofing tiles. A large palo verde tree shot up from behind the wall. An open chain-link fence with red plastic strips woven into the links could be closed to seal the driveway. Twin Death Heads faced each other over the porch, engaged in a nonstop stare-down. Painted between them in the flared Hells Angels typeface was the red word MESA.

Five Hells Angels came out to greet us. Rudy called them Ghost, Trigger, Bighead, Stroker Dave, and Rockem, who was a prospect. All were armed with guns, and each carried a favorite fighting tool: a Buck knife, hammer, sap, or set of brass knuckles. They led us to a side entrance. Rudy entered with Trigger, and I followed Ghost, who wore a ballistic vest. When he reached the door, he turned, put a hand on my chest, and said, "Sorry, Bird. Those gotta stay outside." He pointed at my Glocks.

We had to keep our guns; if the Angels wouldn't allow us the freedom to carry, then the case simply could not progress. Our thinking was that if we relinquished our guns we'd be doing ourselves a disservice. If we said OK, we'll leave them behind, but just this once, then they might have wondered if we were the badasses we claimed to be. That couldn't happen. Every word and action had to be devoted to gaining credibility. We decided we'd insist on staying armed—the alternative wouldn't just be foolish, it would look weak. It's a cliché, but it's especially true for undercover operators: You can only make one first impression.

I said, "Ghost, no disrespect, man, but I don't take my guns off for anyone, not even HA. It's nothing personal, it's just that we're just like you." Ghost looked over my shoulder. "My boys will say the same thing." Carlos, Timmy, and Pops nodded solemnly.

Ghost frowned and cocked his head. I couldn't get a bead on his eyes because, even though it was nighttime, he wore dark wraparound shades. I had on a pair of clear prescription wraparounds that were good for night riding. He took his hand off my chest and grunted, "Uh-huh."

I continued, "Hells Angels ain't the only ones with enemies, dude. We got 'em too. If you insist we disarm, then we'll gladly wait for our P out here. You know Rudy can't carry, and if you guys were to get ambushed by those Mongol faggots, then we need to be with him to protect him."

Ghost said, "OK, Bird, I hear you, but I don't make—"

"—the rules." The voice slithered from beyond the threshold. It was Bad Bob.

Robert Johnston Jr., at six foot five and 230 pounds, took up the entire doorway. I recalled his rap sheet: arrests for extortion, assault, reckless endangerment, narcotics distribution, and felon in possession of a firearm; felony convictions for criminal enterprise, RICO, and, of course, felon in possession of a firearm. His appearance said something else. He had a neat, round, brown and yellow goatee and long, healthy brown hair that fell onto his shoulders in waves. You could tell he took pride in his grooming. He looked like Barry Gibb's badass, long-lost brother. He had a barrel chest and catcher's mitts for hands. His leather vest, which was tastefully adorned by dozens of patches, parted around his round torso. He looked down on us, beaming.

He repeated, "I make the rules." His drooping brown eyes looked like they'd seen enough. I sometimes thought I'd seen enough too, but I didn't have drooping brown eyes. Mine were blue and lit-up. With Bad Bob I figured, He's a Hells Angel, how many times has he really feared for his life? Not as many times as I had. Bad Bob said, "It's OK, Ghost. These guys are OK. They're our guests." He opened his long arms and we all moved up the stairs.

As we walked into the main room, Trigger latched a series of deadbolts behind us. It didn't feel so much like we were being locked in, but that the rest of the world was being locked out. We'd taken steps that we'd never be able to take back. The sense of the unknown was almost crippling—*almost*. Sure, we'd kept our guns, but all that guaranteed was that we could fight back.

I lit a cigarette to cloak my fear. I told myself that this was it. I didn't know how yet, or who would do it, or if it would happen then or later, but I was suddenly convinced I'd die in a Hells Angels clubhouse.

We were inside.

There was a bar on one side with a small triangular stage wedged next to it. A twelve-foot-long Death Head painted on one wall, an adjacent wall covered with trophies and memorabilia. A jukebox, two TVs, and a red neon sign that buzzed HELLS ANGELS. The windows were either boarded or covered by red-and-white vertical blinds. The place smelled like a bar. Steppenwolf played on the juke.

At least one person had already been killed on the floor of the Mesa clubhouse. In the following month, ATF would finally learn why Mesa Mike had decided to turn on his brothers. On October 25, 2001, a forty-something woman named Cynthia Garcia was partying with the boys at Mesa. During the course of that night she had the drunken balls to insult the Angels on their home turf—a major no-no. She was beaten unconscious by patched members Mesa Mike and Kevin Augustiniak and a prospect, Paul Eischeid. She lay sprawled out on the clubhouse floor while her assailants got drunker and higher. When she came to, she had the temerity to disrespect them again for beating up an unarmed woman. They lit into her, this time with steel-toed vigor. It was a textbook case of them feeding off each other for each other, as Slats so accurately put it.

Mesa Mike, Augustiniak, and Eischeid hauled the body, which was still technically alive, into the carport and dumped it in the trunk of a car. They drove Garcia out to the desert. They did some off-roading. They dragged her into the brush. She grabbed a cuff of Mike's pants.

Eischeid had an old Buck knife. It wasn't sharp. They stabbed her repeatedly. They took turns trying to cut off her head, which they wanted to leave on a fencepost for the vultures. Her spine gave them trouble. They hacked and wedged the knife's point into the vertebra, but it remained stubborn.

Cynthia Garcia, a mother of two, had made a bad decision, and she was dead for it.

Unable to take the guilt, Mesa Mike flipped.

I looked at the floor as we walked in. At the time, I knew that Mesa Mike had a secret, but I didn't know what it was. The floor was clean and white.

I told Bad Bob that I liked their place and that I liked that he kept it trim. He smoothed the front of his vest, thanked me, and directed us to the bar and told Rockem to serve drinks. Bud bottles and shots of Jack. We all did the shots, and the glasses got refilled. Bad Bob gave Rudy a piece of paper.

Bad Bob went behind the bar and rummaged through a shoebox. He found what he was looking for and closed the box and put it back under the bar. He fanned out a handful of HAMC support stickers and patches.

"I want you guys to take these. Put them on your bikes, your vests."

We took them and said thank you.

Carlos asked Rockem why they called him that. He said I got a brother called Sockem. Carlos asked so you're Rockem and Sockem? Rockem said yeah. He said we like to fight. Carlos said I like to fight too.

Bad Bob said Rockem was an America West pilot, a dude with a warped mind devoted to free pussy. Bad Bob lamented that we hadn't been there the night before. Rockem, whose name was Ralph, had brought a female flight crew to the clubhouse so they could put on a show. He said they rolled in with their pencil skirts and bad stockings and before anyone knew it they were all-the-way drunk and twirling around in their underwear. Pops said he would've liked to have seen that. Bad Bob said stick around and you will. He said one of the girls did a lot more than work the floor. Ghost and Trigger giggled like schoolboys. Trigger pumped his fist in the air as if he were pulling the cord that sounded the horn of a big rig.

This is the universal biker sign for gang bang.

My phone rang. I had the ringtone set to Nelly's "E.I.," which confused the Angels. To put it lightly, Hells Angels don't like black people or rap music. The only Nelly they know is Willie Nelson.

I ignored them. I flipped open as Nelly spat, *Somebody probably jealous cause they bitch got hit—*

"Yeah, Bird." I answered the phone the same way every time.

It was Jack. "Hi, Daddy."

I said, "Whassup? Big Lou there?" That was our code for "Put your mother on the phone."

Jack said, "Hold on."

"Cool, dude. Let me talk to him."

Gwen got on the line. I heard Jack running away, yelling something to the dog. Gwen said, "You're busy."

"Hellooo. What's shakin'?" I mashed out my smoke in a glass ashtray and lit another. I got a perverse enjoyment from talking to Gwen when I shouldn't have been. Like the bullet that had once punctured my chest, Gwen's voice gave me a feeling of invincibility.

Gwen said, "You're smoking."

I didn't say anything. I took another pull and exhaled into the mouthpiece.

"I wish you wouldn't do that. It's disgusting." Her dad had succumbed to smoking-induced emphysema. She was serious.

"I know. What's up?"

"Nothing. Jack and Dale just wanted to make sure you were coming home this weekend."

I paused to make it seem like I was getting instructions. I nodded and said, "Right." On the other end, Gwen hummed the *Jeopardy* tune. Then I said, "You got it, Big Lou. Nothing I'd rather do more. Nothing at all. You can count on me."

"Good. See you then. I love you."

"Right. Me too." Gwen made a kissing noise and hung up. "Right. They won't know what hit 'em. I'll contact you when the gig is up. Right. Later."

I flipped shut and put the phone on the bar. As I turned back to the boys, Trigger passed me a joint. I took it, but didn't put it to my lips. My cigarette was still going. Trigger asked, "Who was that?"

I told them about Big Lou and went into my Imperial Financial debt-collecting spiel. As I talked, I pulled hits from my cigarette and waved my arms around so much they mostly forgot about the joint. We were all various degrees of drunk, anyway. I stuffed the joint in my mouth, not inhaling, and drew out a business card. I handed it to Rudy, who handed it to Bad Bob. He looked at it and slid it into an inside pocket. Pops's eyes craved the weed. He said, "Bird, you gonna Bogart that roach all night or you gonna share?" I pulled the joint from my mouth, exhaled the remainder of some Marlboro smoke, and passed it to Pops, who covered me by coolly taking a long pull.

Real cops can't do drugs unless our lives depend on it. If, down the line, a defense attorney got wind of any drug use—or any sexual misconduct, or a short temper, or anything that might make us look like assholes—then they could discredit us as witnesses. We were, after all, professional liars who constantly misrepresented ourselves—a fact every half-witted defense attorney never let a jury forget. But Pops, our paid informant who was in no way a bona fide law enforcement officer, was our narcotic exception. He was in a gray area, and he partook sparingly to serve our purposes.

Bad Bob said, "Sounds like a good job, Bird."

"Yeah, well, pays the bills. Keeps the lawn green and all of that."

"Good stuff. I got a good job too." We knew Bad Bob worked at a car dealership. Trigger passed Bad Bob the joint and he inhaled sharply. He looked bored. Out of the blue he said, "Hey, let's hit Spirits."

We went outside, assed up, and started our engines.

Rudy wasn't lying; the Mesa boys rode like fearless banshees on crack. Jesus Christ himself could not have ridden a motorcycle better, faster, or tighter than Mesa. True to Rudy's warning, they kept no more than eighteen inches off the wheel in front of them—and they were often closer than that. By the time the lead riders had banked into a turn, the guy three bikes back had already leaned his shoulder into the thin air. They moved like a snake chasing a rabbit through its burrow. They blew lights and ignored traffic. The rabbits—everyone who wasn't on a chromed-out Harley-Davidson, everyone who was ensconced in the "cage" of a car or truck, everyone unfortunate enough to be a pedestrian, everyone who was not a Hells Angel—ran scared. We rode like no one's business but our own mattered, which is the way the Hells Angels always ride, because no one else's business *does* matter.

Spirits, in northern Gilbert, was Mesa's spot. There were parking spots permanently reserved for the boys, right near the entrance where the bouncers—two lumps built like ice cream trucks—could keep an eye on them.

Bad Bob led us in. I wasn't quite inside, but I could hear the music come to an abrupt halt. Then a bad Michael Buffer impersonator boomed over the PA:

"This is Good Time Charlie the Outlaw DeeJay here to tell you we got more Heeeeeelllllllsssssss Angeeeeeellllllllssss in the Housssssssssssse-ah!" Spotlights hit the entrance as we walked in. "Baaaaaaad Bahhhhh-hhhhhhb! And his Angels broooooohhhhhhhhhhssss!!!!!!" The crowd, which was respectable but not enormous, parted like the Red Sea for Moses. As we Solos walked in, the DJ added, "And guests!!!!!!"

The music—"Enter Sandman" by Metallica—fired back up. It was like stage night, and I thought, All that's missing is the smoke pots.

Even for a guy who'd played to stadiums full of screaming football fans, I had to admit that this ceremony felt good. It must've felt incredible to the Angels. These were guys who, if they didn't have the Death Head stitched to their backs, would be broke-dick drifters sitting alone at the end of the bar counting quarters to see if they could afford another can of Bud. Instead, the drinks were free and the women lined up. This goes a long way toward explaining the appeal of joining the Hells Angels: It's where guys of a certain stripe go to feel good about themselves. Once members, they are offered universal respect—which they undoubtedly deserve since they are, as a group, a fearsome bunch. They get treated like kings because in their world they *are* the kings. And since they are instantly recognizable wherever they go, they get this respect everywhere. Their world travels with them and for them, a bubble made of leather and motorcycles.

We were led to a VIP area that was occupied by a few other Angels and a snarl of scantily clad women. Some were attractive, some looked like mudflaps on a snowy day in March. We were introduced.

After the intros, we broke up. Timmy periodically checked on our bikes and talked with the bouncers, Pops hung with Ghost, and I huddled with Rudy and Bad Bob.

"I know you been doing business with Cruze down in Tucson," said Bad Bob.

Rudy said, "I'm glad you do. If you didn't, it'd mean he wasn't on the level, and that'd mean I'd have to stop working with him."

"It's my business to know these things."

I said, "It sure as shit is."

Bad Bob puffed up. "That's right." He turned to me. "I want you to know you can do your thing with Cruze and whoever else with my permission. So long's I know about it, it's cool. Man's gotta put bread on the table." An unknown prospect brought each of us a brown bottle of beer. The bottles were sweating, their labels peeling.

Bad Bob swigged his beer. He was reading from the script. We all were. He said, "I hear good things about you, Bird. Only good things." A little ball formed in my stomach, but Bad Bob smiled and it went away. He appeared to trust us. A more astute criminal might have caught the implication of those words: Sometimes the personas we undercover cops create are *too* good. I hoped this wasn't the case. I hoped we weren't moving too quickly. Bad Bob said, "I gave Rudy a list of phone numbers. We can help you. You can help us."

"You're talking about the Mongols."

"I am. But we prefer 'Girls.'"

"OK. I got your back on those bitches. Me or my boys see any of them—down in Nogales, on some dirty cactus road, in a fucking Mexicali saloon, wherever—you'll be the first to know."

"Thank you, Bird."

"Don't mention it."

He didn't.

We went back to the clubhouse around 1:00 a.m. In spite of being drunk, the boys still rode tight and fast. Stroker Dave was in front of us, and at one point he spread-eagled his arms and legs. He looked like a four-pointed star doing 90 mph down the Superstition Freeway. Timmy looked at me and shook his head. I knew what he meant. I was exhausted, and we still had to write reports and get up the next day and do it all over again. And it wasn't even that late. We were still warming up.

Rockem served another round of Jacks and Buds at the clubhouse. I poured back the shot and nursed the beer. Then I said we have to go. Bad Bob, ever the host, asked, "You sure you're good to get home?" I thought he was going to offer a ride with a designated driver. Instead, he removed a plastic Ziploc filled with white powder from behind the bar. "'Cause I can offer you each a little road bump if you need to fly right."

Pops said he was reformed, Rudy said he'd already had some, I said that Timmy and Carlos and I had a job early in the morning, and that I'd had enough of that stuff for three lifetimes. Bad Bob shrugged. "Suit yourselves. I'll see you soon."

Yeah. Soon.

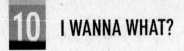

10 I WANNA WHAT?

AUGUST 2002

HELLS ANGELS LIVE for their club and their brothers. One of their credos is "Step down or aside for no man, no law, no God." They are free men unto themselves. At the root of this liberty is the experience of riding a bike. Their Harley-Davidsons are the vehicles of their emancipation. Emancipation from society's rules and expectations; from a life of work and obligations; from other men, wives, girlfriends, and family. Of course, they have jobs and wives and girlfriends, but these things are secondary to their status as Hells Angels. The things that the rest of us depend on for safety and consistency were never there for these men. They're outcasts. The way they see it is, why should they return any favors?

For these men it is the smallest of steps from outcast to outlaw.

The irony is that while their appearance and lifestyle are clearly set up in opposition to those of us who live straight lives, they are hardly distinguishable from one another. Their individuality is confined by a rigid conformity. All wear the same kind of clothing, ride the same brand of bike, and adhere to the same set of club rules. All must report once a week to "church" meetings, and all must pay monthly dues. The cuts forever remain the property of the club, as do the "skin patches," the tattoos that each new member must receive. If for whatever reason a brother quits the club, then the Hells Angels are bound to go to his residence and remove every article of clothing, furniture, and memorabilia that contain any reference to the Hells Angels—not merely to punish and divest him, but because the stuff simply is not his. If the man in question leaves on good terms, his skin patch gets an "out" date; if he leaves on bad terms, then those tattoos are carved off—in some cases taken back with a cheese grater, or with a clothes iron on the linen setting.

I eventually learned from Skull Valley Angels Teddy Toth and Bobby Reinstra, whom I had not yet met in August of 2002, that the Hells Angels' rules were legion and covered damn near everything. They made a D-I football playbook look like a pamphlet on buying a Jacuzzi. The Hells Angels have rules that govern their bikes, their appearance, their behavior, their old ladies, their engagement in criminal activity, their handling of rivals. If you become a Hells Angel, everything else about you becomes moot. You're no longer John J. Johnson—you're a brother. A soldier. A unit of fear. A spoke on a wheel of violence. Drinks become free, and pussy is never more than a dick's length away. You're the rock star and *both* of his bodyguards rolled into one. You're suddenly capital-R *Respected*. If you're done wrong by someone, the whole club is duty-bound to do wrong back to that person.

For example, see Cynthia Garcia, God rest her soul.

In spite of all this, they apparently lacked a rule that prevented us from gaining easy access. That or Bad Bob was gullible or desperate enough to vouch for us statewide within a week of our visiting Mesa that first night—which is exactly what he did.

We were exploiting one of the Angels' few weaknesses. In the wake of Laughlin they needed allies and potential recruits. They looked at us and saw kindred spirits, guys who were tough, cautious, business-minded, and willing to use violence. The Mongols situation was real and the Angels, while prepared for their adversaries, could never be prepared enough. The bottom line was that the Hells Angels knew a good thing when they saw it, and we were a good thing.

The day after our first Mesa visit, I made sure to call home ASAP. The next morning I rolled over in bed, opened my phone, and dialed home. I told my kids I was sorry I couldn't have been with them the

night before. I told them they were the most important things to me in
the entire world, and that I'd never cut them short if my life hadn't
depended on it. I told them I loved them. Then I told them I loved
them again. I told them that I was their father before I was anything
else. I wasn't naïve enough to tell them what I was doing I was doing for
them, but I was naïve enough to believe my own lies.

I apologized to Gwen for having to pretend she was a mobster.

"No worries, honey. It's not the first time it's happened. I know it
won't be the last. Besides, like I said, it gives me some kind of a rush."

"I like hearing your voice too. When I'm around guys like that."

"It's the closest I ever get to visiting you at work." She laughed. Gwen
has a way of laughing at jokes she makes for her own benefit, whether
they're funny or not. It's something I've always loved about her.

Fair or not, I've always kept her out of my work. I needed to know
that my family was distinct from my job, that the two would never
cross into one another. I didn't have the heart to tell them the ugly
secrets the world had shown me, and I needed to believe that decent
families like mine were what I was fighting for. I needed sanctuary,
which is exactly what they'd been for me.

I wanted to go back to them, but first we had to do a gun deal that
Rudy'd set up. It was in no way associated with the Angels, but it was all
part of the show, so we saddled up.

The deal was in Apache Junction. The neighborhood was a blank,
garbage-strewn expanse of neglected suburbia, which is too kind a term
for it. Not a lawn in sight. Dotted with dilapidated trailers. Rubble and
litter and dust everywhere. Vast, worthless, vacant lots. One of those
broken places on the fringe of what we think of as America, but which
is every bit American.

Carlos, Timmy, Rudy, and I pulled up to a white trailer around five
in the afternoon. Carlos brought up the rear. He lost control of his bike
a little and skidded to a stop, nearly bowling me and my bike over. No
harm done: We laughed. Rudy put his head in his hand. He still
couldn't believe how lame his crew members were at handling their
bikes. I couldn't half blame him.

There was a white, late-model BMW 325i with filthy, illegible license
plates in the driveway, along with three cars on blocks. On the porch of
the trailer was a ratty, stained love seat. Sprawled across the love seat was
a shirtless man with tattoos of a pentagram around his bulging belly-

button, a hand with its middle finger extended over his heart, and a necklace of satanic-looking letters. He was passed out. Around his right wrist was a hospital outpatient band.

Rudy said, "That's Nathan."

A woman opened the door. "Hey, Rudy."

"Hey, sweetie."

Sweetie was the last word that came to mind as I gazed on a classic meth tramp: lined face, shattered teeth, sunken eyes, bleach blond hair, her waist bulging over her cutoffs.

"Hey. This your crew, huh? I'm Iwana."

All I could think was, I wanna what? I lit a cigarette.

I should have had sympathy for people like Iwana, but the simple truth was that I didn't. After a certain age, after so many miles, after so much drugs—and after I'd seen so many people like her in my work—it was easier to think of people like her as lost causes. I knew this was a convenient lie I told myself. I wouldn't hesitate for a second to use a person like Iwana as a snitch if I thought she could be useful. Rudy was a prime example of just this kind of arrangement. What we dangled in front of him was not merely a pass on jail but a final way out. Often the opportunity to flip—and be remade in relocation—was the ultimate chance in a life of repeated disappointments. All involved silently agreed that these changes were unlikely—cops held them out as fantasies, and perps clung to the hope that there was something pure left in their hearts. We knew that even with the best intentions, the odds were stacked against the Iwanas and Rudys of the world. Habits die hard, money is tough to come by, and temptation is a bitch.

A kid appeared at Iwana's bare thigh and tugged at her shirt. It was a boy, maybe five years old. He looked as though he hadn't bathed in days.

Iwana swiped at him and said, "Not now, Dale, we have guests!" He ran away.

He shared my daughter's name. My heart sank as he hung his head and scampered off.

We went inside. There were two others—Rudy intro'd them as Mark and Sharon. Sharon said, "I'm Nathan's old lady." She added, "He OD'd last night."

No shit.

Timmy asked, "He need anything?"

"Naw. They already gave him some stuff."

Rudy said, "Mark's your guy," and we went with him. He led us to a dark, one-room apartment that could only be accessed from the backyard, where little Dale rolled a tire around. As Carlos and Timmy followed Mark, I went up to the kid.

I said, "Whatcha got there?"

He stopped, the tire twirled to the ground. Dale said, "You wanna see the new toy Nathan got me?"

"Sure, kiddo, where's it at?" I expected him to tug me around the side of the house to show me a Big Wheel or a Slip 'N Slide or a Super Soaker. Instead he walked up to the tire, knelt, tilted it up, and pushed it toward the side of the trailer. It hit the wall and twirled to the ground once again.

Dale turned to me, smiling genuinely. "Pretty cool, huh?"

I smiled. It hurt. "Yeah, that's great, kiddo. I gotta go talk to Mark."

"OK. Later, mister."

Later, I thought. I added myself to the long list of people who had abandoned him.

Inside the apartment, Mark was handing Timmy an H&R .410 sawed-off shotgun. He told us Rudy had already given him fifty bucks for it. I looked for Rudy and asked Timmy where he was. He shrugged. Timmy cracked the gun to confirm it was unloaded, then snapped it shut.

"I got this too." Mark faced a low counter and his back blocked what was on it. He wheeled around, brandishing an AK-47.

Carlos, who was off to Mark's side, said, "Whoa!" and grabbed the rifle's wooden grip. I put a hand on the rubber stock of one of my Glocks, but didn't draw.

Mark said, "Chill! It ain't loaded!"

Carlos pointed the barrel up. "Yeah, heard that before. It's all fun and games until someone puts an eye out." I released my pistol.

Mark said, "I thought you guys might be interested in this. Damn. That's what you do, right? Buy guns?"

I said, "We buy certain guns, dude. Let's have a look."

Mark handed it to Carlos, who exited the apartment to inspect it in the remaining sunlight. It was Chinese, no serial number, no magazine, nothing in the chamber. It was in bad shape and probably hadn't been fired since before it left Beijing on a cargo boat.

"I'll give it to you for a hundred dollars. That's a hell of a deal."

"We know what's a deal and what ain't," said Carlos. "This is shit, a relic. Mount it on your wall and tell people your dad was in Korea or something."

I said, "There you have it. We'll stick with the shotgun. Anything else?" I wanted to get out of there.

Mark said, "I don't think so. Let's go ask Nathan." We humored him. All of a sudden I wanted a taco. Good taco stands in Apache Junction.

When we got back to the trailer's living room, Sharon and Nathan were on the floor. Nathan moaned and Sharon appeared to be trying to help him. Rudy and Iwana were nowhere to be seen.

Timmy asked what happened.

Sharon looked over her shoulder. Her eyes were wide and desperate, like she'd just flung herself off a balcony. "He fell down."

Nathan said, "Fuck that."

From a back room a woman screamed, "Yes. Fuck. Oooh, yes. Yes. Yes! YES!"

The kid wandered into the room and stopped in front of me. No one said anything to him. He was bored. He'd seen it all before.

I felt filthy. I moved out of the boy's way. He passed, leaving the room.

Nathan still lay on the ground. I pointed at the pentagram on his stomach. "What's with the tattoo?"

He sat up. "This?" He grabbed his belly with both hands and shook it like a Jell-O ring. "I'm the fucking devil, man."

"Really?" asked Carlos. Timmy huffed. "Well, you got any guns you want to sell us, Beelzebub?"

"I got a pistol in the car. Shit, I'll *give* it to you."

Mark said, "Fuck that, Nathan. These guys deal." He turned to us. "I'll go get it." He left. Timmy took a knee next to Nathan and asked if he had to go back to the hospital. Nathan said fuck no. I asked him if he was hungry. He said you got a line for me? I didn't say anything to that.

Mark came back holding a greasy rag. He unwrapped it, careful not to let his fingers come in contact with the pistol, which was a very small, battleship-gray .22 derringer. Carlos took it, unloaded and inspected it. Carlos said, "This isn't a gun, it's a paperweight."

Timmy looked at it and laughed.

"How much you want for that?" I asked. It wasn't worth more than ten bucks.

Nathan said, "Twenty."

Sharon said, "Fuck that. Just take it."

Nathan said, "No, Mark said these guys deal." He looked at me. "Twenty bucks."

Sharon got up and pleaded, "Please, take it." Apparently she didn't want the devil to be armed. Timmy helped Nathan to his feet. He took two steps toward Sharon and slapped her hard across the face. "I'm sell-ing that fucking gun if they want it, OK?" Sharon started hitting Nathan on his shoulders and chest with both hands. He reeled back a little, but was otherwise unfazed. Timmy got between them. They calmed down just as quickly as they'd started up.

I lit another cigarette and took a deep pull. The thought drifted through my mind of my blue pool in my shady backyard with my great kids playing in it before they ate the dinner their mom had cooked for them.

This was bullshit. I started to leave.

I didn't see Carlos give Nathan twenty bucks in exchange for the der-ringer. I addressed Mark. "Well, that about takes care of everything. We're gonna wait outside for Rudy. Nice doing business with you, dude."

"You too."

As we were leaving, two small girls appeared in the adjacent kitchen. Neither one was older than four. They both looked scared and hungry. The younger clung to the older, who clung to a naked, hairless plastic doll. I wanted to take the kids outside, call social services, come back inside, and beat all of these people to a pulp.

As I stood staring at these little creatures, Nathan and Sharon started to get into it again. Apparently, Sharon didn't want Nathan accepting any money for the gun. I asked Carlos if he'd paid for it, unaware that he had. Carlos said, "Sure, I gave him the money, it's only twenty bucks."

I said, "Fuck that, if she wants us to have it, then we're just going to take it." I took the twenty dollars that clung to Nathan's fingertips. I didn't want to give these assholes any money to blow up their noses so they could not feed their children. I pointed at the two girls, whom Carlos hadn't noticed. He looked at them, looked at Nathan, looked at Sharon, and said let's get the fuck out of here. Timmy was already open-ing the door.

We went to the bikes. When we were out of earshot I said, "Jesus Christ."

"Motherfuckers." Carlos rubbed his cheek.

Timmy leaned against his bike. We were all pissed. We weren't here to stand by while Rudy fucked a meth whore. Minutes passed.

Timmy said, "Sun's still strong." It was almost six, but it didn't matter. He took out a tube of sunscreen and placed it on his handlebars. He took off his T-shirt, squeezed some cream into his hand, and started rubbing it into his chest. "Got aloe in it. Cools you off."

Carlos asked, "Really?" and peeled off his shirt too.

I took off mine. We all started to rub it in. Carlos asked if I'd do his back. We laughed uneasily. We'd seen it all before too, but that didn't make it any easier. We still wanted to forget. I did his back. He did mine. We laughed a little harder, a little easier.

Rudy walked out of the house, buckling his belt. Iwana stood on the porch, waving like a wife whose husband was off to work. He walked up to us—three bikers rubbing sunscreen into each other on a hot Phoenix night.

"What the fuck?"

I asked, "What the fuck with you?"

"Had to get a piece. You know how it is. These hens can't get enough of this old rooster."

I didn't like Rudy's behavior, but I couldn't call him out on the spot. I had to maintain the appearance that he was the president of my club. I wanted to tell him he had to stop acting the way he was acting. I wanted to push him out of the way, march back into the trailer, and arrest the losers we'd just dealt with. But I couldn't. An undercover constantly trades his or her ethics for the greater good of a case.

I knew this kind of thing wouldn't stop on its own, though. Barely two months on the job and Rudy needed to be reined in. Old dog, old tricks.

New problem.

11 WHY'D JACK GIVE ME THAT ROCK?

THE NEXT DAY was Saturday. I went home. I needed to.

When I pulled into the driveway, my job was jammed inside me like a kidney stone.

It dissipated quickly.

I was greeted at the door by a postcard: my wife, my children, a dog. Smiles and waves and hugs. The weekend passed in a blissful flash. The kids laughed around the pool, Gwen pointed me to the yard work. I love yard work. Everything is self-evident and rewarding. The lawn needed a trim, I trimmed it. There were flowers on the verge of the backyard that needed pruning, I pruned them. I put some of the clippings in a Southwest-style vase—red desert pottery painted royal blue with yellow sun discs—and put them in the middle of our heavy oaken table. I played flashlight tag with Jack and Dale on the golf course, we went to the movies, we played chicken in the pool. That weekend the heavyweight burdens of the job succumbed to the featherweight joys of home life.

Gwen's birthday was coming up, and we knew I wasn't going to make it—I had to go to San Diego for an ATF training session—so one night all the grandparents came over for dinner. Gwen broiled shrimp and I grilled T-bones. We talked about Jack starting slow-pitch baseball that fall. No more T-ball. My dad said I'd teach him all about getting it going under pressure. I said hell yeah, I would. We talked about what I'd do in San Diego, and I said aside from listening to lectures and hanging out with my partners, I was going to surf.

At night, in bed, I'd run through the case in my head. We'd made good progress, but I was still insecure. The fear I'd felt as we rolled up to Mesa was subsiding and beginning to congeal into confidence, but I still wanted to take it pretty slow. We'd go full-bore later, once we knew that we had a reasonable chance of getting away with riskier questions and activities. If you don't wait until you have enough credibility, then cases can go bad fast.

My most recent bad experience was on a Sons of Silence case. The Sons were a minor biker gang in Colorado Springs. We were running around as a made-up club called the Unforgiven—all the members were cops, our center patch was Saint Michael—and we wanted to further demonstrate that the Sons used intimidation and the threat of violence to maintain their turf. If we could do this, we could roll it into the RICO case being built against them. We wanted to do it that night by putting the screws to them, by hanging out in their place and showing them up. They were small-time and my confidence was high.

My partners, John "Babyface" Carr and Chris "Chrisser" Bayless, accompanied me to their bar. We sat in their place and drank and waited. We didn't have to wait long.

A guy asked me who I was and I told him I was the Unforgiven, who the fuck are you? He said he was the Warlord for the Sons of Silence. I lied and told him I'd never heard of them. He knew I was full of shit. He said we needed to take off our cuts, sit tight, and wait for the ass-beating that was on its way from his brothers. I told him fuck you, we stay or leave when I feel like it, not when ordered.

That was stupid. The place was suddenly pin-drop quiet. The only sound was the deadbolts turning on the front door.

Most of the time, after taking a beating, a man will bullshit about how big the other guy was, how he didn't have a chance in hell. I'm no small fry, but this guy was legitimately huge. According to the marshal's processing, he was six foot six and a shade under 300 pounds.

He reeled back and hit me with a no-shit-for-real knockout punch.

My head whipped like a rag doll's. Babyface later told me that as the guy hit me he watched my eyes roll into the back of my head. I fell, and the only thing that kept me on my feet was a column in the middle of the bar.

Not five seconds later, Babyface was chicken-winged while Chrisser and I fought for our lives as the whole bar whaled on us—guys, chicks, everyone. Pool cues, shot glasses, steel-toed boots, flashlights. We had a couple guys locked outside who eventually came in and helped put a stop to it, but we took a licking. We'd made such an impression that when the Sons' president learned of the fight, he said, "I don't know who those dudes are, but they should be in our club." The only price I had to pay for that kind of respect was pissing grape juice for about a week.

That's why I love yard work, and I had plenty of it that August weekend.

But the weekend had to end, and as I loaded the Merc, Jack ran up to me. He looked up and held out his hand, giving me a small, smooth rock from the backyard. He placed it in my palm and folded my fingers over it. He held my fist in his hands. It was a mature gesture for an eight-year-old. I wondered what exactly the rock was for as I smiled at Jack, but I didn't ask. I pocketed it and kissed his hair and left.

THE TRIP TO San Diego was a week away, and before we left, I had to see Smitty.

Throughout the Riverside case I'd run with Sugarbear, I'd maintained that I was *not* a One Percenter. As far as Smitty knew, I was a freelance roughneck. I was afraid he'd be suspicious when I revised my line and told him that I'd been a Solo Angeles Nomad all along.

I knew Bad Bob had called Smitty and told him that the Solos were a new club with permission to fly their colors in Arizona. When Smitty told Bad Bob he knew who I was and that I was no One Percenter as far as he knew, Bad Bob assured him I was on the level. He agreed with Smitty that I should've told the truth from the beginning, but he vouched for me in the same breath, saying that my dishonesty would be compensated for by my loyalty. Smitty told him fine, but he still wanted to talk to me.

On August 9, Carlos, Timmy, Pops, and I met Smitty, his wife,

Lydia, and Dennis at the Inferno in Bullhead. We were led upstairs to a private room that had been set up with empty glasses and a few bottles of Crown Royal.

I apologized quickly and said I'd lied out of necessity and respect. I said, "I held out so long because the last thing I wanted to do was challenge the Hells Angels. I'm sorry I wasn't honest, but, hindsight being twenty-twenty, I think it was best for everyone."

Smitty mulled this over. Lydia and Dennis sat off to the side whispering to each other. After a minute or so Smitty cracked the seal of a bottle of Crown and poured out half a dozen shots. When he was finished he looked at each of us with hard eyes. He lifted his glass and indicated we should do the same. We did. He took a sip. As he removed the glass from his lips, he cracked that mile-long grin of his. Even his beard got happy. Smitty put a hand on my shoulder. He wagged his finger at all of us like we'd been bad, bad boys. Then he said, "You did all right, Bird. Not *right*, mind you, but *all* right. From now on you be on the up-and-up with the Eight-Ones and all is forgiven." Eight-Ones was another of their nicknames, referring to the eighth and first letters of the alphabet: H-A.

I choked back my Crown and said, "No sweat, Smitty."

Smitty then launched into his welcome-to-Bullhead speech. He said do your thing. He said I have guns if you want them. Said I got guys all over the state with guns for you. Said I got chicks with guns. To that Carlos cupped his hands and jiggled them in front of his chest and said I hope so! Smitty laughed, his grin never breaking stride, and said not just those kind, but the kind that go pop, too! Carlos said that he'd once had a pair of titties go pop on him. Said it wasn't pretty. We all laughed. Lydia laughed the hardest.

Then, unprompted, Smitty offered up that he had fled California for Arizona after he'd committed an arson. He said he'd torched a bar, an adjacent business, and a motorcycle garage.

"It was just too hot, you know?"

No one pointed out the bad pun.

He went on. "Hey, man, Arizona's good stuff. Good stuff. Sonny's here, Johnny and Hoover and Bad Bob too. Teddy's here. Crow's here. Lots of old-school headbangers. We got this state locked down. Arizona is Red and White through and through. Bad Bob did right. We're thin up here and we're happy to have you. You guys are good fucking stuff.

Now let's go eat dinner." As we left the bar, Smitty flashed the butt of a gun at me with a wink and handed it to Dennis, a convicted felon. Dennis took it and stuffed it in his pants.

We consummated our friendship with burgers, beer, and milkshakes at the Mad Dog Tavern.

Everything was delicious.

Things were going well.

Which meant we were due to hit our first speed bump.

12 TEACHING TEACHER

"THE FUCK DO you mean we're 'not official'?!" It was Slats. He had Rudy in the crosshairs.

Rudy was strung out. His eyes were as beady and black as a teddy bear's.

We were getting ready to go through one of our gauntlet sessions at the Patch. At these get-togethers, undercovers and informants sat at one end of the room while Slats and the support agents grilled us as mock Hells Angels. It was role-playing designed to keep us sharp and in character.

Rudy shuffled and looked down. "I mean, you know, I haven't paid my membership dues."

Slats was livid. "We gave you money, why didn't you pay them? Pops, weren't you down in Tijuana with Rudy?"

Pops said, "Yup."

"And so? Didn't you pay up?"

Pops said calmly, "I thought we did. Rudy handled it."

Slats turned on Rudy. "You get on the level right now or I'm calling the paddy wagon and someone other than Iwana is going to be soaping up your ass tonight."

Rudy spoke into his chest. "It wasn't enough. I owed three years of back dues. They wanted more for the start-up in Arizona. It wasn't enough," he repeated.

Slats stepped close to him, took out a tin of Copenhagen, loaded his mouth, and spoke very quietly. "You unfuck this ASAP, understand?" Rudy watched the ground like he expected it to open up and swallow him whole. Slats continued, "I find out you're blowing the money we give you on crank and trailer-trash pussy, I swear to God Almighty I'll bump you faster than you can say 'recidivist.' Got it?" I leaned into Pops and reminded him quietly, "Dude, don't fuck with Slats on this case." He nodded reassuringly.

Rudy said, "Yeah. But, I might need help."

Slats said, "What. The. Fuck."

That's when Rudy told us that not only were we not official at Solo Angeles world headquarters in Tijuana, Mexico, but that we weren't even supposed to be organized in Arizona. He said it wasn't like they said he *couldn't* do it, it's just that they said he didn't have permission on account of the money he owed.

We had to get creative, fast.

First stop, Los Angeles, Solo Angeles U.S. headquarters, to meet president Dave "Teacher" Rodarte.

Rudy, Carlos, and I went to Rodarte's house and sat down in his living room. At first, Teacher wasn't too happy. He called some of his friends over and we punked them down. He had them wait outside while we told him how it was. We basically cross-arm-eye-fucked the guy into submission. We told him Arizona was already set up and we were sorry we weren't on the level, but we'd promptly take care of whatever Rudy was short on. We said we were doing good and we wouldn't miss another payment, ever. We told him we'd followed local protocols and gotten the blessings of the Hells Angels.

Strong-arming the U.S. president was a risky tactic, but we had to do it that way. We didn't have time to screw around, because if the Angels caught wind that we weren't official with our own damn club, it was going to look fatally suspicious. We also could use it to gain more credibility. The last thing a criminal—even a half-assed biker like Teacher—expects of an undercover cop is to be out-toughed by him. The logic was, yeah, maybe we messed up, but look at us, we're more real-deal than you are, so shut up and give us what we want.

He did.

As a token of our appreciation and commitment, we gave him $500 in cash.

He told us the only catch was we had go to Tijuana immediately to meet with the head Solo, a wiry Mexican-Japanese cat called Suzuki.

Fair enough.

We sent Rudy and Pops down once again. Only God could give us special agents permission to leave terra Americana, and we didn't want to bother God. Our bosses could've also done it, but then they'd probably shut us down for lack of due diligence with Rudy, so that was out too. Before they left I told Pops not to let Rudy screw the pooch. We gave Pops an extra $1,000 that Rudy didn't know about, just in case. Carlos and I went back to Phoenix and waited.

Pops told us about it afterward. He said they were all happy to see Rudy again—all of them except for a Solo named Alberto, who kept to himself and shunned Rudy and Pops. They paid Rudy's back dues and were told that from then on at least one of us would have to come down for their monthly church meetings. We were also ordered to purchase genuine Solo cuts with the Nomads rocker in Spanish—*Nomada*. Lastly, Suzuki demanded that we bring him a Harley Evolution Sportster on our next trip. Rudy and Pops agreed to their demands, but we never bothered to heed them since they couldn't reasonably enforce them. Instead, to maintain our Solo Angeles membership, we kept throwing token amounts of cash at them and never missed another dues payment. By the time the case ended, they'd collected something to the tune of $3,000 from us. Credibility can literally be bought from minor clubs like the Solos.

Pops and Rudy spent the night in a Solos' safe house with security cameras and high walls and a methamphetamine lab on the second floor. Pops couldn't understand a lot of the conversations because they were in Spanish. Before they left, I'd taught him all the Spanish I knew: *Tiro el gringo en la cabaza*—shoot the white boy in the head. That wasn't very useful, so Pops settled down with a few SoCal members and bullshitted with them.

They told him something interesting. They'd heard that there was an undercover cop or informant running with the Red Devils in Tucson, or maybe with the Phoenix metro charter of the Hells Angels. This was a hard-to-crack charter that consisted almost entirely of former Dirty Dozen members, including the dangerous Robert "Chico" Mora, whom Mesa Mike had warned me of at the Florence Prison Run. Pops said thanks and he'd pass it on.

Which is exactly what he did as soon as he got home.

13 FEEDING SMITTY HIS CAKE

THIS INTELLIGENCE COULD'VE referred to Rudy himself, or any of us, or Mesa Mike. It could also have simply been an inconvenient, baseless rumor. Bikers always think they're being infiltrated by someone—it confirms that they're big shots who need to be checked. They don't *want* to be investigated—that'd be a real pain in the ass—but they always want to *believe* they're being investigated.

It's a strange psychology.

The task force discussed the issue at our headquarters, the Patch. Since we couldn't come up with a way to make it work to our advantage, we decided to let it play out. In the meantime we were off to San Diego for our annual undercover operators' conference.

ATF training sessions are not known for their entertainment value, but this one was a blast. The speaker that weekend was Michael Durant, the Black Hawk helicopter pilot who got shot down over Mogadishu, Somalia. His lecture was truly inspirational. The specifics of his ordeal were more harrowing than I could imagine. He spoke at length about the generalities of perseverance in the face of lethal odds—a thing the UCs at the conference understood completely. His words sent a charge through the crowd.

After Durant spoke, I decided to clear my head and hit the surf. I rented a long board and headed down to a popular Mission Beach break. The beach was lined with bars looking over the water. I zipped up my wetsuit and paddled out. I waited with the local kids on the line and caught a few waves.

The ocean did its rejuvenating thing. The salty air erased a carton of cigarettes from my lungs, and the water scrubbed my nicotine-stained fingertips clean.

When I was done, I trotted up the beach to the boardwalk and turned south to where I'd parked my car. As I passed the Lahaina Beach Club bar, I heard shouts of "Baldy! Hey, Baldy!"

I turned to the bar's patio. Sitting in the best seats in the house—in a bar that is notoriously difficult to get good seats at—were Smitty, his wife, Lydia, and Pete Eunice, the Dago Angel we'd met at the Laughlin Flamingo and who'd been a shooter that night at Harrah's.

I walked onto the patio and joined them, leaning my board against the wooden rail of the terrace. Smitty asked what brought me to Dago, and I said I was in the area on a collection and after that I was going down to Tijuana on Solo Angeles business.

After we'd talked for a while, Pete barked, "What the fuck, Bird? You surf?" He said the words as if he were confirming that I'd been to the moon. Things like surfing, especially for the old-school guys like Pete and Smitty, were basically off-limits for Hells Angels.

I said, "Fuck yeah, dude!"

"Where'd you learn?"

"I know these crazy Mexican cats down in Puerto Vallarta, drug dealers. They like to do half a dozen lines and dive in the ocean with their long boards. They get so jacked up that half the time they're just falling into the drink, but they have a hell of a time. They taught me." I'd actually learned while in college.

Pete said, "Crazy wetbacks."

"Yeah, well. They help me out, I help them out. We have a good time. So, you guys here on pleasure?"

"Business and pleasure," answered Smitty. "I got your call. Was gonna get back to you later." He pointed his beer at Pete. "We got some serious club shit to go over. And Lydia came out too, so we could celebrate my birthday." I recalled the Laughlin surveillance tapes showing how Smitty had backed up Pete while Pete plugged away with his pistol. I assumed they were getting their stories straight for when they got served by the grand jury, which hadn't happened yet.

I mentioned that a bunch of friends and I were planning on having dinner later on. I insisted that I treat them to surf-and-turf at Jose's, up in La Jolla. Smitty and Lydia accepted. Pete said he wouldn't be able to make it, but told me to stop by his bar, Dumont's, if I had the time.

I grabbed my board and decided to head back into the water to show them what I could do.

I paddled out and turned around. I could see them as I bobbed up and down, my feet dangling below me in the Pacific. Lydia waved. I couldn't tell if Smitty or Pete did anything, but they were clearly looking in my direction. I waved back—a big, goofy kid's wave. I was having fun sticking it in their faces. I couldn't see the point of being a Hells Angel if it meant you couldn't enjoy things like surfing.

I dropped into a lazy four-foot wave and glided along its face. Before it petered out, I threw the board over the edge of the wave and grabbed the rail and fell into the water. I came up and looked at the bar. Lydia was waving again.

I could even see Smitty's cocky, big-ass granddad's smile from all the way out there.

AS SOON AS they left the bar, I got out of the water and headed to the Holiday Inn where the conference attendees were staying. I grabbed Carlos and we gathered a bunch of agents, including the young female operative who'd been at Laughlin, Jenna "JJ" Maguire. JJ would be my girlfriend for the night.

I knew I'd eventually need a full-time girlfriend on the case. Whoever this woman was, she'd need a take-no-shit mentality in order to survive—and thrive—in the biker world.

There aren't too many female street agents—the ratio of men to women is somewhere in the neighborhood of twenty to one—so we were lucky to meet JJ when we did. JJ's main drawback was that she was a complete greenhorn, but she had a ton of things going for her. She had brains, ambition, a positive and sunny attitude, fearlessness, and self-control. She was also very attractive, which couldn't be overlooked since it was the first thing any Hells Angel was going to notice about her.

I spoke with her a few hours before dinner. I didn't want to pop into the restaurant with her on my arm; I wanted her introduction to look spontaneous. We decided to station her at the bar, where I'd notice her as a onetime flame, and I'd send her a drink and invite her over. This "chance encounter" would give her an out whenever she wanted it—if she got uncomfortable or if I thought she was in over her head, she'd simply excuse herself for having made other plans. It also gave me a good out if Smitty or Lydia decided they didn't like her.

That didn't happen.

Smitty took right to her, first because of her looks and then because of her personality. JJ was all smiles and kept Lydia occupied. I think if she could have, Lydia would've taken her back to Bullhead that night.

Carlos and I intro'd everyone as Solos associates of one kind or another. The team was practiced and professional. They deflected all attention to Smitty and Lydia. All of them told Smitty how honored they were to have the chance to sit down and hang out with a senior Hells Angel, and for his birthday no less.

Smitty happily accepted the attention. He told us he'd been in Vietnam, had killed lots of gooks, and had extensive military training. He made it sound like he was a Ranger, Marine, and SEAL all wrapped into one lethal package. I thought of Scott Varvil, and for a moment it seemed like Smitty was no different from that broke-dick school nurse with the gun and bike fetishes.

But once he got rolling he talked about Laughlin and whispered about how much he hated the Mongols. He told us everything we already knew: that he'd been arrested at Laughlin and was likely to face a murder rap, and that he was still without his dear old cut, which had been impounded. We gasped at this, as if impounding a Hells Angel's cut was not only unreasonable but downright un-American. He appreciated our outrage.

At the end of the night I took the waitress aside and told her to bring cake for everyone, and to put a candle in the slice for the Hells Angel.

The cake was vanilla with white icing, the candle was red. By that point in the evening, JJ sat between me and Smitty. Lydia had gone home relatively early. Smitty smiled and blew out his candle. JJ interrupted his hand and grabbed his fork. She cut into the cake and held a chunk to Smitty's mouth. Smitty took the bite and chewed, smiling all the way. JJ fed him a few more bites. Smitty said, "Shit, my wish just came true."

It was a good performance, one I didn't expect from such a young and inexperienced agent. JJ was a natural.

After dessert, Smitty leaned into my shoulder and asked if I'd do a collection for him in Bullhead. I said sure, no sweat. Smitty also said he had some shit for me when we got home, pulling his finger like he was firing a gun. I said cool, dude, you know me. I said it was too bad we didn't hook up before Dago, since Carlos and I'd be running to Mexico in a couple days. I said he could've had a little extra birthday cash to throw around. He lamented, saying, well, next year, next year.

I doubted that.

WE GOT BACK to Bullhead refreshed and ready to roll.

Slats and I agreed that Smitty's collection was a gift, a perfect opportunity to gain more credibility. In fact, it was ideal since we'd be protecting the guy from an otherwise certain ass-whooping. We decided to slow-play it to see if we could get any more information out of Smitty. We were professionals. I wanted it to look like we knew how deep the pool was before we dove in.

A few days after getting back from Dago, Timmy and I met up with Smitty one evening in the parking lot of the Sand Bar Tavern. We shook hands and Smitty told us to follow his white pickup over to his house.

The Smiths lived in a nice working-class neighborhood of double-wides and simple ranches. Their street was named Swan Road. I liked that.

We pulled up to the house around eight-thirty in the evening. It had been another scorcher—115, 120 degrees. Light still hung in the sky, as if trapped by the heat, and Lydia watered her plants in the front yard. It was a nice yard. Sea-glass wind chimes, eccentric whirligigs, painted stones, and garden gnomes. There was a large neon red-white-and-blue peace sign propped against the side of the house. None of the decorations was expensive-looking.

Lydia waved as we kicked the bikes down. Timmy and I waved back. She looked happy, not strung-out or hungover. She had on dark denim shorts and a light denim shirt knotted below her sternum. Her black hair was pulled back in a ponytail. It was her gardening uniform.

I said, "Hey, Lydia. Yard looks good. Love the gnomes."

"Thanks, Bird. Hey, Timmy."

Timmy said hey and we walked up the wooden steps to the doorway, which was occupied by a beckoning Smitty.

The inside of the trailer was neat and orderly. Angels memorabilia were strewn across the walls and coffee tables—plaques, trophies, framed newspaper clippings and obits, drawings—and in the living area, next to the television, was a single black-and-white monitor whose image was split into quads. Three of the quads had images of the outside of the Smith residence—the fourth was black. Lydia busied herself in the yard in the lower-left section.

Smitty directed us to the dining table while lifting two Coors Lights from the fridge. He passed them out and we each popped one open. He then mixed himself a Crown and Coke. Smitty sat down with us. Lydia walked in and did stuff in the kitchen.

Smitty complained about an argument he'd gotten into at work about a co-worker's son who'd died on a motorcycle Smitty had sold him. He looked into his Crown and Coke like it was an oracle and said, "Man, I been around too much death lately. Laughlin, a brother's son got killed recently, this kid. Too much, man, too much."

We didn't say much. We were tough guys, used to death and death's senselessness. As far as Smitty knew, we were hit men—what did we care about a few random deaths?

He caught on to our indifference, straightened up in his chair, and said, "I don't like death, you know? Unless I'm the cause of it. You know."

He changed the subject and told us about the collection. It was over a disputed eight grand a guy named Porter owed to a woman Smitty kept calling "Crazy Carol." The dispute was currently in court, with Carol as the plaintiff and Porter defending. He gave us a docket number and the guy's home address.

Suddenly, Dennis whisked in without knocking.

No one seemed surprised. Maybe Smitty had caught sight of him on the surveillance system. Dennis moved into the kitchen, got a beer, and settled down. Smitty asked him if he knew this Porter guy, and Dennis said he didn't.

Dennis was sweating and on edge. He took his beer, opened the front door, looked outside in three directions, and walked down the steps.

With Dennis gone, Lydia asked, "Bird, you know what they call Dennis?"

"Nope."

Smitty said, "They call him Chef-Boy-Ar-Dee."

Lydia asked, "You know why they call him that?"

"No. Why?"

"Because he cooks the best rock you can find. The absolute best," said Smitty.

Lydia said, "Make Jesus jealous, his shit's so good."

Dennis came back in. No one asked him anything, but he trilled, "Naw, I don't know no Porter. Why the fuck would I know some Porter guy?"

Smitty said he messed around in the drug game. Dennis ignored him and started to bitch about seven grand he owed the county. Apparently his residence had incurred some taxes while he was in lockup.

Smitty went to the kitchen for another drink. When he returned he said, "You know? I got another thing for you. Bail bonds place has about three hundred grand out and they need it back. They wanted me to help them, but I just can't do it now, not with all this heat from Laughlin. You should take that action, Bird, it could really help set you up."

I lit a cigarette and pretended to think it over. No way could I, a federal agent, start collecting debts from low-lifes for some broke-dick bail bondsman. On the other hand, I couldn't say no right away. I said I'd think about it, I was pretty busy with my Vegas work and the guns— but the percentage on three hundred grand was nothing to shake a finger at. I also said I'd do the Porter thing, but that I needed to do it my way, which was methodically and by the numbers. I said I needed to case him a little and that it might take a few weeks. He said he didn't care as long as it got done.

I squashed out my smoke and Timmy and I got ready to leave. Dennis plopped down on the couch and squealed, "Later." Lydia gave both Timmy and me a kiss on the cheek as we passed the kitchen. She told me to say hi to Carlos. Smitty said, "You know, Bird, I was thinking. You oughta move that little blonde number out to Bullhead."

I told him I'd been thinking that too, I really had.

14 "FUCK YOUR GUNS!"

THE NEXT WEEK was busy as hell. Flew to New York on September 9 to be part of an ATF peer support team and to go to some 9/11 memorial events. While I was there I hit a local biker bar named Hogs and Heifers to throw back drinks with other agents, including Karen, a female special agent based in New York. I was extra cocky that night. I put a call in to Bad Bob saying I was in New York on a collection. I asked if I could visit the boys at the Third Street clubhouse. He told me he had to make some calls. He called back fifteen minutes later. He said I should call Branden, the New York City P, at such-and-such a number. I did and Branden said, "Fuck yeah, come over!"

I was dumbstruck. The New York P was a guy known around the biker world. He didn't owe me—a nobody from a nothing club—a damn thing. Bob's willingness to vouch for me opened that door.

As I left, Karen implored me not to go, saying it was stupid to go without any cover. I asked, "Go where?"

She said, "You're going to meet the Hells Angels, Jay."

"I don't know where you got that from, and besides, fuck the Hells Angels. I'm not worried about what they're going to do to me. They should be worried about what I'm going to do them!"

She looked me dead in the eye and said, "I'm glad I'm not working with you. You're out of your mind. If you leave, I'm going home." This was probably the first time during Black Biscuit that my desire to succeed overcame my common sense.

I flagged a cab and said, "Take me to the Hells Angels, dude!" He didn't know where that was. I said Third Street between First and Second avenues.

I was scared—I'd been scared a lot lately and I was getting kind of used to it—Jesus Hates a Pussy!—but I couldn't believe what I was doing. As the cab crossed town I told myself I couldn't chicken out. I thought of the time I went bungee jumping, of how terrified I was at the thought of jumping off a bridge only to be saved by a glorified rubber band. I remembered how every nerve in my body told me not to jump, while my mind screamed, "You need to man-up and just do it, dude!" I threw myself off that bridge. It was almost more than I could handle, but it was exhilarating, and worth the fear. That's what it came down to: Were the risks taken worth the fear? Would I be able to live with myself if I'd given up? No. I'd have no self-respect. How could I expect people—my family, my partners, even the people I investigated—to respect me if it was obvious I didn't respect myself?

We pulled up. I paid. I got out and lit a cigarette. I crossed the street.

The New York Hells Angels lived on arguably the safest block in New York City. They owned an entire tenement building. It was painted black. The sidewalk in front of their building was cordoned off with barrels and bikes. There were plenty of cameras trained on the front door and street. The sidewalk was so clean it looked like someone had polished it. I knocked. A small shade slid open. A pair of black eyes. A voice asked, "Who is it?" I said, "I'm Bird, Branden's expecting me." The door opened. A big dude, like five-bushels-of-wheat big, blocked the opening. He said he was Lumpy. I held my smart-assed tongue, shook his hand, and went inside for the nickel tour.

The place was a museum. HA paraphernalia everywhere, going way back. Pictures, plaques, flags, framed in-memoriam cuts and tabs, old guns, a battle ax, helmets, knives, newspaper clippings, even decommissioned bikes. It was Hells Angels heaven. I was zooming.

I'd fallen under my own spell.

I didn't stay long. I only wanted to pay my respects. I bought some T-shirts to show the boys out west. I met a few guys, one of whom was among the scariest dudes I've ever laid eyes on. He was only five-eleven, but he weighed about 300 pounds and didn't have an ounce of fat on him. He was an Illinois Angel named Mel Chancey. The scariest thing about him wasn't his size, it was his smile and easy laugh. It looked and sounded kind, but what it said underneath was, "Hey man, nice to meet you, I'd love to bash your head in on the curb. Wanna go outside?" I steered clear of him. Branden asked if I wanted a sausage from a fair on First Avenue, said they made them real nice, Italian-style, with peppers and onions on soft bread. I declined. I left not twenty mintues after having arrived.

I decided to check out Ground Zero. I wanted to do a right thing, for the right reasons. Something in me had to push back against the impulsiveness and recklessness of Bird. I got there around ten at night.

The streets were quiet. There was the pit, still in disarray, flooded with lights. High fencing cordoned off the area, with pieces of paper and photos and posters laced into the lattice of the fence. A small group of people huddled at the corner of Church and Vesey—they looked like Mennonites—the men bearded, the women in bonnets and wearing dresses that looked like nineteenth-century kitchen aprons. The previous night, two columns of blue light had shot up from a huge array of spotlights, reaching for the heavens, honoring the souls lost that day and the ghosts of buildings gone. Everything felt respectful. I forgot who I was and who I was pretending to be, who the Angels were and who they were pretending to be. I was in the biggest, busiest city in the country and it was almost entirely silent. I stared at a fluttering American flag. For a few minutes I put everything aside.

Then I got on the train and went back to my hotel in Brooklyn.

I FLEW HOME on September 13. I landed in Tucson, got in my car, and drove home. I never settled in. The things I did around the house I did poorly. I mowed the lawn, neglecting whole tracts, leaving mohawks in the grass. Gwen scolded me. I knew something wasn't right. The old me—the real me?—would've been correcting mistakes. My current incarnation didn't care. All I wanted was to go back to work.

The afternoon before I left, Dale had some friends over for a pool party. I watched them in their bathing suits—twelve- and thirteen-year-old girls on the verge of growing up—and all I could think about were the women the bikers hung out with. The old ladies, the daughters, the whores. I could confidently guess how the lives of women like these had differed from Dale's and her friends', how it was that some women ended up in a Hells Angels clubhouse as drug mules and dealers, waiting for their old man to come around so he could demand—and get—a blow job or whatever else he wanted. I knew with dead certainty that these women had fathers who were never there for them, who never showed them any love (or showed them too much of the wrong kind of love), who never told them they were valuable in any way. It hurt to watch my daughter play with her girlfriends as these specters hung over me. It hurt to think that, given some bad breaks and poor decisions, it was possible, though unlikely, that any of these girls splashing in my pool could be in similar circumstances in only a few years.

I called Dale over, interrupting her fun. She had to get out of the pool and wasn't happy about having to do something for her dad. She pleaded, "What is it, Daddy?"

As she stopped in front of me I said, "This is important, Shoey"—when Jack was a baby he pronounced "sister" as "sheshu," which Gwen and I changed to Shoey and which stuck—"so listen carefully, OK?" She threw out an impatient hip and rolled her eyes. "Just hear me out, OK? I need to tell you this."

"Right now? Is this about boys?"

"It's not about boys, not really. It's more about you. Just listen. Never, ever do anything that you don't want to just because someone else says so. If someone wants something from you that you don't want to give, then you don't give it, understand?"

She didn't say anything. It was too awkward. Even as the words came out of my mouth I knew Gwen would have to clarify the message later.

"What I'm saying is, you're the most important person in the world to yourself. If you carry yourself with respect and determination, you'll be fine. Other people won't respect you unless you respect yourself first, understand?"

"I guess so, Daddy."

"Just don't forget. You have only one reputation, so guard it and protect it. Don't let anyone tell you what to do."

She straightened up with a quirky smile. "But you're telling me what to do right now!"

"Smart-ass. Listen to your old man on this one, OK?"

"OK." She turned and ran back to her friends, her wet feet slapping the patio.

"I love you, Shoey." She stopped, turned around and shot daggers at me, and ran off that much faster. Her friends giggled.

The rest of the day and night dragged on. I couldn't stop thinking about the case. That evening I played catch with Jack and actually dropped a couple of soft, high-arcing pop-ups. Later that night Gwen and I didn't have sex, which wouldn't have been that unusual except that she had to point it out to me. Sex hadn't even crossed my mind.

As I got in the undercover car the next morning, Jack handed me two more of his rocks. He smiled and repeated the gesture of folding my fingers around them. I kissed his head, put them on my dashboard, told him I loved him, and left.

I MET CARLOS to do some Tucson gun deals that Timmy and Pops had set up. It was going to be our first big day of dealing, which was good, because Slats was getting anxious. He'd been putting the screws to us to procure some evidence. We knew that all the protocol stuff we'd gone through—all the approvals and permissions—were good background for the RICOs, but none of it meant anything if we couldn't demonstrate that the Hells Angels engaged in criminal enterprise.

Carlos and I met at one of the Solo "clubhouses," a Waffle House at Grant Street and I-10. We chowed on the Solo Angeles Special: pecan waffles with fried eggs and bacon. We waited for our contact, Doug Dam, a Tucson Hells Angel, to give us a call and get things rolling.

We ran recording devices that day, but they weren't transmitting wires; in order for the cover team to follow us, we'd have to call and let them know where we were headed.

Doug called Carlos. He told us to meet him at his place. We paid the waitress—who, no joke, was named Flo, and who had a flowery platinum explosion of a hairdo—and left.

We met Doug in his front yard. He was six feet tall and a shade under 200 pounds. His eyes looked like windows into the soul of a very intense or very stupid individual. He sported the standard Hells Angels facial hair and wore a thin silver chain and cross around his neck. His rep was that of an unstoppable street fighter. He routinely traveled the country to resolve Angels problems with his fists.

He shook our hands. He said we had a lot of running around to do and he needed to eat first. Carlos suggested Waffle House number two, this one at 22nd Street and I-10.

Ah, the Waffle House. A finer undercover cop restaurant there never was. Bad coffee, below-average service, good waffles, easy on the wallet and hard on the digestive tract. Smells familiar, just like the funk underneath your big toenail does. Has practicality written all over it, especially since, for some bizarre reason, they always have open parking lots with views in three directions, the fourth being blocked by the Waffle House itself. Good for surveillance and a lack of surprises. Yes, when I or any of my law enforcement brothers are cruising down the road and see those eleven yellow squares containing those eleven black letters, there is little we can do but be drawn to them. Like moths to a porch light, except that we crave a cup of coffee in a questionably clean mug.

We told Doug we'd pay, and Carlos and I had seconds of pecan waffles. Doug actually finished his meal with ice cream.

Spooning scoops of vanilla into his goateed mouth, he said, "Here's the deal. I got a .38 and a .40 semiauto back at my place. The .40-cal isn't clean so don't get caught with it. I got another gun too, but can't sell it." He wiped his mouth with the back of his hand, smearing white cream into his mustache. He leaned in and whispered, "It was used in a serious crime and it has to go in the river, so . . ."

I whispered back, "We understand. Occupational hazard."

"Right." Doug was a talkative son of a bitch. Getting info out of him was like fishing with dynamite. "Thanks for moving this stuff today. I really need the dough."

Carlos stepped in. "Hey, we thought you guys were doing pretty good down here." We knew they weren't.

"Not really. I had a nice bulk pot thing going, but since I got picked up on it last year, it's been pretty dead. But, man, those were the days. I could get shit down here for about four hundred dollars a pound, drive it to Maine, where I used to live, and sell it for three times as much. Used to move shit for a supplier—five hundred pounds a trip—but I got wise and started taking smaller loads of my own stuff so I wouldn't have to pay anyone else. But like I said, that's stopped for now."

I said, "Sounds like our thing with the iron. We got those Mexican boys by the balls with one hand and the throat with the other."

"How d'you mean?"

"Man, I'm the source and the distributor. No middleman. The Alpha and the Omega, baby. I show up with a load of pistols and I set the price. Supply and motherfucking demand, econ one-oh-one."

"Sounds just like my pot thing," he said longingly. Then he added, "'Cept I didn't have no border patrol to fuck with me."

I said, "Yeah, well. Occupational hazard."

Doug laughed as he souped up the melted ice cream. "Naw. We don't got it as good as Mesa, I'll tell you that. Tucson's had some tough times. First, we only got six members, not counting the couple guys in prison on some ATF bullshit. Then we got one member, our tattoo guy, Mac, who's got a nonassociation clause as part of his probation. And we got JoJo who just got out of the joint and whose leg is all fucked up. We got me who just got my bike's license plates revoked for lack of insurance and who barely beat out a third-strike felony for the pot thing last year. I acted as my own lawyer, I tell you that?" He hadn't. Carlos said wow. "And then we got Fang who did a sixteen-year murder lick and who doesn't want to go back to prison but who still doesn't give a fuck—you'll meet him later. He's got some goods too. Anyway, I'm telling you, man, if the fucking feds wanted to throw a RICO our way it wouldn't take much but some Scotch Tape to make it stick."

Sweet. Slats would like the sound of that.

Carlos looked at Doug, nodding seriously. In the meantime he played a subtle game of footsy with me under the table, like we were teenagers macking on the same girl. Carlos got off on making light of any situation.

I told Doug about our cash contributions to Mesa and said if things worked out then we'd throw them some proceeds from the Mexican markup, that it was the only decent thing to do. Doug said he and all the boys—who he insisted never did anything without group approval, an important point for our records—would really appreciate that.

And so we began to deal. Before we left the second Waffle House, I called Slats from the bathroom and gave him Doug's address. Slats said he'd park the van four blocks away and could be there in a flash. I said good, but I didn't think there was much to worry about. I said, "Sit back and pound the Diet Cokes."

"Shut up." He coughed.

We went to Doug's and he gave us a .38 Taurus blue steel five-shot revolver and showed us the dirty gun—a 9 mm of unknown make—that he couldn't sell. He said the .40-caliber was at Fang's and that we'd have to go over there to get it, but that he would take the money now. Carlos gave him $800 for the two pistols, plus a fifty-dollar commission. Doug put the $800 in his back pocket and the fifty in his wallet. He told us that was all he was going to make for the day's work.

I thought, Dude, one day you're going to go to prison for a long time on a third strike because you were jonesing for fifty bucks. Pathetic.

Doug got in his car and we followed him to Fang's. Carlos called Slats and told him where we were headed. He told him we'd have these guys all prosecutable by three in the afternoon, that things were going easy, which they were. We were veteran ATF agents doing our thing. Over the years, Carlos and I had bought so many guns between us, it was like picking up milk on the way home.

We pulled into Craig "Fang" Kelly's driveway at 1501 South Winmore around one in the afternoon. He offered us beer and we took him up on it. I asked him where the .40-cal was and Fang said it wasn't here, that he'd had trouble getting it and that we'd likely have to pick it up at the house of Tucson Angel Mark McPherson, but that he and Doug had to make some calls first. He said we could wait outside if we wanted.

Carlos pulled the shade aside. In the backyard was a metal table and a basketball hoop. Carlos and I looked at each other and nodded. OK, we'd wait outside.

As we walked toward the table Carlos said, "I got fifty bucks says you can't dunk anymore, Bird."

"And you can?"

"You know it." Carlos was a Division II All-American defensive back and punt returner.

"Dude, no way you dunk and I don't."

"All right, let's find out."

"All right, then."

We looked for a ball. No surprise that there wasn't one. Can't imagine the Hells Angels squaring off for a game of shirts and skins. The hoop must have been left by the last tenant.

I held up my car keys. "We'll use these."

"All right. Who goes first?"

"You do, shorty."

"Bet. I'm on it."

Carlos stripped to his undershirt. I didn't have to since that was all I was wearing, but I did put my shoulder holster on the table. We both had on jeans and motorcycle boots. I threw Carlos my keys. He walked under the hoop, held up his arm to measure the distance, which was about three feet from his fingertips, and then stepped back several paces. He got in a ready position and rocked back and forth, jangling the keys in his right hand. I was glad Slats wasn't on the wire. He would've been calling us right then to tell us to stop. But we couldn't. That was a big reason why I loved working with Carlos. He kept me light on my feet.

He jumped and was well short. His boots skidded on the ground. He said, "Best of three!" and tried two more times, never getting closer. I said, "Give me those and let me show you how it's done." In my day I could throw down with both hands. I didn't bother measuring the distance—either I'd make it or I wouldn't. I took a running start from the side of the rim. When I got to about three feet I leapt, my left arm extended. I touched the rear of the rim, but I couldn't get above the cylinder. I came down in a graceless thud, my boots also skidding along the ground. My back shot through with pain. Nothing serious, just a reminder that I was old and no longer cut out for things like dunking.

The keys, however, stayed put, wedged between the rim and the backboard.

Carlos laughed his ass off. He said he'd give me twenty-five for my efforts. I said that I didn't think I could get back up there. He said, "Well, we'll just give the Merc to Doug for payment—he can scrap it and turn it into Hells Angels T-shirts or an eight-ball or whatever." I said shut up. Carlos laughed some more.

I tried to jump and retrieve the keys, but my bounce was all gone—I couldn't touch the rim. I was glad Jack wasn't there to see me. Carlos took four running jumps but was still a mile away.

I said, "All right, get on my shoulders."

"Fuck that."

"Fuck nothing. Get on my shoulders. I'll pay you twenty-five bucks to do it. We'll be even."

"Fine."

I took a knee. Carlos got behind me and straddled my shoulders. I stood up, legs creaking, and we teetered back and forth before Carlos grabbed the rim and went to work on the keys.

"Damn it, Bird, you really jammed these things good."

"Just like Shaq."

We faced the house. As Carlos said, "Got 'em!" we both caught

Doug on the phone watching us from behind the shade. Presumably he was talking to McPherson. He was probably saying that he had a couple of clowns who wanted to do business, that maybe they'd heard of us, the badass Solo Angeles, Jay "Bird" Davis and Carlos Jimenez, who at that moment happened to be playing chicken with an old basketball rim.

Not exactly respectable biker behavior. Which is exactly why we laughed so hard about it later.

Carlos grabbed the rim, did a pull-up and swung over my head, let go, and landed hard on the pavement. We walked back to the table and picked up our beers. I put my guns back on. We went inside and no one said anything about it. Doug said we'd have to go to see Mark for the .40-cal, but that he'd make it worth our trouble.

I said, "No trouble."

We left Fang's and didn't bother to call Slats. Everything was under control and the day was almost done. As promised, the .40-caliber pistol was at Mark's, as were two other guns: a Chinese Model 213 blue steel 9 mm semiauto and a Hi-Standard Model A .22 long-round semi-auto target pistol. Mark said the 213 was legit, but that he was unsure of the .22 so be careful with it.

As we inspected the guns, I noticed two Silver Star medals mounted on the wall of McPherson's living room. I asked who they belonged to. Mark said they were his. I asked, Vietnam? He said yep.

I had to hit an ATM to get enough cash to finish the deal. Doug accompanied me to a nearby Safeway, asking if I had any meth hookups because his stupid wife had done his last rail the night before and Tucson was drier than Death Valley. He also said the Tucson boys had ordered him to not cook or sell meth anymore, even though he still needed half an eight-ball to get by every couple of weeks. I said I'd let him know if I heard anything, that maybe Rudy could help him out.

I took out $600. It'd be fun explaining that to Gwen later on.

Doug and I went back to finalize everything. Dealing with McPherson gave me a bad feeling. He owned a legitimate bike repair shop that we never got any dirt on, and he was a decorated Vietnam vet. I later discovered that one of the stars was given to him for jumping out of a departing chopper to grab a fellow platoon member who'd been shot right before he made the helicopter. Mark had defied a direct order from his CO, who wanted to take off right away since they were taking fire. Mark grabbed the guy and got back on while the pilot waited for them. He came up for both a court-martial and a Silver Star, and the brass had the good sense to give him the latter. I was not into busting guys like McPherson; it wasn't what I was on the job to do.

Regardless, it was a good day for Black Biscuit. Carlos and I pulled out of McPherson's $1,500 poorer, but that much richer in the way of small arms and evidence. Carlos called Slats. We decided to meet at a shopping center about three miles away.

After he hung up Carlos said, "Slats sounds steamed."

"Well, we got a trunk full of guns. He'll be OK."

"I don't know, he sounds pretty steamed."

We got there first. We parked by a Dumpster. Carlos opened the trunk and arranged the firearms to show the boys that we'd had a good day at the office.

Slats pulled up, jumped out, and slammed the door. He was with two other task force agents, but they got out of the van more slowly. As Slats walked toward us he picked up an empty green beer bottle that lay on the ground. He threw it hard at our feet and it shattered into a thousand pieces.

I yelled, "What the fuck?!"

"What do you mean what the fuck? Where were you?"

"Buying guns, dude."

"Oh, really? Where were you buying these guns?"

"At bad guys' houses. Lighten up. We did good."

"Fuck you, lighten up. You were off the map half the day! You know what that does to my heart?" He pounded his chest. "Jay. Anything happens to you it's my ass, you hear me?"

Carlos and I held our tongues, not pointing out that if something happened to us we were pretty sure it was *our* asses.

I said, "But we got a trunk full of guns!"

"Fuck your guns!"

A young black guy wearing a straight-brimmed Phoenix Suns cap and a leather shearling bomber coat that was way too hot for the southern Arizona climate suddenly walked into our circle from behind the Dumpster. He surprised Slats, who jumped back. Carlos and I couldn't help but chuckle. Slats didn't like that.

He turned on the guy. "What are you looking at?" Slats pulled his jacket aside, unsnapped his holster, and pulled his revolver half out. "I repeat, what are you looking at?"

Who knows what went through the poor guy's head? He probably thought we were doing a deal. He sure as shit didn't think we were cops. I begged him silently, Don't say anything, dude, just keep going, just keep going. It must've worked. He turned on his heel and disappeared just as quickly as he'd shown up.

"Jesus." Slats looked like he was about to suffer a coronary.

Carlos said, "Take a breath, Joe. Come see what we got."

Slats mumbled, "Fuck your guns." Then he walked up to the open trunk and looked inside. He nodded. He spat out a strand of brown chaw and stared absently into the trunk. "All right, good work. Try not to go off the map again. It really kills me. I need to know you're safe." In spite of his anger, I knew he'd been really worried about us. He said quietly, "Jay, you know me and the guys in the van are responsible for you. I know you think you can climb Everest without help, but I won't let anything shitty happen on my watch." Slats looked hard at me. "I'm not pulling into your driveway to tell Gwen you're not coming home because I couldn't keep track of you."

Carlos and I said, "OK." I added, "We won't go off the map again." I knew I was lying. Our ditching Slats wasn't conscious, it was just that we had too much experience and were too used to running our own games—it was bound to happen again. Besides, I really didn't like being minded all the time.

Slats turned and walked back to his car. "Drive the stuff to the Patch for processing." He got in. As he was about to close his door he leaned out and said, "Oh. I almost forgot to tell you. Carlos, as of next week you're off the case. The Miami SAC wants you back."

He closed his door and backed out of the lot while Carlos and I stood there staring at each other.

15 GOOD-BYE, CARLOS

WELL, THAT SUCKED. We knew that Carlos was on loan to us, but we'd hoped that our early successes would convince the special agents in charge that we needed Carlos more than anyone else did. No dice. He was headed back home and he wasn't excited about it. None of us were.

We were convinced we were being screwed in the usual way that certain ATF bosses screw street agents: Carlos was being reassigned simply because someone had the power to reassign him.

The truth wasn't far away. Slats, having worked in Miami, was on good terms with the SAC there. But our assistant special agent in charge wasn't. Our ASAC penned the request for Carlos's extension in a terse e-mail that rubbed the Miami boss the wrong way. Carlos's extension was turned down and his reassignment to his home district was expedited, effective October 1, 2002.

His imminent removal presented an imminent challenge: how to extract him from the case without it seeming rash or out of character?

The task force had a brainstorming session at the Patch. Carlos could have a motorcycle accident—everyone knew he wasn't much on a bike, just like me—but putting him in the hospital would require a bunch of makeup and effort, and it wasn't likely to justify his disappearance from

Arizona. We could arrest him, but we couldn't figure out a way to do that without arresting any other Solos. We could say he was ordered to relocate to Tijuana by the Solo brass, but since we knew that there already existed murky channels of communication between the Mexican Solos and the larger biker world, that would be too risky.

For a few days we were at an impasse.

To distract ourselves, Carlos and I decided to do Smitty's Porter collection.

Slats suggested we do it at Porter's job, so as to maximize exposure and lessen the risk of it going bad, which we could not let happen. As an undercover you have to do your best to control situations while giving the other party the impression they're the one in control.

We decided to show up in numbers. That way we'd be intimidating *and* deterring. We recruited two of the larger task force agents to join us: Nicolas "Buddha" Susuras, who had neck rolls that recalled loaves of white bread, and Chris "Elvis" Hoffman, a hulking Tempe cop.

Porter worked in residential construction. As we approached him he drew his framing hammer from its belt loop and flipped it so the claw would be on the offending side of a power swing. Gotta love that.

We were all openly packing, and Carlos carried my Louisville Slugger.

Porter and I spoke. He repeated what Smitty had told me, and that the matter was in the courts. He didn't understand why he should be collected for money that he didn't technically owe, not yet anyway. He also called the woman we were ostensibly collecting for "Crazy Carol." He was calm and tough, especially considering that, as far as he knew, he was explaining his way out of a beating or worse. I found him believable, and I told him I'd have to ask my boss whether or not we'd be paying him another visit. He said he understood, then thanked me and we actually shook hands. If I could have, I'd have bought him a beer.

I called Smitty later that night from the Verano Circle undercover house and told him what Porter had told us and that he didn't back down or act pussy. I said I believed him and we let him off the hook. I told Smitty no problem paying him another visit if he wanted me to. Smitty said, "Naw, I trust you, Bird. That Carol's a crazy old bitch anyway."

We never heard about Porter again.

Smitty's words echoed in my head: "I trust you, Bird."

THE NEXT MORNING as Slats sat over his cup of coffee reading the *Arizona Republic*, he came across a story about a Phoenix landscaper who'd been arrested in Chicago for large-scale cocaine trafficking. His last name was Jimenez.

As far as the Angels knew, Carlos' last name was Jimenez too.

On September 26 we arranged to meet Smitty at the Inferno for drinks. He sat at the bar with Lydia when Carlos, Timmy, and I walked in. Lydia had her hand on Smitty's thigh and her eyes were as big as lily pads. We said hi. She smiled at us like a little girl being given lemon drops. They didn't know what we were there to tell them.

Smitty said, "Hey, boys."

Smitty pointed at Dennis, who was playing pool. Dennis held up his bottle of beer. We settled in at the bar and bought a round. Crown Royal and a water back for Smitty, Cuervo 1800 and a ginger ale for Lydia, whatever Dennis was having. Beers for us Solos.

Carlos sat next to Smitty, and Timmy and I sat next to Carlos. Smitty asked what we'd been up to. I told him that Timmy and I had been doing a job in Vegas, that it was easy and we got some good scratch out of it. Timmy said that for a couple of guys who looked like us, doing collections was sometimes too easy. I agreed. Carlos didn't say anything, just stared at his drink.

I said, "I caught up with some chick who wants me to do some work for her." This was true. During Operation Riverside, a woman had offered me a murder-for-hire to knock off her old man. Apparently he'd been beating her and sniffing her powder and she was tired of him. "Her best friend's on the Laughlin grand jury, and I talked to her. She ran down a list of names and yours came up." This was also true—to a point. Having good knowledge of the Laughlin case, it was safe to assume that he'd been spoken of during the Nevada grand juries. But I really had met this woman's friend and she really was on the grand jury—call it fate—though she hadn't told me anything.

"And?" Lydia asked impatiently. The grand jury had been taking its sweet time. There were a ton of witnesses, and the marginal quality of the surveillance footage made it difficult to work with. The case seemed as though it would be cut-and-dried, but the attorneys were taking their time handing down indictments. They wanted airtight federal cases before they went to court. There was also some pressure to see what our investigation could add. At that time, no Angels had been formally served. Those involved were waiting for the other shoe to drop and the marshals to show up at their doors with warrants and shotguns.

I said, "And that's it. She just had names, nothing solid. She mentioned Dago Pete and a couple guys named Calvin Schaefer and George Walters." This was also information I knew as a fed but played as if I'd heard it in confidence.

Smitty said, "Schaefer's Casino Cal. He shot some of those Mongol bitches. George is Joby. Skinny guy. Mullet."

I remembered him from the Flamingo. The Nestlé Quik Rabbit. "Well, I told him to get what he could on you and Pete. I can tell him to listen out for others, too."

"Yeah. Do that."

Lydia asked Smitty, "Whaddaya think, sweetie?"

"I think if those bastards bring me up on RICOs, you and I are moving."

Still staring at his beer, Carlos asked, "Where to?" They were the first words he'd spoken since we'd arrived.

Lydia announced, "Brazil!" as if she'd already punched her ticket. Living in Bullhead for as long as she had, I couldn't blame her one inch.

Smitty looked at me and said, "I'll need some help from your connections in Mexico to make that happen." Then he turned to Carlos and asked, "What's up, 'Los?" Carlos didn't say anything. "Hey, Carlos, you listening to me?"

Carlos asked, "What's that, Smit?"

"What's with you, man?"

"You read the *Republic* yesterday?"

"Nope. Won't read it tomorrow, either." Lydia giggled.

"Well, there was a thing in there about a cousin of mine. He got popped a couple days ago."

"No shit?"

"No shit." Carlos tossed the newspaper clipping down on the table.

Smitty looked it over. "I'm sorry to hear that, Carlos. Real sorry."

"It don't matter. He was a piece of shit. But he was into some things, and I helped him out from time to time." Carlos pretended to change the subject. "Brazil, huh?"

"Yeah." Smitty didn't bite. We didn't want him to. "What're you talking about?"

I leaned back and looked at Smitty. "We're losing Carlos, Smit."

"What?" Smitty half stood out of his seat. Lydia let out a little gasp. Dennis looked our way. I was a little jealous. Smitty and Lydia really loved Carlos. I didn't think they'd feel so strongly if I was the one leaving.

Carlos said, "Yeah. I can't hang around here, Smitty. The cops are going to be looking for me—just questions, but you know. There's gonna be some heat. If I stay, I'll be putting my Solo brothers at risk. I'll be putting you guys at risk. I can't do that."

Lydia said, "Oh, honey."

Smitty wasn't smiling. He settled back into his chair. He poured back his Crown Royal and signaled for another. He put his hand on Carlos's shoulder. "That's the way it is, then that's the way it is. I'll tell the others."

"Thanks, Smitty," I said.

Carlos said, "Yeah, thanks, Smit. I'll come back when I can."

Smitty said seriously, "You do that. Make sure you do that."

But Carlos never would.

16   WE WANT YOU

I SOMETIMES THINK things would've been different if Carlos had stayed. We had the kind of relationship where we could be fistfighting in the morning and sharing ice cream by lunch. He had the same size balls I did, but was more easygoing. On off days I fretted about who we could work, and drew up lengthy lists of impossible missions that Superman on crack wouldn't have been able to complete. Carlos, on the other hand, would sit back and watch a *M*A*S*H* marathon on TV. He was a twelve-year-old boy in the body of a goateed five-foot-ten, 200-pound ball of muscle. He'd say to me, "You think you're the hardest-working man in ATF? You're not. And even if you were, no one would care, so sit down and watch TV with me and maybe you'll learn something." He balanced me out. If he'd stayed he would've reminded me to take it easy now and then—something I wouldn't do on my own.

October was party month. There was an Arizona Nomads rally on the fifth, a couple of Mesa support parties in the middle of the month, and a party commemorating the Angels' fifth year in the state of Arizona on the twenty-sixth. We hoped to go to all of them.

Before the partying started, however, Smitty called and said we needed to meet. It was September 27. I said I'd be right over.

When I got to the Smiths', Lydia was in the yard, as before. She had on a wide-brimmed hat to protect her from the sun. I said, "Yard looks good."

She thanked me and pointed to the house. "Old man's inside," she said.

I knocked and Smitty let me in. He didn't wear his cut, he held a bottle of Bud, he smiled that winged smile of his. The Smiths looked like they were having a nice day at the old homestead.

"Having a nice day at the old homestead, huh?" I asked.

Smitty smiled some more. His eyes turned to slivers. "You bet. Beer?"

"You bet."

We went inside. He ushered me to the table off the kitchen, went to the fridge, got out a beer, and popped it with an opener on his key chain. He handed me the bottle and sat down.

"This is gonna be quick. I gotta leave for church in an hour."

"No worries. What up?" I drank. The beer was sweet and cold. I held up my pack of cigarettes and raised my eyebrows, making sure it was OK if I smoked.

Smitty said, "Of course." I lit up. "Two things. First, I really need to know what you can tell me about Laughlin, from that gal of yours on the grand jury. If Lydia and me need to get out of the country, I gotta know ahead of time."

I nodded and smoked and said, "I'll keep on her. Soon as I hear anything, you'll know."

"Good. The other thing is I'm this close to getting approval to start a Mohave Valley charter of the Eight-Ones. It'll be me, Dennis, Joby, a couple other Arizona Nomads, a brother from Barstow who's gonna open a tattoo shop, and a couple of prospects."

I nodded. "That's good news. You need more representation around here. I been hearing about some Mongols setting up over the hill in Kingman." Kingman was just east of Bullhead.

Smitty grimaced. "Joby said the same shit. Ain't good. You tell me anything—*anything*—you hear about those bitches, got it?" I nodded deeply. This was serious business.

Smitty reached for a hard pack of Marlboro Reds. He flipped the top and drew one out. My lighter was lit as he slipped it between his lips.

He pulled on the cigarette, the tip flared up. He nodded, I clicked my Zippo shut. He nodded again. "That's what I'm talking about, Bird. You guys know how to act."

I nodded again.

He smoked with conviction. He inhaled a large blue puff and it didn't come out. "Here it is, Bird. We need more people like you. I want you, Timmy, and Pops to come in with us at Mohave Valley. I've spoken to Dennis and he approves." He didn't mention Rudy because we'd kept him on a short leash and Smitty hadn't met him. Rudy was too unpredictable to be gumming up the works all over the state.

This was a very exciting development, but I couldn't accept for a few reasons. Joining while the case was still in its early stages wasn't feasible, let alone advisable. I knew that as an Angel prospect I wouldn't be able to operate with the same freedom I had had as a Solo Angeles Nomad. Not to mention that Slats—and our bosses—would have to approve such a move. I decided to offer Smitty a non-denial denial and consult with the rest of the Black Biscuit task force.

But I still took comfort from Smitty's overture. The emotional way he'd received the news of Carlos's departure and this sudden recruitment were excellent signs that we were being accepted—even coveted. They were proof we were doing a very good job.

As I mulled over his offer, I must've paused for a moment too long because Smitty demanded, "Did you hear what I just said, Bird?"

I lit another cigarette. "Hear you? You kidding, Smit? You're asking if I wanna become a Hells Angel?"

"Timmy and Pops too. I want the Arizona Solo Angeles Nomads to patch over."

I drank my beer. It was hot and the beer was already getting warm. I gave Smitty my considered, and technically honest, answer: "Look, Smitty, no disrespect, but I gotta think about this. I have to talk to my P, Rudy. Bob knows him. I got loyalties to the Solos and I can't just give up on them."

"Loyalty is trump. I understand." He flicked a fragile column of ash into a Hells Angels ashtray. "Of course. Think about it, you have to. I know you have what it takes, but remember—it takes a lot." He tipped back his bottle, I finished mine. "Now I gotta go to church." He stayed seated. Our meeting was over. I stood up.

I stuck out my hand. "Thank you, Smitty."

He grabbed my hand from his chair, smiling. "I'll see you soon, Bird."

OCTOBER 5. ON the way to the Patch I stopped at a Starbucks. They already had the Halloween seasonal, a pumpkin-flavored latte with brown sugar cinnamon sprinkles. I love the seasonals at Starbucks—I get them with extra foam and low-fat milk. Totally lame, but there you go.

As I walked through the Black Biscuit headquarters, Slats asked, "What the fuck is that?" He pointed at my coffee.

"A triple Venti pumpkin spiced latte, extra foam, extra sprinkles. What's it look like?"

He hung his head and turned around.

The agents were getting ready to head to an Angels Nomads rally in Bellemont, a town west of Flagstaff. It was an afternoon run, not a ton of partying. We planned on dropping in, paying our respects, and coming right back to Phoenix.

We did a mini-gauntlet. Slats fired questions at us: Where you living these days? Solos, huh? Never heard of 'em. Where they from? Where'd you say your business was again? What's that tat for? Where'd you say you used to live? What kind of bike is that? Who's your president? Where is he?

Slats barked at me, "Where's your old lady?"

"You're looking at a freebird, dude."

"That so? I got some choice pussy I can hook you up with." Slats played a convincing dickhead biker pimp.

"I'll be the judge of that."

"Follow me."

"That's OK. You wanna bring 'em around, do that. I said I was a freebird, not desperate. I do good enough I don't gotta follow you around to look up some skirts."

Slats spat into a Coke can and broke character. He leaned into a metal folding chair, the hard gray back pressed into his chest. "I dunno about that."

"What am I supposed to say?"

"Not that."

"Dude, I think that's pretty good. Besides, they're already calling us the gay Solo Nomads. Something's gotta give."

"I know, but you gotta make a better show than that."

"Well, I could always fuck my beer can." I inhaled sharply. "Get me a girlfriend, dude."

"Working on it."

"Work harder."

"Working on it."

A little clash of cop egos.

I knew Slats had hit a glass ceiling with the brass in securing a female operative. Like it or not, this business takes place in a man's world. I'm of the minority opinion in law enforcement circles that women are as capable and essential as men are in undercover assignments, but the truth is that they have a hard road to walk. Most of the time they play girlfriends, runners, or mules. What I needed was a woman whom the Hells Angels would actually respect. Slats had brought a few women in to assist for short periods, but circumstances had kept them from being able to commit. I wanted Karen from New York, but her boss adamantly refused her participation.

I became convinced that Jenna Maguire was the best alternative. Her contact with Smitty and Lydia had been impressive, and her youth, good humor, and attractiveness were solid pluses. The problem was getting her. Her superiors and more experienced co-workers had been warning her not to go with me, who had a reputation for wild impulsiveness, into the violent, misogynistic world of the Hells Angels. Her reply was that at least the Angels wore their sexism on their sleeves. JJ's bosses didn't much like that.

There was nothing we could do about it before the Angels Nomads rally, so we suited up. I insisted we trailer the bikes to Flagstaff and ride the final few miles to the actual rally. Neither Timmy nor Pops put up much of a fight.

Pops was our designated driver. He pulled the truck around to the back of the Patch. Timmy and I pushed the bikes into position. Pops got out of the truck and opened the trailer, not paying attention to where his bike was parked. As he dropped the truck's gate, it hit the top of his bike's front wheel and the bike fell over. Pops said shit, Timmy and I laughed. Pops pulled the truck forward and we picked his bike up and strapped it in. Timmy went to use the head while Pops and I finished. As we pushed my bike into the back, I turned my ankle slightly and momentarily let go of my side of the bike, suddenly transferring all the weight to Pops, who was not in a good enough position to hold it. The bike rolled back, over my other foot, and fell into Pops, who managed to keep it upright. I cursed and helped him out. He wasn't amused. We strapped my bike in as Timmy began to roll his bike up the ramp. As I've said, Timmy was a big, strong man, but he'd misjudged the weight of his bike on an incline. He got it halfway up the ramp, lost momentum, and held it there. He asked for help.

Slats watched the whole thing, chewing chaw like cud. Most of the task force agents stood behind him, shaking their heads.

As we walked down the ramp, Slats spat and said, "You guys look like a bunch of zoo monkeys trying to fuck a football." Everyone behind him howled. We did too.

From then on, in all of our coded conversations, reports and correspondences, we were code-named the Monkeys. For brevity's sake, I was M1, Timmy was M2, and Pops was M4. We reserved M3 for the dear departed Carlos, should he ever return.

WE RODE TO Flagstaff, parked the trailer north of town in a Waffle House lot, got out of the truck, rubbed oil on our foreheads, and rolled around in the dirt to make it look like we'd just ridden 150 miles.

The rally was at the Bellemont Harley dealership and Roadhouse Tavern. The cynic in me couldn't help thinking that a bar and a bike dealership were the perfect combination of symbiotic enterprises—kind of like a jail and a bail bondsman, or a gun shop and a liquor store.

Billy Schmidt, a hangaround who wanted to prospect for Dennis, worked the ticket gate with Dolly, Dennis's platinum blond, near-toothless fiancée. We said hi to them and started to pay. Dolly told us not to worry about it, but I insisted. We went back and forth. Ultimately we each paid five bucks and got our hands stamped with the number 81 in blue ink.

We sauntered into the parking lot where a few barbecues were smoking, a large tent was erected, and Hells Angels posters flapped in the breeze. The Harley dealership had lined up a phalanx of fresh floor models and the tavern end of the operation had set up several kegs in iced garbage cans. Everyone milled around drinking beer, smoking, and bullshitting. No one was openly armed, us included, as the warning had gone out to be clean for the rally.

Smitty greeted us and led the way to a group that included Dennis and Turtle. Other clubs in attendance were the Red Devils, the Spartans, the Rough Riders, and the Desert Road Riders. Pops went and got as many beers as he could carry and we commenced drinking and standing around. Traffic whisked by on the adjacent I-40. There was a line of smoke-colored ponderosa pines to the north. I noticed two black vultures drawing lazy spirals in the sky.

We were living the glorious, free life of the Hells Angels.

I asked Smitty if there was anyone doing any business that day. He said no. He said this was a public rally and we couldn't be sure of who was in attendance—the implication being informants or even, perish the thought, undercover cops. He said the uniforms were parked out on the interstate, waiting for an excuse to pounce. I agreed we shouldn't give it to them.

Unsurprisingly, a couple of old buddies were in attendance too: Varvil and Abraham. Sugarbear hadn't arrested them yet. I thoroughly and completely blew them off. I was hanging out with the Angels—with their local hero, Smitty—and they no longer deserved my attention. I could see them eyeing me jealously from across the parking lot and I fought the urge to fall down laughing.

I told Smitty we weren't staying long, that we had a job the next day and wanted to get back to Phoenix. He told us to stick around, spend the night, get a room at the Geronimo Inn.

We made a snap decision and stayed.

At some point Steve Helland, an Arizona Nomad and close friend of Smitty and Dennis, came over with his wife, Cheryl, and a couple of girls who looked to be about sixteen. The girls were attractive—both wore cutoff jean shorts and HA support T-shirts. They reminded me, as all young women did, of my daughter. Helland said to me, "Hey, Bird, this is my daughter, April, and her friend Michelle. They've been wanting to meet you."

Smitty said, "Yeah, Bird, you should hang out with these girls, get to know them." Cheryl Helland nodded, a smile plastered on her face.

I was being offered the flesh of a minor—and that of her friend—by her own father. I didn't know whether to laugh at or simply assault the Hellands. In retrospect, I think they were offered to me because, while I was a biker and a debt collector and a gun runner and a supposed hit man, I had my act together, wasn't a drug addict, and treated myself and others with some measure of respect. In the biker world I was a catch.

Sad.

I declined, saying I was plenty capable of getting in trouble without involving a fourteen-year-old. Everyone chuckled. April said she was eighteen, which gave me zero pause. She was still a girl. Helland leaned in and growled, "If she's old enough to sit at the table, she's old enough to eat." He smiled at his wife, who shrugged. April and Michelle stood around for a couple minutes and then wandered away. Lydia, who'd heard the whole thing, asked if I'd spoken to JJ lately.

I said I could speak to her right now. I flipped open my phone and dialed her up.

She wasn't expecting my call, but I didn't have to speak any code to let her know what the story was. JJ immediately fell into role. Lydia demanded the phone. They gabbed about the rally, Bullhead, San Diego, and me. I heard Lydia say, "We love Bird."

That's damn right.

Lydia passed the phone to Smitty, who spoke to JJ for a few minutes. He mentioned his birthday and the cake she'd fed him, how he'd never forget it.

Smitty handed me the phone. I said, "Take her easy, sweetheart. I'll be seeing you soon."

17 GIMME A B! GIMME AN I! GIMME AN R! GIMME A D!

OCTOBER 2002

I'VE MAINTAINED A good relationship with Slats in the years since the case ended, and he's recently likened my demeanor and intensity during Black Biscuit to that of a fight-trained pit bull with him as my handler, holding the leash as best he could. Any good dog handler knows that even when holding back, you have to let the dog get an occasional taste of blood in order to keep him fierce. He did a good job. I wanted to bite, bite, bite all the time. I wanted suspects. I wanted all of the Angels to be prosecutable. I wanted better evidence against the people we already had, and I wanted new evidence against those we didn't. We'd gotten a lot of information that could be used against Smitty for both the Laughlin riot and a potential RICO charge. I'd continue to work on him, but I had to spread my wings and branch out.

It was time to head south. To Phoenix. To Mesa.

These were bigger hunting grounds—Mesa claimed at least twenty full patches with a large contingent of prospects and hangarounds— and things were going to heat up. We expected to have women pushed on us more often than they had been in Bullhead. Timmy prepped a female Phoenix cop for action, while I waited for Slats to get JJ. Progress on this front was slow—JJ's ASAC wanted her to attend an advanced undercover class before he released her. This was fine, except that the class *started* in January. We couldn't wait that long.

A return to Phoenix also meant we had to take a good look at Rudy, who was in the wind and useless. Every now and then we'd hear about him running around Apache Junction with Iwana, strung out or on the hustle. For Rudy, the worst had happened. His demons had re-sunk their addicted, criminal talons deep into the thick of his back. His nature had beaten his better intentions. Slats was figuring out what to do with Rudy—whether to cut him loose and pick him up later, or force the issue and sweep him away. It came down to whether or not we thought Rudy was dangerous to us—we weren't convinced either way. Not yet.

Timmy, Pops and I went with Mesa to a support party on the seventeenth at Spirits Lounge. We got the standard welcome—a booming intro over the PA by Good Time Charlie the DJ—with a special flourish for us Solos, who were by then a name-brand local club. That night Bad Bob offered Timmy a pretty blonde with hoop earrings, saying she liked to "blow out-of-town bikers." Timmy said that sounded great but declined, telling Bob he had a woman and that she'd be coming to the support party on the twenty-fourth. Bob let up.

That same night, Mesa Angels Kevin Augustiniak, "Casino" Cal Schaefer, and Nick Nuzzo nudged a three-sheets-to-the-wind blonde at me. They'd fed her boilermakers, tequila, and beer and decided that I should have the pleasure of taking her home. She tottered up to me and did a little curtsy. I stood with Bad Bob, who was accompanied by a young, attractive blonde wearing glasses and overalls, and who was completely inked from her neck down. The curtsying woman was cute. I never caught her name, but I'll never forget what she did next. She took three steps back, shook off the cloud of alcohol that surrounded her, and began to kick and pump her fists in the air.

"Gimme a B! Gimme an I! Gimme an R! Gimme a D! What does it spell? BIRD! BIRD! That's my man, if he can't do me, no one can!" She was actually pretty good. She jumped high, her toes were always pointed, and her smile had the quality of being attached, like she was a Mrs. Potato Head toy.

Casino Cal and Nuzzo nearly fell down laughing. Bad Bob grabbed the tattooed blonde's slender waist and squeezed, toasting the cheerleader with his beer bottle. I smiled and shook my head.

I took the cheerleader on. I let her sit on my lap and hang off my arms and shoulders. At one point I gave her a piggyback ride around the pool table.

We all went back to the clubhouse and horsed around some more. The Angels fed her more booze.

ATF had recently discovered the secret that Mesa Mike, the informant being run out of LA, had been keeping: He'd admitted and alleged that he and two of his Mesa brothers had beaten Cynthia Garcia on the clubhouse floor and killed her in the desert.

We were at the clubhouse for fifteen minutes before I realized what I'd potentially done. By allowing this cheerleader to come back to the clubhouse, I'd delivered an arguably innocent, if foolish, woman into the mouth of the lion. The beast hadn't bitten yet, but there was nothing saying he wouldn't.

I had to get both of us out of there. Pronto.

I grabbed her and went up to Timmy, Nuzzo, Augustiniak, Bad Bob, and his skinny blonde. The cheerleader tugged at my arm. I said, "I gotta roll this honey outta here right now. She's gonna be no good to me in thirty minutes."

Bob said, "Shit, Bird, stick around. Looks like the little girl wants to have some fun. The party's just gettin' started." We had to go. If she passed out, I'd have been responsible for facilitating a gang bang.

We turned to leave, and everyone gave us a hearty good-bye.

Outside, I squeezed her for her home address, put her on my bike, and took off. She barely held on. I took it slow. When we got to her house she was asleep on the back of the bike. I hauled her off, fished her keys from her pocket, walked her upstairs, and dumped her into bed. She was very unconscious.

My mind raced. Was this chick a setup? Who knew what else besides liquor was in her system? My paranoia said roofies. I looked at her lying in bed. She looked dead, but her chest rose and fell shallowly. I left her room convinced I was in a bad spot, that the Angels had followed me to make sure that I'd screw this woman and leave.

Therefore, I couldn't leave. I had to maintain my cover and play my role. I'd been in similar situations, and they raced through my mind. One stuck out.

I was working the Iron Cross MC in Georgia with Vince Cefalu. Vince was one of the few UCs who outshone me in terms of performance and aggression. I learned a lot from him. In addition to being a hell of a UC, he's got a PhD in psychology, which I can only assume has helped him in his undercover work a great deal.

The leader of the Iron Cross MC was a guy named Li'l Rat. He was being bad-mouthed by a local nobody who owned a tattoo shop. Li'l Rat wanted us to work over this rival and tell him to shut up. We knew it was a mud check—a test of will to make sure we didn't "drop our mud" in serious situations—and we knew we had to do it in order to maintain our cover story.

We went to the guy's shop. It was dusk, and the guys Li'l Rat sent to follow us did a poor job of concealing it. We'd have to have big words with the guy, maybe knock him down and rough him up a little.

We pulled into the parking lot. The guy's shop looked shut down. Vince walked up to the door and pounded it with the fleshy side of his fist. He dragged hard on a cigarette before pulling it from his mouth to shout, "Open up!"

No answer. Another drag as he pounded some more. He yelled, "Open up, get out here, and take your ass-whooping, you chickenshit cocksucker!" Vince put on a good show for Li'l Rat's spies.

Eyes appeared through some blinds. A voice said, "Give me a minute." Vince turned to me and winked.

The door opened, and before either of us could react, the Tat Man had lowered a double-barreled crack-back shotgun in Vince's chest. I thought, Shit. I also thought, Shotguns throw a wide pattern, I better step to the side. I did. I put my hand on my pistol but didn't draw.

Later on Vince told me all he could think was that he should've been a fireman.

Tat Man was clearly scared and tweaking. All three of us were in a jam. Vince was dead and so was Tat Man, as I was going to kill him right before I stooped to the blasted body of a dear friend in a futile attempt to save his life. Also, the case was as dead as Vince.

Then Vince did one of those things only Vince would do.

He took a final drag on his smoke and let the hot, pinched butt drop to the ground. He grabbed the bad end of the shotgun, removed it from his chest, and guided it onto his forehead, keeping his hands on the barrel. As he did this he turned to me slightly and winked again. The message was clear: *If I die tonight it won't be like a punk. Tell my sons I died like a man, not like some loser begging a drug addict to spare his life.*

The Tat Man didn't know what to think. Truthfully, neither did I.

Vince spoke clearly and calmly. "Few things. One: If you're gonna shoot someone, shoot them in the head. Two: You put a gun on me, you better intend to use it. And three: Fuck you, do it now or I'm going to beat you with your own gun and fuck you in the ass over the hood of my car."

As Vince finished his words, he quickly jacked the gun into the shoulder of the Tat Man. Then he yanked it back. In less than a second Vince had reversed roles. He was holding the gun and Tat Man was looking for a place to hide. I thought, How did he do that?

Vince broke open the breach and pulled the shells out, putting them in a pocket. Then he did something else only Vince would do: He didn't beat the guy. He handed him back the gun, still open, and said, "You can't bad-mouth Li'l Rat anymore. He's my friend and I won't have it. The next time you open your mouth and 'Li'l Rat' comes out, you better start with 'I'm sorry' or 'Forgive me.' You got a pass tonight, but you'll only get one."

With that he turned and left. I followed him like a shocked puppy dog. The Tat Man just stood there, trembling lightly. He was probably pissing himself.

The guys Li'l Rat had sent to see how we handled ourselves had already scurried off to report what they'd just witnessed.

This episode ran through my mind as I wandered through the cheerleader's apartment. I knew that mud checks came in many forms, and that when given one, one should always, at minimum, give the impression that one has followed through. The Angels still made me insecure. Was this a test because I'd been avoiding women? Was it Cal, Nick, and Kevin's joke on me? Was she the old lady of an enemy and I a pawn in some payback game?

I wandered into her kitchen, not turning on any lights. I phoned Tom "Teabag" Mangan, a task force member and close friend who was on the cover team that night, and told him the situation. He broke off from the team covering Mesa and cruised over to the cheerleader's neighborhood. He looked around and gave the all-clear. He asked how she was doing. I said she looked fine. Teabag asked, "That girl got lucky tonight, huh?"

"Yeah. Real lucky. Instead of one of those assholes fucking her, she gets me *pretending* to fuck her."

Teabag laughed a little.

I told him I was going to hang around for a while, just in case. He said OK and hung up. I opened the fridge, made myself a turkey sandwich with some slightly moldy cheese and brand-X ketchup, and settled down in the living room in the dark. I ate quietly, and when I was finished I closed my eyes.

I knew I'd be slammed in the future for my mishandling of the cheerleader. I could see myself in the witness box, questions being fired at me. I'd remind the court that undercover operators like me were consistently thrust into situations that forced us to question our individual ethics and morality, and that in this instance I'd made a poor on-the-spot decision that I'd tried to fix with limited success. But I'd also remind the court that I didn't have sex with the cheerleader, and that would be the God's honest truth.

I knew I'd be held accountable. But being second-guessed and spoken poorly of is a cost of doing business as an undercover.

THAT NIGHT BAD BOB handed Timmy written invitations to the remaining October parties. We'd go to Mesa's support party on the twenty-forth and the anniversary party on the twenty-sixth.

We rolled up to the Mesa clubhouse around nine-thirty on the twenty-fourth. As promised, Timmy brought his "girlfriend," an undercover Phoenix metro detective.

There were guys there we'd seen and never seen. In addition to the Mesa regulars were John "Joanie" Kalstedt, the Phoenix charter P; George "Joby" Walters, the Skull Valley Angel who was at Laughlin; and a couple dozen more members sporting bottom rockers that read Alaska, New York, Connecticut, South Carolina, Colorado, and Belgium. There were California members from San Fernando, Dago, and Berdoo (San Bernardino). There were also a few members from other Arizona support cubs. At least nine of the men, not including us, were openly armed with pistols. One such person was Joby Walters.

Bad Bob showed us around. We met everyone. At one point I stood with Bad Bob, Bruno from the Spartans, and "Dutchman" Keith from the Lost Dutchmen.

We talked about nothing in particular when I noticed Bob staring at my chest.

As good-naturedly as possible I said, "Why you staring at my tits, Bob?"

He barely giggled. Bruno and Keith waited for his reaction before doing the same. I just stood there.

Bob said, "I noticed you got some new flash. JHAP."

"Jesus Hates a Pussy. The Solo Nomads' motto."

"Well, I think you could use some more. I think you should sport a Hells Angels support tab like these guys." He pointed at Bruno and Keith, who both looked down at their cuts. You could've run a finger up their noses, they looked so gullible.

I didn't smile. I said to Bob firmly but respectfully, "Can't do that, Bob. I'm a Solo and I'll never sew another club's name onto my cut. It's a Solo cut, you know what I mean?" I meant the cut wasn't mine, it was my club's, just like an HA cut belonged to the Angels, not to the guy who wore it. I also meant I wasn't like Bruno or Keith. I wasn't going to roll over for the Angels like they had. It was ludicrous to suggest, but I was trying to cast the Solos as the Hells Angels' equals. I was also saying that I was loyal above all else and, like an Angel, I'd never substitute loyalty to my club for allegiance to another.

I continued, "These guys, no disrespect or nothing"—I nodded at them—"they choose to support you with those patches. Me? I support you with these." As I said that I pulled back the front of my cut, revealing my ever-present Glock 19s. Bob smiled, and I did too. I looked at Bruno. He practically blushed. Keith didn't seem to mind even though I'd punked him bad.

Joby walked by as I finished saying this. He nodded in my direction. Apparently he'd overheard everything and liked it.

Good.

A few minutes later Bad Bob announced that we were all going to Spirits.

We rolled. It was the largest group of Angels we'd yet ridden with. The Mesa guys rode tight at the front, but down the line things were looser. We, being non-Angels, rode at the back, which suited me fine.

We blew traffic lights, ignored laws and courtesies like signaling and yielding right-of-way, and roared into the parking lot at Spirits, forty strong. It felt damn good.

As we walked in, a South Carolina Angel said, "Damn, these Arizona brothers press it hard. Shit, I ride like old people fuck: slow and sloppy." That gave me some comfort. I wasn't the only one who was scared of riding like Mesa.

A VIP section was hastily cleared by prospects and bouncers, and free alcohol began to flow. Women popped up like mushrooms. Lynyrd Skynyrd's "Freebird" played over the system.

This has been my song since junior high school, a song I took to heart from the first time I heard it. There are songs you respond to because they tell you something about yourself that you already know but were maybe unable to articulate, and there are songs you respond to because they help mold your image of yourself. "Freebird" was both. As practically everyone knows, the lyrics talk about the impossibility of a stable love between a woman and the Freebird, who is a restless, wandering soul. This restlessness is what has always spoken to me. It recalls my inability to reach any kind of lasting satisfaction, and reaffirms, in a cruel twist, that I can only ever remember my failures and never my successes. Looking in on myself, especially since the case has ended, I regard this trait to be one of my weakest.

The irony is that satisfaction is all I really want. This is where my restlessness comes from, and where it turns into action, into wandering, into searching, more often than not in the wrong places—I *am* an undercover cop, after all. Therefore, I'm just like the guy in "Freebird," who cannot stay, who cannot change, and whose Lord knows he cannot change.

Nothing changed at the bar, either. It was the usual scene. We left around eleven and rode back to the clubhouse, bringing a cache of women with us.

The party never stopped. The jukebox was fired up and the sound system was turned to the front yard. I could only imagine what the neighbors thought.

I went to take a piss and Joby, whom I was yet to formally meet, was standing at the urinal next to me. He nodded to me as we went about our business. He finished before me and went to the sink. Before I zipped up I let a drop of piss hit each of my boots. When I turned to wash up, he was looking at me quizzically.

He said, "You're Bird, right?"

"Yep. It's Joby, yeah?"

"That's right. What the fuck was that about?"

"What? The boots? An old bullrider told me it was good luck."

He smiled wide, his buckteeth shining. "I like that."

"Hasn't failed me yet."

We stepped back into the party and went our separate ways.

I stood around the yard with a dozen other guys and half as many women. The Mesa clubhouse had a "front house" that was for members only. Occasionally its door would swing wide and one of us would get a glimpse inside. All we saw was more of the same.

Joby came up to us. "Hey, Bird."

"Hey, Joby." We shook hands. Timmy and Pops were with me. I introduced them.

Joby said, "I heard a lot of good things about you guys. A lot of good things."

I said, "Glad to hear it. It means the world to us that you guys think well of us."

He nodded. I could see over Joby's shoulder a little commotion breaking out. A drunken woman in high-waisted, too-tight, acid-washed jeans pestered two Mesa Angels. Joby glanced over his shoulder and looked back at us. He said, "Smitty and Bob both spoke to me. Dennis too."

Timmy said, "Cool. We love those guys." Pops said nothing.

"It sounds like the feeling's mutual." Joby spoke with a quick High Plains twang, but it didn't change the feeling that he was a smooth customer. He sounded smart to boot.

The woman in acid-washed jeans had moved on to a group of Angels standing next to us. She was begging for a bump of meth. Her voice was shrill and her words were pathetic. Bad Bob emerged from the front house, followed by the tattooed girl. His face was pinched and red. As he walked by, he looked at me and spurted, "Shit, Bird!" He sniffed hard and his eyes were tearing. The tattooed girl was laughing. Bob grabbed each of her butt cheeks.

The acid-washed tweaker, instinctively aware of the proximity of some good crank, begged more. Joby cringed but otherwise ignored her. He said, "The Chief moved me out to Kingman a few months ago. We need more numbers in that area." The Chief, I assumed, referred to none other than Ralph "Sonny" Barger.

I said, "Yeah, I've been hearing some shit about Mongols in Kingman."

"Heard that too. Heard there's four or five of those motherfuckers around there."

Timmy said, "Well, there shouldn't be."

"Goddamn right," Joby sputtered. He got angry just thinking about them.

The tweaker squealed, "I need a rail! Who's got a rail?"

Joby said, "I'll kill those motherfuckers on sight. I don't give a fuck. Courthouse steps or out in the desert, I see a Mongol bitch and I'm shooting her off her bike and selling it for scrap. I don't give a solid fuck."

I believed him.

The tweaker, failing with everyone, turned to us. Joby eyed her peripherally. She bent her knees slightly and bounced, bringing her hands together in a plea. Her face was red and tired-looking. She had shopping-bag eyes and rotten teeth. It looked like she'd been pretty before the crystal. Pops turned to go inside. I could tell he was disgusted. He'd seen this kind of woman one too many times. Timmy and I watched Joby.

The woman got out two words: *I need.* Then, in a fluid motion, Joby turned on her, unholstered a hip-belt .380 semiauto, and pushed it into her forehead. She stopped talking and went cross-eyed.

Joby barked in a sudden, deep tenor, "Bitch, I will kill you if you do not leave me and my brothers alone right now!"

The only sound was music. Time crept. Some nearby Angels looked at Joby, others didn't even bother. The woman had already ceased to exist for all of them. It was like Joby had drawn-down on a ghost, or a patch of sunlight in a living room.

Joby was serious and, by the look of it, acquainted with homicide. The woman had to leave or he'd keep his promise. I took note of it.

As cops, neither Timmy nor I could let this happen. I made a snap decision to grab Joby and stop him if necessary. I'd have to tell him she wasn't worth it, which she clearly wasn't. I hoped he'd have sense enough to hear my words and forgive me the offense of touching a Hells Angel without permission. Joby continued, "You're talking to a Hells Angel, bitch. Lesson number one: We don't give, we get. You ever ask me or my brothers for anything ever again"—Joby pressed the gun harder into her forehead—"and you'll find out in a real bad way what happens."

Luckily for us and the tweaker, another woman materialized, grabbed her arm, and pulled her away. She disappeared and I never saw her again.

The music hadn't stopped and everyone resumed whatever they were doing.

The woman gone, Joby turned to us and holstered his gun. He said calmly, "Let me give you my cell. Next time you're up Kingman way, you give me a shout."

We said we would.

Joby left us. We stood around in the yard. A girl I hadn't noticed strutted out from the clubhouse. She was followed by five Angels I couldn't ID. Bringing up the rear was Bad Bob, who wagged his tongue at us. He pumped his fist in the air, pulling that imaginary train whistle.

That night's gang bang was on.

We left not too long after that.

18 FIVE YEARS IN THE DESERT

THE TWENTY-FIFTH WAS a hotwash day. Hotwash is when you try to take everything that's "hot" in your memory and "wash" it out clean into reports. Slats knew our nighttime activities were hectic. He insisted we reset our memory banks to zero before going out for more.

The Patch was buzzing with activity. Cricket and Buddha worked on our bikes. Our tech guy did routine maintenance on our temperamental recording devices. Other guys processed mugshots and rap sheets and added surveillance photos to the suspect matrix. Timmy and I typed reports and went over op plans with Slats. Slats had some good news: He'd been able to secure JJ for a couple nights. She'd sit in the surveillance van and get a bead on what we were up to. She hadn't been approved for action, but Slats said he was getting closer to a green light. I said, "Great."

The overall mood at Black Biscuit headquarters was euphoric. Our plan was working well. This was the first time in the case when we started to overachieve as a unit. My confidence was rising, and since I was one of the case's chief barometers, the whole team's confidence rose too.

I called Gwen after completing reports. She didn't want to hear from me. Dale was having a tough time in the beginning of the school year.

Some problem with math that I didn't take the time to understand. Jack was doing fine, but he was still a kid who wanted his old man more than he got him. Gwen was pissed because she was tired of playing Mom and Dad. She was stressed. I tried to explain to her that I was too. I told her a little bit about what I was doing—she knew I was trying to get in on the Angels—but she thought all I did was party all the time, hang out with loose women, ride a bike, and have fun. That pissed me off and the conversation ended quickly. She said she needed some time to herself. I said that I did too, that it wasn't like my life was all roses. Gwen couldn't hear that. She was holding our family together with dedication and spit and I was being ungrateful. We didn't quite hang up on each other, but we didn't quite say good-bye, either. I didn't speak to the kids.

After that, Timmy, Slats, Cricket, and I discussed Rudy. At one point during the festivities of the twenty-fourth, Bad Bob had asked me if I'd heard from Rudy. I'd done what every undercover operator should endeavor to do whenever possible: I'd told him the truth, that I hadn't heard from Rudy and that it was worrying me. I told Bob he'd gotten his nose deep in the bag and had gone off the map. Bad Bob asked me if he was cooking, and I said I didn't know but if I had to guess I'd say yes. Bob's concerns were mixed. There were security issues, but he was also being opportunistic: Bad Bob was always looking for a tweak. Regardless, he acted concerned about Rudy. He asked if I was using and I said no way. By that time Bad Bob had seen a set of tattoos emblazoned across my pecs: GDJ on the right and DOA on the left. He knew that GDJ stood for God Damned Junkie (actually, it stood for Gwen, Dale, Jack), and that DOA stood for what DOA always stands for; in my case it commemorated the fact that Brent Provestgaard had essentially rendered me DOA back when I got shot as a rookie agent. It's located over the exact spot that his bullet exited my chest. I'd told Bad Bob, however, that DOA referred to the time I'd overdosed and nearly killed myself. I said these tattoos were constant reminders to stay clean. No one doubted my story one inch, including Bad Bob.

But we were talking about Rudy. Bad Bob laid it out simple: "You gotta bring Rudy back in."

We decided to take Bad Bob's advice literally. As soon as we got a chance, we were going to arrest Rudy Kramer.

PARTY NIGHT. SERIOUS Hells Angels heaven.

The local cops secured the street. It was a comical scene. On one side of the barricade were marked units with twirling cherry lights and uniforms posing tensely. These cops were outnumbered on the other side of the barricade by relaxed Hells Angels, prospects, and hangarounds. The guys lounged in folding lawn chairs and drank beer, leaned on their bikes, and sat on the curb. It was, from the Angels' point of view, a perfect example of their existence beyond the system, a picture of their out-of-bounds status. The cops were there to protect the outside world from the Hells Angels, but they were also there to protect the Angels from the outside world. In a sense, the cops were working for the Angels that night.

I arrived forty-five minutes after Pops, Timmy, and Timmy's female partner. A prospect I'd never met stopped me at the police barricade at the end of the block. The cops looked at me sideways. I nodded to them, openly mocking them. They were used to it. They'd been getting it all night.

I showed the prospect my invite and he let me in. I was stamped in at the clubhouse gate.

It was a bona fide convention. Bikes constantly hummed, music constantly pounded. You could have resurrected a herd of cows with all the leather in evidence, or created the world's largest pair of jeans with all the denim. Every shape, color, and length of beard was present, from the ZZ Top to the flavor-saver. The pungent smell of marijuana hung over the whole place, as if smoke rose from the storm drains on the street and the vents in the house, as if every step taken was on an inch-thick carpet of perfumed buds. Women laughed, men scowled; men laughed, women scowled. Beer was the water of life, whiskey man's surest elixir. A circus tent their neighbor had allowed them to place in his backyard underscored the party's surrealism.

Smitty was near the entry gate when I walked in. He gave me a big hug. I congratulated him and the Angels and said it looked like everything was going well. He pulled me aside.

"Bird. Gotta tell you something I just found out. One of my contacts in the Bullhead police told me that they're looking into you guys up there. They wanna know what you're up to, bad. They've assigned a gang task force to you, they're handing out flyers with your picture on it and everything. So, you know, be careful, all right?"

From innocence to experience. Who knew an all-American kid would end up being so good at busting gun- and drug-runners?

Case agent Joseph "Slats" Slatalla. Always a friend, sometimes a rival, Slats ran our Hells Angels investigation, code-named Operation Black Biscuit, with an unwavering hand—even when we butted heads about how to achieve our objectives.

Rather than endear ourselves to the Hells Angels as freelance bad guys, we formed a legitimate charter of the Solo Angeles, a Mexican motorcycle club, and cozied up to the Hells Angels as peers.

I never got a single tattoo specifically to enhance my undercover work—but they sure did help. And as the Hells Angels case progressed and I lost myself more and more in the role of outlaw biker, my love of ink went to the next level.

(Right) Our act was so convincing, it fooled not only our adversaries, but also local law-enforcement agencies ignorant of our operation. In fact, it fooled the local cops so badly they started investigating *us*.

LAW ENFORCEMENT BULLETIN

***** DO NOT CONTACT ***** ARMED AND DANGEROUS *****

INTELLIGENCE REQUEST

The Arizona / California / Nevada Tri-State biker intelligence group, the Bullhead City Police Department and the Mohave County Sheriffs Department are seeking identification and intelligence information on a newly formed OMG (Outlaw Motorcycle Gang) calling themselves the

Solo Angeles Motorcycle Club (SAMC) Nomads

The SAMC is based in Tijuana, Mexico. A newly formed Nomads charter is allegedly establishing a U.S. base of operations in Bullhead City, AZ. Known members are *Jay Davis* (D.O.B. 08-19-61), a.k.a. 'Bird', 'Jaybird'; and, *Timmy Davis* (D.O.B. unknown), a.k.a. 'TD' (6'3" 270 BR(BD) BR). As many as eleven members of the charter may exist. Jay Davis and Timmy Davis are believed to be half-brothers. Both are known to be armed and dangerous. SAMC is allegedly involved in firearms and stolen motorcycle trafficking.

The SAMC clubhouse / residence is located at 1793 Verano Circle, Bullhead City, Arizona. Members are associates of the Hells Angels Motorcycle Club and the Vagos Motorcycle Club.

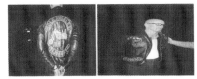

Solo Angeles MC
club vest orange over black
motorcycle outline center patch

Jay Davis
08-19-61
6'1" 215 BN(BD) BL

Call the Bullhead City Police Department (928-763-9200) with information.

FOR LAW ENFORCEMENT USE ONLY

(Below) Undercover every day. Even the kids who lived near our Phoenix undercover house got the Jay "Bird" Davis treatment.

Line 'em up!

Kevin Augustiniak

Dan "Dirty Dan" Danza

Paul Eischeid

Duane "Crow" Williams

Ralph "Sonny" Barger

Dennis Denbesten

Rudy Jaime

Mug shots of the principal Hells Angels we investigated

Robert "Mac" McKay

Robert "Bad Bob" Johnston

Robert "Bobby" Reinstra

Robert "Chico" Mora

Theodore "Teddy" Toth

Donald "Smitty" Smith

George "Joby" Walters

(Above) Pops (at left) hanging out with the late Daniel "Hoover" Seybert, the Hells Angels heir apparent to Sonny Barger. Not two months later, Hoover was shot dead in a parking lot.

We flew our Solo Angeles colors at the Florence Prison Run, seamlessly joining the rumbling horde.

Looks fun, right? Wrong. You try convincing yourself that, at heart, you're still the good man you think you are, even as you fall deeper into the rabbit hole of a deception that was increasingly becoming a self-deception.

Finally, I was on my way to becoming a full-patch Hells Angel as a Skull Valley prospect. The case was coming full circle, and my dark, dangerous biker life had become all-consuming. I'd become the man I was pretending to be.

Not happy with our prospecting duties, my partners and I became determined to get our patches as quickly as possible, and at almost any cost. Making the Hells Angels had become an obsession . . .

. . . an obsession that compelled us to attempt the ultimate push for membership. The Angels hated rival motorcycle club the Mongols with a passion. How could they turn their backs on us after we showed them a dead Mongol in a desert ditch?

I gripped his arm. It was the first I'd heard of this, and I was sincerely grateful. I'd have Shawn Wood from the Arizona Department of Public Safety check on it the next day.

I stayed with the Bullhead gang for a few minutes, then excused myself to find my crew.

Timmy and Pops were hanging out with a Red Devil named James. Timmy told me later that they'd been discussing large-quantity marijuana buys, gun deals, and moving stolen cars. James had given Timmy his cell number and told him to call him the following week. Timmy said he most definitely would.

James wandered off, and we Solos were alone for a few minutes. We stood by the bar in the common area of the clubhouse. A topless stripper in gold bikini bottoms and another stripper in a tight, torn T-shirt with a screaming eagle on it giggled at the far end. Ghost, who'd broken his leg when he went OTB—over the bars—in a traffic accident, talked to these women along with Rockem and Sockem.

We were approached by Dennis, Dolly, and another couple in their early fifties. Dennis intro'd them as JoJo and Tracey Valenti. The guy was a monster. Weighed in around 300 pounds, his bald head smaller than his neck, which was smaller than his upper arm. He had a doughnut-sized Death Head tattooed above his right ear. His flared-out, bushy beard was as big as his face. His cheeks were clean-shaven. He had on black leather spiked cuffs that covered most of his tatted-out forearms. He sweated and breathed like a fat man. He was past his prime, but it was obvious that back in the day he was a flat-out wrecking ball.

JoJo was the Tucson vice president, one of the guys with Doug Dam and Fang. He was on crutches. One of his legs was in a cast. The other was a prosthetic. The story of his remaining leg had recently become infamous. JoJo'd broken his ankle in a motorcycle accident and gashed it pretty badly. They stitched him up, put him in a cast, gave him crutches, told him to keep off the leg. He didn't listen. He should have. Considering he was diabetic, he really should have. He took bad care of the cast, let it get wet in the rain and in the shower, walked on it, rode, everything. Everyone noticed that JoJo had been smelling bad lately, but no one talked about why. He was a fat guy, fat guys don't always smell like roses. JoJo complained of pain and severe itching. One day, as he sat on the toilet, blood started to ooze from the cast around his foot. His toes were as black as the leather of his cut. Tracey took him to the hospital. As they cracked the cast open, a swarm of young black flies buzzed out. The gash was full of maggots. The doctors cleaned them out, gave him a new cast, and told him to take better care of it. He said he would.

We moved on and met more Angels. One was Duane "Crow" Williams, a Mesa member who was old and senile, and mumbled everything he said. He was always armed, even though he barely seemed to register what went on around him. His wife led him around the party by the arm and propped him on bar stools and fetched him drink after drink. She was more of a chaperone than a spouse. From the first time I met Crow he called me Pruno. I insisted I was Bird, but he said that was bullshit, I was Pruno. He said that I was Pruno because I made the best jailhouse wine he'd ever tasted. Months after the anniversary party I bought a Taurus pistol from Crow. Before he handed over the piece, he pointed out blood splatter on the muzzle. In a burst of clarity he told me he'd tried to scrub it off, but could never get it all the way clean. I told him it didn't matter, it was a gun, right? He smiled and told me he liked me, and gave me a little necklace with a dagger pendant. I asked him what it was for. He said, "Because you're the real deal, Pruno." I told him for the thousandth time that I was Bird. He shrugged and said, "Well, keep it anyway." Months after *that*, as the case was coming to an end, Crow would be the last Hells Angel we'd have contact with.

We met Daniel "Hoover" Seybert, the president of Cave Creek. He told us to come visit him at his place, the RBC Tavern. We said we'd drop by for sure.

We met Robert "Mac" McKay. He was the Tucson member with the nonassociation clause in his probation—a probation he'd received for beating down the ex-president of the Tucson charter. He wore a phony long gray beard and a brown wig—two tones of hair that belonged on separate heads—so the cops wouldn't mess with him. His real beard bled out from beneath the fake, and as the night went on and the beer kept flowing, he looked more and more ridiculous. I wasn't sure why he wore the disguise inside the clubhouse, since there was no one there he had to fool. Like everyone else, Mac said he'd heard good things about us Solos. I was typically gracious and humble. He seemed to be a nice guy, and was, as I'd find out, a damn good tattoo artist.

It was a whirlwind. At one point Pops stepped away to get some beer. As he crossed the room an older Angel—tan, trim, wearing eyeglasses—stepped into his path and grabbed his arm.

I immediately recognized him as Ralph "Sonny" Barger.

This was the first time I'd laid eyes on the man. He was around sixty-five, but looked to have the health of a vibrant man in his mid-fifties, a remarkable achievement considering the paces he'd put his body through over the decades. He had close-cropped white hair, was clean-shaven, and looked more like a Marine drill sergeant than a life-long outlaw. He moved with all the confidence and sureness of a sultan in his harem.

For those who don't know, this was the man—the legend, really—who molded the Hells Angels into what they are. It's not a stretch to say that Sonny Barger is a visionary who essentially created the image of the outlaw biker as we know it. He had help, to be sure, and the names of his cohorts dating back to the late fifties through the present are legendary in the biker world: Johnny Angel, Terry the Tramp, Magoo, Junkie George, Mouldy Marvin, Cisco Valderama. Together and with a host of others, these men created the image—the leather, the hair, the grime, the hardness, the silence, the impenetrability, the bikes—everything that constitutes an outlaw biker.

Especially the bikes.

Without the Hells Angels we wouldn't have floor-model Harleys that look like stripped-down scream machines. No ape hangers, no flared fenders, no bitch bars, no spool wheels, no front-end extenders. There'd be less chrome, less-creative paint jobs, less style. The HA were obsessed with going fast, and without this obsession bikes would be slower. They were relentless in stripping their bikes of all but the barest essentials. The formula was simple: Less weight plus bigger engines equaled more speed. Every pound they shed gained them two miles per hour. Thus, "choppers"—chopped-down motorcycles. What they did was mimicked by everyone who wanted to be a Hells Angel but couldn't be. Their influence is seen today in bikes designed by Jessie James of West Coast Choppers and the Teutuls at Orange County Choppers.

Bikes aside, a world without Sonny Barger would look pretty much the same, but the world of the outlaw biker, if it even existed, would look a hell of a lot different. He is *the* iconic outlaw biker, and all members of every club look up to him as the godfather of their culture. He's respected for who he is, but he's also respected for his vision. He saw that the Angels could go international, that though American in origin, they needn't be limited to America's borders. As I've said before, I believe that the Hells Angels, and to a lesser extent all American-style biker gangs, are this country's only organized-crime export. This is the doing of Ralph "Sonny" Barger. He embodies everything about the Hells Angels, from their unwavering image right on down to their contradictions.

Those contradictions fascinate me. The Hells Angels are separate from society, but they're rooted in it; they're nonconformists, but they all look the same; they're a secret society, but also flamboyant exhibitionists; they flout the laws of the land, but they're governed by a strict code; their name and their Death Head logo represent freedom, individualism, toughness, and lawlessness, but both name and logo are protected by legal trademarks.

The way these contradictions manifest in the real world is what really pisses me off. These guys shouldn't be able to have it both ways. I mean, if you don't respect the law, then why use certain laws to protect yourself? Why conduct toy runs and other charity drives to bolster your public image if you don't care what the public thinks? Which is it? Are you misunderstood bike enthusiasts, or violent hoodlums? Why do you care if anyone likes you? When the Angels are at their criminal best, they embody everything an outlaw ought to: fight first and ask questions later. Better yet, don't ask questions. Take what you want: turf, pussy, beer, bikes, drugs. Be violent and don't apologize. I never apologized for being an undercover cop, even when it put me in life-threatening or ethically compromising positions. I never apologized for arresting people who deserved it, whether I liked them or not. I never apologized for being on the other side of the Hells Angels' coin.

Like me, most of these guys had a chip on their shoulder—but unlike me, they all thought that society unjustly discriminated against them. Like me, they had no interest in a regular job or lifestyle. Maybe I cherished my family and friends more than they did—but didn't they cherish their brothers and their club in the same way? They knew they were outcasts, so why not be outcasts together? Maybe the essence of their alienation was a question of nature versus nurture. Maybe, just maybe, they *did* get a raw deal. Did the Hells Angels shun the world, or did the world shun them?

These armchair reflections never crossed my mind during the investigation. All I thought as I watched Sonny approach Pops was, Wow, there's the Chief. The fucking Chief is here! With us! I'd told myself I wouldn't be impressed by his presence, but I was wrong. I was starstruck.

Pops was too. All of Sonny's movements and gestures were charming. I couldn't hear him, but I could tell by the way Pops turned his ear to him that Sonny's tracheostomy hole made no difference. There was nothing funny about Sonny's cancer kazoo. In fact, it made him more formidable. They'd carved his throat out thirty years back and the guy hadn't missed a beat. Sonny was the king of the outcasts and he knew it. We all did.

Sonny checked out Pops's Solo cut and gave him a hearty hug and they parted.

Pops told me later that Sonny had said, "Thanks for coming out. Thanks for showing respect. You should come visit us at Cave Creek. We have a charter up there, too."

The Solo Angeles Nomads had the blessing of the godfather, and it felt good.

We hung out. Bad Bob looked more like Barry Gibb than ever. His hair was immobile—perfectly frozen in place with a net of hair spray. Doug Dam wanted to know if I wanted "any of those things," referring to more guns. I winked and told him we'd talk later. I hung out in the front yard and watched the members-only door swing wide. Inside, on a low table, I saw a rock of crystal the size of a baseball. Next to it was a mound of ground meth several inches high. Members came and went, their women came and went (women, exempt from ever being members, were allowed to enter the front house with permission from a patch). All leaned over the table to snort. All came up zooming.

At some point during the evening I remembered that I'd brought a donation. I found Bad Bob and handed it to him. He peeked inside at five crisp hundred-dollar bills and removed a Solo Angeles business card (we'd had a thousand printed—black and orange, FSSF). On the back I'd written "Love and respect, Solos." He put it in his vest. We shook hands and ended up hugging.

Everyone was happy. They were happy because they'd made it five years in the desert. We were happy because we thought they'd never make it to ten. Success and smoke and that dank smell of beer infused everything.

The haze never lifted. The party wasn't going to end. I have no idea when we left.

19 ARRESTING RUDY KRAMER

NOVEMBER 2002

ANOTHER DEVELOPMENT ADDED to our high-flying attitude. As promised, JJ was in Phoenix the night of the anniversary party, listening in with the cover team. On her way back to San Diego the following day she got a call from her ASAC. He said, "Maguire, you got what you wanted. You get to run with those crazy bastards in AZ. Have fun."

Her part-time reassignment started on November 5. From then on, JJ would be available to Black Biscuit three glorious days a week.

I went home on Sunday, October 27, for a couple of days of R&R. I only went because Slats ordered me to. Had he said nothing, I would've stayed in Phoenix.

Pops's wife and daughters lived in Tucson too. We decided to ride our bikes home, flying full Solo colors down I-10, running side by side through the Valley. I had my cut on over nothing—just my bare torso, the leather vest open and flapping in the wind, my Glocks sticking out of my waistband. Cold as hell but I didn't care. I was showing off for anyone to see. Pops had on a long-sleeved orange T-shirt under his cut. We both had orange bandannas tied around our heads. I rode on the left, he rode on the right. I was getting better on a bike: We rode around

85 or 90 mph. Cars got out of our way. The country around us was wide open, the highway seemed to exist just for us. I felt free.

We peeled apart at the edge of metro Tucson. All we did was wave. We'd see each other soon enough.

I stopped at a flower farm owned by an old friend. He sold his goods on the honor system, leaving cut flowers in vases in the front of his house. You paid by dropping money in a little wooden box. I took three bouquets' worth of flowers and stuffed a hundred bucks into the box. I strapped them to the backseat with black and orange bungee cords. Neighbors gave me sideways looks, trying not to be noticed by the badass biker with the flowers.

I pulled onto my street. It curved this way and that through the desert. A roadrunner sprang across the pavement, his tail pointed straight up. A long black snake slithered into a patch of cholla like an animated *S*. My bike was loud, people knew I was coming. Gwen stood by the front door when I pulled in.

I fired down. "What's up, honey?"

She eyed me hard. Real hard, harder than any of the guys I'd been hanging out with could ever have hoped to. I didn't like it. I unstrapped the flowers.

"I got you and the grandmas some flowers."

She didn't look at them. "I'm going out. Jack's in his room playing video games. Dale's at Mel's."

"Who's Mel?"

"A new friend. The number's on the fridge." She walked toward her car and repeated, "I'm going out."

"This Mel, he a boy?"

"No, Jay."

I'd been holding the flowers out to show her. As she moved to her car, I let my hand fall limply to my side. "Where're you going?"

"Just out. I'll be back. Don't worry."

She got in her car and left.

I went inside and took my cut off. I hung it on the coatrack. It looked out of place next to my family's outerwear. I caught my image in the hall mirror: topless, tattooed, muscles bulging, arms and face dirty with the road. I was wrong. *I* looked out of place.

I moved around the house. It was a mess. Piles of dirty clothes on the bedroom floors, piles of unfolded clean ones on the beds. Unrinsed dishes in the kitchen. Little pools of water on the tops of the bathroom sinks. Gwen knew I had a compulsion for organization and cleanliness. The mess was probably unintentional—I knew she was overwhelmed with being everything to everyone while I was away—but I couldn't help wondering if the state of the house meant that she didn't care to make me comfortable whenever I happened to come home.

I took a shower. When I was done I put on a pair of swim trunks and went to see Jack in his room. Clothes lay on his bed, too, but they were folded. By the way they were folded I could tell he had done it himself. His TV was on. A frozen image from a Madden's NFL 2001 game was on the screen. Jack was hunched over his desk, writing.

I said, "Hey, kiddo."

He turned. He looked surprised and frustrated. He hadn't heard me come in. When he realized it was me, his features softened. He was a good kid. Too good for me.

I asked him what he was doing.

"Well, homework right now. I was playing Madden's, trying to learn all the offensive sets so I don't have to think about it so much, you know?" I told him I did. I knew he had limits on how long he could play video games, but I was happy to hear he was trying to learn all the sets. I'd played the game with him in the past, and even I was shocked by the number of plays the computer had, and how hard they could be to execute or defend. Sad to say, but I looked at his playing of Madden's as a kind of education, which I fully supported.

I asked, "Hey, you hungry?"

"Yep."

"Why don't you bring your homework to the dining room. I'll make some lunch."

He said OK and gathered his stuff up.

In the kitchen I got out a can of tuna, opened it, drained it, and put it in a bowl. I added mayo and pepper. I cut up a small onion and a sour pickle and put them in the bowl. I added dill. I got out four slices of bread and put them in the toaster. I mashed the fish mixture with a fork. I looked over at Jack. His shoulders were gathered around his ears, his tongue was out. He was trying really hard, striving to do his best. I was proud.

I put the bread on a big plate and divided the tuna salad onto two pieces of golden bread. I got out some lettuce and put it on the salad.

I squirted yellow mustard on the other two slices of bread and folded them onto the lettuce. I pushed them into place and cut the sandwiches diagonally.

I watched Jack some more. He was erasing some of his letters. No—he was erasing a lot of them. I could see the side of his face. His concentration had crossed back into frustration. I grabbed the plate and walked over to the table.

He'd been erasing to the point where he was eating holes in his paper. I asked him if he was having trouble with an answer.

He said, "No. The answer's right."

"Then what's the problem, kiddo?" I sat next to him, put down the plate, and grabbed a wedge of sandwich. I bit into it.

"It's my handwriting. It's all wrong. I can't get it right. I hate it."

He dropped his pencil and hung his head. The tuna tasted good but I felt sick. I knew immediately that I'd screwed up something in my son's head.

I said, "It looks good to me. I can read it."

"That's not the point, Dad, it's not *right*, you know? I can do better."

"You're nine years old, kiddo. You'll get the hang of it."

"But it's not right." I knew what he meant. I recognized them as a paraphrase of my own words, repeated to him and Dale who knew how many times, in all kinds of contexts: sports, schoolwork, chores. I'd drilled it into them: "Everything you do—*everything*—do it to the max. This is the key to success in life and personal satisfaction. Nothing short of everything you have is acceptable. *That* will make you a winner." I felt like a worm. I should've been there to tell Jack that it was his effort that was important, not the result. But I wasn't there. I mean, I was there in the sense that Jack was trying to make me happy, by getting his letters right—but I wasn't there physically to tell him that no matter what, Jack always made me happy. He'd confused effort with result, just as I always had.

A worm. A worm split in two. I writhed, but I wouldn't let him see it.

I said, "Hey, kiddo, I know I've said otherwise, but what really matters is that you try your best. You give a good effort—your best effort—and there's no reason why you shouldn't be satisfied with what you get. Got it? That's what's important. Try hard. Effort is its own reward."

He said OK, but I didn't believe him. Why should I? I barely believed myself. Results were all that mattered to me, all that had mattered to me for years. I handed him a sandwich wedge. We ate and talked about Little League and the Arizona Cardinals. I promised I'd take him to a game. He said, "Really?"

I said, "Really."

GWEN CAME BACK later. She'd gone shopping at Old Navy and had an early dinner with some friends she hadn't seen in a while. Jack was already off to bed, and Dale, who'd had dinner at Mel's, was in her room reading.

Gwen wasn't happy. We went to our room and argued. She told me she didn't want me showing up at home looking the way I did. She said it was hard enough for the kids my not being there, that I didn't have to confuse them by looking like a damn biker in my own home. I said Jack didn't see me decked out. She said he just as easily could have. She was right; I said I wouldn't wear my UC clothes home ever again. She said that wasn't the point. She said she was getting worn down. I asked her if she thought I wasn't. I asked her if she knew the kind of shit I dealt with every day. She asked me the same question. Neither of us knew what the other was dealing with, and we both felt underappreciated, but neither of us was going to concede that the other was more correct. I asked her why she'd had to go out so quickly, why we couldn't have had some time at home together, with the kids and all. She yelled my full name—Jay Anthony Dobyns! I said, "Hey, I'm not a detective."

She said, "No, you're an undercover." She changed gears, said, "I know you have a woman on the case, I just know it."

This shocked me. I hadn't told her anything about JJ, who had yet to work even a full day. Woman's intuition, I guess. She asked if I thought it was fair that she had to stay home all the time with the family while I did whatever the hell it was I did with whomever the hell I did it with. I didn't like the implication. I hadn't slept with another woman and I wasn't planning to. I told her that was my job, and that, by the way, when I'm working I'm running with thugs in Bullhead, not sipping mai tais on Kauai. She said that when I came home, whenever that happened to be, I could expect her to take off for a while. She said she needed a break too. I agreed. She said it may be my job to do whatever, whenever, with whomever, but it was her job to look after our family. She put a particular emphasis on that word, *our,* as if I'd forgotten a fact. Maybe I had. No—I'd definitely begun to forget by then. Once again, I felt like a worm. But, more than that, I felt angry for being made to feel like a worm. I was just doing my job, and I was good at my job, and I wasn't going to stop doing my job.

I had to cool down. I went out to the pool and listened to the desert. There were crickets and coyotes. There was no moon. The stars were bright. Jack's light was out. Dale's and Gwen's were on. I lit a cigarette and smoked it. I lit another and smoked it. I lit another, and smoked it.

NOVEMBER 2, AND I was back on. I left the house wearing a tank top. Jack had given me two more rocks as I got ready to leave—both were gray—one looked like a fist, the other like a fish. I stuffed them into my pocket. As Gwen had requested, I did not wear my cut. I waited until I got a safe distance from my house, pulled over, unstrapped it from the backseat, and put it on. I tied on my bandanna. I got out my Glocks.

I was Bird.

I hooked up with Pops and went over to Doug Dam's to buy more guns.

We hung out with Doug, his girlfriend, and a prospect named Hank Watkins. Hank had been a Tucson Red Devil who'd been requested to patch over. He was in his late forties, more of an old-school guy than an up-and-comer. He'd had some preliminary dealings with Rudy, but since his Angels prospecting phase had begun, he'd been ordered to cool it: Prospects are not allowed to conduct any illegal activity without the express consent of their Angels superiors. Doug was his sponsor, and since they were together, nothing stopped them from selling us some iron.

They had two choice pieces. An Intratec AB-10 9 mm Luger semi-auto pistol and a Heckler & Koch blue steel semiauto 9 mm pistol. They wanted $1,600 for both. It was more than I thought they were worth, but I agreed to the price. The H&K was a very nice gun. I went to the bank to get some extra cash and paid them.

Pops and I hit the road. We rode hard through the Valley once more, 90, 95 mph. Towers of red rock watched over us. Near Picacho an ostrich farm stretched out to the west. The bike felt good between my legs. She was humming along. I'd gotten some ape-hanger bars at the Motorcycle Shop in Kingman, and they were really comfortable to ride with.

I thought about the case, about Bird, about being in role. I thought about what was coming later that day.

Other than Jack's rocks, I didn't think about home much at all. The plain truth was that in those days I didn't reflect much on my family. I knew they were there, at home, and that was enough. I knew I wasn't there, but I believed in my reasons. Still, I couldn't help thinking of Jack's handwriting and how it frustrated him. I was frustrated too. I knew I had to do a better job on the Angels—not for ATF, not for Slats, not for Gwen—but for me. I knew I had to work harder. I knew I had to hang my ass out even more. I also knew I had lied to Jack when I told him that it was only his effort that mattered.

But I didn't dwell on it.

We went to the Patch. We dropped Hank and Doug's guns in the evidence vault. I filled out a voucher. Pops drank a Coke and fiddled with his fuel-intake valve, which had been giving him trouble. Slats told me that the Phoenix UC house was ready to go. He said I could spend the night there. He said it was over in Vattoland, South Central Phoenix. There were good taco stands out that way.

Timmy showed up at the Patch with his female partner. They were in role. Timmy had been teaching me some martial-arts basics and we sparred lightly. This was a big part of his cover—a martial-arts instructor offering private lessons. He twisted me up, threw me on the ground, and choked me out. Fun stuff—for him. When the time came to leave, we all tied black bandannas around our biceps.

We were off to a funeral.

I DIDN'T KNOW the guy, but Rudy did. Some dude he rode with back when they were in a minor club called the Loners. Most recently the guy had been a Spartan Rider. He'd been hit by a semi while blowing a red light—all kinds of nasty things in the grille. Rudy had come to us for support, said we needed to go as a club, to show our respects to a fallen brother. We agreed, but not for his reasons. All we wanted was to draw Rudy out into the sunshine.

The funeral was at the Church of the Sun in Cave Creek. There were Loners, Spartans, Lost Dutchmen, Bonded Slaves, and Limeys in attendance. There were three Hells Angels flying Phoenix tabs—none of whom we'd met.

The ceremony was brief and unceremonious. Words on death quickly passed the lips of these men. There were the usual platitudes of a life lived the right way, of a loyal brother, of a man who might not have been a good son but who was a righteous outlaw. Eulogy was not their strong point. They grunted, they nodded, they hung their heads. They prayed—to what god one can only guess. They saluted. They all wore their cuts. They were good Americans, good friends. They believed in the soul. They believed in redemption, in ultimate relief from a world of judgment and harassment and incarceration. They prayed that he find a bike in the afterlife.

We left in a single-file column. We roared our engines, sending his spirit to wherever it was destined to go with a final flourish, with an announcement.

Maybe it was pathetic, maybe it was profound, maybe it was nothing. I watched it all, but didn't much care. I had other things on my mind.

Rudy looked like shit. He'd completed his journey home to Methopotamia, the cradle of crystallization. I'd told Bad Bob that his nose was deep in the bag. From the look of his eyes, that wasn't all. He'd put his whole head and body into the shit.

We went to the Spartan Riders' clubhouse on East Van Buren in Central Phoenix. More of the same, this time with beer and smoke.

We Solos left close to 7:00 p.m. We rode down Van Buren and turned onto Seventh Street, headed toward I-10 and the Bank One Ballpark, where the Diamondbacks play. We were in standard formation, Rudy and I up front, Timmy and Pops directly behind us.

Two marked units pulled nose-to-nose onto Seventh Street in front of us. Rudy slowed to a stop, and I followed his lead. A helicopter came in from the west, dipping low fast, a million-candlepower "night sun" spot illuminating the scene. The marked units' doors opened. Rudy was backing up in a three-point turn, telling me to follow him. I said, "Today ain't my day to die, Rude. These dudes don't look to be fucking around." I glanced over my shoulder. Three more marked units blocked our rear. We were trapped in the middle of the block.

The police moved quickly. I knew their orders. Knock down the Solo Angeles Nomads, execute the warrant on one Rudy Kramer, a felon in possession of a firearm.

From a side street, two tactical SWAT members jogged toward us, all in black, helmets with blacked-out eye shields, muzzles pointed down, the Darth Vaders of law enforcement. The uniforms got out and approached quickly. We were ordered off our bikes. We got off. Guns were drawn, but not ours. In fact, none of us was armed that night.

Heston Silbert, a Phoenix SWAT lieutenant who knew our status, ran the op, but the officers who carried it out knew nothing about us. They were very professional, surgical, and speedy. They concentrated on Rudy.

They laid us out—facedown, hands on the neck, ankles crossed—in neat rows. Rudy was next to me. I looked at him. He didn't look at me. He looked calm—it wasn't the first time he'd been through this. As they pulled Rudy to his feet, I said, "I love you." He looked at me and said, "I know." I held back a burst of laughter. He thought I meant it. Irony was lost on the old addict. I looked back at the ground. I wasn't sorry it hadn't worked out for him. It was my job to put guys like Rudy away, even if I had to use them first. Still, I would've thanked him if I could.

They cuffed him and hauled him up. He spat on the ground, not out of rage but just because he had to spit. He was taking it easy. A good perp. The guys found a loaded pistol and a three-ounce bag of meth in his saddlebags. They put these into separate evidence Baggies, then stuffed Rudy into one of the units. A panel truck pulled onto the block. Two guys loaded Rudy's bike into it. The truck left. The SWATs disappeared. The car doors shut, the units backed up and drove away. The helicopter banked to the north and peeled toward the highway interchange. We got up.

The strike was so convincing that, years later, defense attorneys insisted Rudy Kramer's arrest was a routine, if elaborate, traffic stop that bagged our P right out from under us. They couldn't believe it was a premeditated part of Slats's plan to cut the weak link from our chain.

Rudy had been removed from Black Biscuit.

I'd never see him face-to-face again.

20 HELLO, JJ

I CALLED TEACHER, the Solo Angeles U.S. president in L.A., the night of Rudy's arrest and told him what was up. I said the second the cuffs got clamped on Rudy's wrists, I'd become the Solo president in Arizona. He said it was fine with him, so long as we kept up with dues and all. I told him not to worry. Then I called Bad Bob and Smitty and told each of them I was interim P until Rudy's situation cleared up. I had to play it like his fate was uncertain, and as his supposed ally, I had to sound like I hoped he'd beat the rap.

I knew he wouldn't. And I knew my new post was permanent.

Next order of business was our new partner. Pops and I picked her up at the Phoenix airport on November 5. We drove the Merc and met her at baggage claim. She wore black jeans, a white T-shirt, and a California smile. Her blond hair was pulled back in a ponytail with a large black scrunchy, her bangs brushed the tops of her eyebrows. A nice-looking, healthy young American woman, equal parts innocence, enthusiasm, and confidence. It wasn't a disguise—JJ was a good woman, and a good woman was what I needed. We felt it would be less convincing if she looked too much like a biker tramp. A cardinal rule of undercover work is to tell as few lies as possible and, in spite of what you think, to be yourself. JJ was genuine, I could see it and I was banking that the Angels would see it too.

Pops waited for her bag while we chitchatted. I said, "You're a sight for sore eyes."

She smiled and said, "You look like shit."

I was in the standard getup, minus my Solo cut and guns. We were inside, but my sunglasses were still on. I had on a black knit ski cap with the words SERIAL KILLER stitched across the forehead. I said, "Great. You're gonna fit right in."

"I hope so," she said.

We'd been briefing her over the phone since Rudy's arrest. She'd gotten the general rundown: our areas of operation, the names of principals, what kinds of deals we'd been doing. During one of the calls, Slats commented that we needed to be bringing in more drugs. I interjected that we'd been doing all right on guns and basic RICO stuff, but that our drug buys were mostly small: teeners of meth, dimes and nicks of marijuana, a few dozen pills. Slats told JJ that he hoped she'd be able to help us secure more junk.

"No problem," she said.

We went over her cover story. We kept it consistent with what Smitty and Lydia knew about her: that we used to date a few years back, and that since we'd run into each other in La Jolla, she'd done a couple runs south of the border for me. The runs had gone well, and we'd hooked back up. We weren't sure we were going to be spending all of our time together, but we were into each other enough that she was going to start spending weekends in the desert, going back west during the week to take care of business for me and my SoCal associates. To lend all of this some credibility and make it look like she wasn't popping out of the woodwork, we decided to run a little longer in Bullhead, where the people who already knew her could get to know her better, and then vouch for her sudden appearance on the scene across the state.

Once she got established, she'd get more operational responsibility. She said she wanted to be treated more like Bird's business partner than arm-candy. We agreed. I knew that if she stood around acting like she was waiting for me to take her home every night, she'd get bored quickly, and she wouldn't be as valuable to the case. We decided to treat her like one of the guys—she'd carry a gun, too—in the hopes that the Angels would respect her as much as we did.

I told her, however, that there would be times when she'd have to act like one of the Old Ladies. It was still a man's world, and she couldn't appear to be privy to everything. She understood—it wouldn't look real if she was always some kind of super-female. I told her not to worry, though, that unlike a real old lady, she'd never be beaten for forgetting to bring home some Taco Bell for dinner or whatever. She laughed and said, "I hope not. Remember, I got a gun too."

We left the airport and drove to the new undercover house on Romley Road.

Timmy was there hanging out with Casino Cal and a Mesa Angel named Mark Krupa, a monster who weighed 260 at just under six feet tall.

I showed JJ to her room and went to use the bathroom. When I got out she'd changed into a black tank top and let her hair down. I shook my head and she said, "OK, I'm ready."

"Lead the way, ma'am." She passed me in the hall and walked toward the living room.

I was ecstatic.

Once in the living room, she asked if anyone wanted anything to drink. Everyone said beer. She turned to Timmy and asked, "We got beer, right, Timmy?"

Timmy, who'd never met JJ in the flesh, said, "Yeah, in the fridge."

She got up, floated into the kitchen, and brought back four cold cans of Bud Light. She handed Timmy one, stuffed two cans under her arm, opened one, handed it to Cal, opened another, handed it to Mark, opened another, and handed it to me. She went back to the kitchen, came back with two more beers, both open, and handed one to Pops. She took a long sip of hers and said, in a measured deadpan, "Well, boys, you do whatever it was you were doing. I'm gonna go unpack."

And she disappeared.

No one said anything for a moment. We all drank. Cal looked at me, eyebrows raised, corners of his mouth turned down, and nodded.

What a difference a woman makes.

WE WENT TO the Patch the next day and loaded the trailer with the bikes. Timmy and I climbed into the backseat. I lit a cigarette and told Pops to drive. Pops told JJ to drive. JJ looked at the trailer and said, "I've never driven a trailer before."

I said, "Well, trial by fire." JJ tried to get out of it. I said, "Pops was at the bottom of the totem pole, but now that you're here he's moved up a notch. Shit runs downhill, sweetheart." Standard rookie hazing.

She drove. Pops warned her not to get caught in any situations where she'd have to put it in reverse, which is exactly what she did in a Denny's parking lot near Prescott. We all laughed as she learned how to back up a vehicle with a trailer hitched to it. As with everything, JJ learned quickly.

We checked into the house on Verano Circle. I made a few calls to the Bullhead locals, telling them we were around and wanted to hang out. I told them JJ was with me. We agreed to meet around nine that night at the Inferno.

Party, party, Bullhead-style. Smitty was happy to see us, Lydia was happy to see JJ. JJ met Dennis and Dolly. We bought a few rounds and toasted the imminent marriage of Dolly and Dennis. Smitty grilled me for more Vegas grand jury info. I said I hadn't heard anything specific, other than that the prosecutors were definitely seeking RICO charges. I assured him I'd told my source to dig deeper for information pertaining to HAMC member Donald Smith. He nodded solemnly, satisfied that I'd kept him in mind.

JJ kept quiet company with Lydia and Dolly. She actually invited them and the boys over for dinner the next night.

STEAK AND BEER and Crown Royal and Cokes and potatoes and a couple pounds of bacon, half of it cooked black and crunchy.

It was Smitty, Lydia, Dennis, Dolly, and Joby, plus all of us Solos and JJ.

It was a fun night. It felt real. I kicked back and bullshitted with the Angels I'd known the longest. Timmy and I arm-wrestled. He won. Joby and Smitty started off talking about Laughlin and spiraled into war stories of fights, beatings, shootings, and near misses. The house was wired and we recorded everything, but it was so much biker smack that it wouldn't have amounted to a hill of beans in court.

Some local biker politics were a high order of business. There was an OMG called the Vagos, a small but strong club that had an on-again, off-again relationship with the Angels. They were commonly called the Green, since their lettering and the background of their center patch was a bright toxic green. In the middle of their center patch was a red devil riding the single winged wheel of a motorcycle, like a genie rising from a lamp.

A few Greens had recently been hanging around Bullhead without the Angels' permission. The main guy was a *barrio chollo* by the name of Nick Prano. Prano was in his mid-forties and had spent about twenty years in prison. Timmy and I had befriended him back in August, when he'd boasted that he'd just gotten off a nine-year stint for shooting a CHiPs cop in the head. He was one of those guys who took real pride in being a criminal, a man for whom time spent in prison was not time wasted but time proven. He'd say, "All I like to do is work, drink, fight, chase pussy, and be an asshole."

Typical biker dreamboat.

It was a condition of his probation that he no longer reside in California, where the Vagos were most prominent. So he'd moved to Arizona. There'd been some beef between him and Smitty, because Prano wanted to put an Arizona bottom rocker on his cut. Smitty wouldn't have it. Timmy and I both witnessed the time Smitty took Prano aside and told him how it was going to be.

It was in late August, and Timmy, Prano, and I were hanging out at a thug bar by the river called Lazy Harry's. Smitty and Dennis came in and walked up to Timmy, who stood by the door talking on the phone. Smitty looked my way and asked Timmy if I was hanging out with "that Greenie, Prano." Timmy confirmed I was. Smitty huffed. He and Dennis came up to us. Neither of them said anything to me. Smitty put his arm around Prano and asked him to step aside. They went and talked for about five minutes by the jukebox. They came back and we all hung out for a couple hours like old buddies.

That was when Prano was informed that he'd never be permitted to stitch an Arizona bottom rocker on his cut, and that the HA would never tolerate the opening of an Arizona Vagos charter. The concession was that Prano would be able to ride freely in the state flying his full colors. Apparently that was acceptable.

This was significant to us for a couple of reasons. First, it showed once again that the HA were in control in Arizona. This would be good for the RICO charges. Second, it proved that we'd done our due diligence, since the Solos had been permitted to operate an Arizona charter, even if we, like the Vagos, also weren't permitted to fly Arizona rockers.

The Vagos were a topic on the night of our dinner party because the Angels had found out that Prano was holding some information from them. Prano was a good criminal politician. He knew when to talk and when to shut up. I'm not sure he wanted anything in particular, but it didn't matter. I think mainly he wanted it to be known that he wasn't a pushover and didn't care who his adversaries were.

The information he held concerned the Kingman Mongols. He apparently had names and addresses, and the Angels wanted these badly. Especially Joby.

"Motherfucker. That Green motherfucker. I don't care. He makes any trouble and I'll shoot him myself." Joby had driven his pickup over from Kingman, and he'd brought a hunting rifle in from his truck. He sighted the gun on the neighbor's house.

Dennis whined inconclusively.

Joby shoved a bloody chunk of steak into his cheek. He chewed it, saying, "And I heard those Mongols over there got some crank operation going. A fucking meth ring and everything. Motherfuckers, I can't wait to kill those motherfuckers. Can't wait!"

Dennis squealed, "Shoot them snitches!"

They were drunk. Joby was in another of his homicidal moods—sense was on vacation. In a twisted way I liked it. I liked that these were the guys we were making. They were the real deal.

I was kind of drunk too.

We capped the night off at the Inferno. JJ, Dolly, and Lydia were like sorority sisters. When we broke for the night, Lydia whispered into my ear, "I just love that JJ, Bird. Just love her."

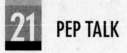

21 PEP TALK

JJ LEFT US for a couple weeks on the ninth. She'd be back for a Nomads party on the thirtieth.

After she left, the task force assessed her inaugural weekend. Slats especially felt it was a success. He was relieved to know all of his wrangling looked to be worth it.

Slats was also relieved to have Rudy removed from the picture. I was too, but the trouble that Rudy had brought weighed more heavily on Slats. After all, Rudy was Slats's responsibility, not mine.

As far as Slats was concerned, we were all his responsibility.

I asked the task force if there was a way we could use Rudy's arrest to the case's immediate advantage.

Slats's quick mind came up with the tack. He pointed out that so far, in spite of Smitty's love for us, it was Bad Bob who'd really put his ass on the line for the Solo Nomads. We agreed. I said I thought it was because both Smitty and Bad Bob wanted us to become prospects— I'm convinced they thought we were the best thing they'd seen in ages—only they took different approaches. I think Smitty thought that since we were Bullhead guys, he'd keep us as his little secret. That hadn't worked. We'd moved on to Mesa, and there it became Bob's goal to fold us in tight with his guys, to use his pulpit as the Mesa P to vouch for us, and therefore make Mesa our de facto charter choice when the time came for us to drop the "Solo" and add the "Hells" to our Angel moniker (and it is "Hells," not "Hell's," the official story being that there is more than one Hell, it just depends on who and where you are). Even though Bad Bob hadn't yet expressed open interest in our patching over, I could feel that was where he was headed. I felt certain that between them, Smitty and Bad Bob were engaged in a quiet battle to win our hearts.

Ah, to be loved.

Since Bad Bob was already a bona fide president, Slats suggested I appeal to him for advice on running a club in Rudy's absence. Slats wanted me to go to him and say, "Hey, Bob, you've been doing this for years. I'd really appreciate it—really be honored—if you could help me out and tell me the things I need to know about running a club. I mean, I'm lucky enough to know you guys, I figure I might as well use you as a resource. If you don't mind."

I thought it was a great idea. I called Bad Bob that day, told him the situation, and asked when we might be able to get together. He suggested the thirteenth, for breakfast at the Five and Diner in Chandler.

I told him that sounded great.

WE SAT IN a secluded corner booth. Our food came quickly—cheese omelets and hash browns for both of us, coffee for me, iced tea for him. After rehashing what had happened to Rudy, Bad Bob laid it down. "Listen, Bird. I'm an officer. I used to be a soldier, but now I'm a decision-maker. Been one for years. And now you are too. It's an honor, let me tell you. You know me, you know us. We run the show. We keep the other clubs in line and make sure we stay on top. Shit, we control this state, you know that. I know you know because you're sitting across from me right now, asking for my advice. Well, here it is: Keep the club strong. Rally around your colors, protect your club and your reputation. You're like a virgin on prom night, man, your rep is all you got." I thought of Dale at that moment, of how I'd told her damn near the exact same thing. He continued, I listened. "Rudy, he fucked up. Simple as that. Took chances he shouldn't have. The shit he's in, it's dirty, you know? You know me, I like to party, but that shit, it goes nowhere. First things first—you gotta get to his place and clean it out. Those maggots around Apache Junction he was with, you don't want them beating you over there. It might take them a week or two to figure out where he went, so get on that. Second, you tell your boys not to worry. Rudy may be gone, but life goes on. You're the P now, and you have my support, you can tell them I said that. You got the Red and White on your side, to the end."

I told him I appreciated his backing and his advice. I asked if he'd give my boys a pep talk in a couple of days, and he said that the next time we were all around Mesa he'd be honored to sit down with us.

"But there's more," he said. "Now that you're a P, you gotta know Hoover better. The P up in Cave Creek, the guy who owns the RCB Tavern."

"Yeah, I remember Hoover."

"Good. I'm gonna call him and tell him to expect you. He's the guy. He's just like me, man—we got our fingers in everything."

I told him that'd be great. Bad Bob called Hoover right then and vouched for us yet again. I was impressed.

When he was done talking to Hoover he said, "Bird—keep up the good work and you'll have free rein in Arizona. Just one thing: Keep me informed. I need to know your business, so I can keep everyone's head clear. I don't like getting blindsided with shit, hear?" He meant: be respectful, keep kicking in those contributions, don't step on anyone's toes. Don't take advantage and don't allow yourself to be taken advantage of.

It made me feel great.

He ate some more of his breakfast and finished his iced tea, slurping it loudly. Then he looked up at me.

"I gotta say this, just so I know I did. Rudy was cooking, right?"

"Yeah, Pops told me like three, four ounces a night."

Bad Bob sighed. He shifted in his seat and pushed his plate back a little. Then he launched into a full-blown lecture about how we couldn't pick that business up. He said the Angels had given it up because they'd gotten tired of shaking down users for money when money was the last thing they had. He said he knew he sounded like he was full of it, since he was a user himself, but he insisted he was different. He wasn't a real down-and-out tweaker who lived for crank and crank alone. He said it was OK for us to dabble here and there—he knew Pops occasionally took a rail—and he said we should go ahead and sell off Rudy's stash, but when that was over, then that was it.

It was good advice. I appreciated getting it and he enjoyed giving it.

The whole time I stared into Bad Bob's eyes. They were serious and sad. Bad Bob cared for me.

I was almost touched.

Almost.

22 "MOTHERFUCKER, IF I EVER
SEE YOU IN THIS TOWN AGAIN
I WILL FUCKING BURY YOU IN
THE DESERT WHERE NO ONE
WILL EVER FUCKING FIND YOU."

DENNIS AND DOLLY got married on November 29.

Biker weddings are like any other—except very few suits, no ties, no expensive dresses, no champagne, no toasts to the parents of the bride, no toasts to the parents of the groom, no cocktail hour at the reception, no sit-down catered dinner, and most definitely no Funky Chicken or Electric Slide group dance. The proper attire was cuts and clean jeans and dirty boots for the men, and anything nice for the women—which meant anything decent that could be bought for less than forty dollars at Wal-Mart or Target.

The Denbesten ceremony was held at the Riviera Baptist Church on Marina Avenue. It's a funny thing to see a bunch of avowed, unapologetic sinners file into a church. It's even funnier when you're pretending to be one of them. The pastor, a short rail of a man in a light blue suit with a dark blue tie, had the eyes of a man created to be confided in. He stood by the door of the chapel and took each of our hands in both of his. He spoke in a near whisper, but each word was clear: "Welcome to the Riviera Baptist Church for this wonderful occasion."

The church wasn't erected on the grand scale of the Southern Baptist churches I'd seen in Georgia. It was spare and unassuming. Like the pastor, it had a border-town feel, a Western outlaw vibe. It was the last place a complicated man came to receive the guidance of God before he did whatever it was he had to do. That little church knew that people weren't as good as God wanted them to be, but that it would never stop with the business of trying to salvage the soul.

The service was brief and practical. Dennis wore his cut over a cheap suit, and Dolly was dressed in a Wal-Mart special, probably with underwear to match. When it came time for Dennis to kiss his bride, he let her have it.

We left and milled around the parking lot. There were over a dozen of us, and we discussed where we'd celebrate. Smitty and Dennis suggested the Inferno.

A sense of propriety overtook JJ. She said, "Hell with that, guys. Let's have it over at our place." The guys said that wasn't necessary, JJ insisted, then I insisted and they said cool. Some of them had other things they needed to do, and Smitty had to go home first, so we split up and agreed to meet at the Bullhead undercover house on Verano Circle around 9:00 p.m.

I went home to set up, and JJ and Timmy went and got a couple thirty-packs of Bud Light, two jumbo buckets of KFC fried chicken, and a few combo platters from Taco Bell: the culinary makings of the perfect HA wedding reception.

The guys showed up.

The rapper Nelly blasted on our system as they walked in. I was in the middle of the room with JJ, dancing like a white boy at a pep rally. No one knew what to do. For a short while they stood there like wallflowers at a junior high prom. Then, between songs, Dennis walked up to the stereo and turned it all the way down. He asked, "Bird, what the fuck is that jungle music?"

"That's my shit, Dennis."

"Well, it ain't mine and this is my wedding day. Put on something else."

I said OK and fired up the same old Steppenwolf crap these guys lived for, and the party came to life.

JJ showed them where the food was, and they dug in. Dennis and Dolly looked happy. They ate the chicken and drank the beer and talked with JJ. Timmy and I drank with a couple guys who'd been at the ceremony—an Angels Nomad named Dale Hormuth and the hangaround, Billy Schmidt.

Smitty and Lydia showed up with Pops a little while later. Eric Clauss, another Angels Nomad who'd been at the wedding, was supposed to be with them but wasn't.

I'd prepped some ruse props for Smitty—some pictures of my old partner, Carlos, and a short personal note from Carlos to Smitty. I also had a ruse e-mail from a guy named "Gato" that discussed the Kingman Mongols problem. Smitty barely looked at the stuff from Carlos, read the e-mail twice, and told me we needed to talk. We went out back.

We each lit a cigarette.

"There's some trouble brewing and you need to know about it. Lydia got a call from an associate across the river. She said there's fifty Mongols over in Laughlin and they're planning on coming over tomorrow to break us up." It was the first I'd heard of that. I immediately thought, Call Slats. He continued. "I sent Eric over there. Lydia gave him her thirty-eight and he left his cut in my car. Incognito, you know?"

"I hear you."

"He'll get back to us."

"Good."

"But we're going to be loaded up tomorrow night at the Nomads rally. Billy's gonna look after the guns, keep all of them in his truck behind the Inferno. Me, I'm bringing two shotguns, a couple pistols, and my Tec-9. Those fuckers come, we'll be ready."

"All right." I paused. "Good."

Smitty raised his eyebrows and said, "Check this out." He pulled a Taurus pistol from his waistband. "This is one of the pistols I'll have tomorrow. Gonna sell Bad Bob one next week." He flicked a switch below the barrel and a red beam shot off it, piercing the dark. He sighted it on a wall. I asked him if he'd sell me one too. He said he sure would, as soon as the Nomads party was over. He said he might *have* to sell it to me if the Mongols showed.

As he turned off the laser sight and tucked the pistol into his pants, he said, "You gotta understand one thing, Bird. You're there for us tomorrow. Things get thick and as far as I'm concerned you fight like you're a Hells Angel. You protect your Solo brothers, but you buck up for us."

I stood tall, didn't smile, and nodded. I said, "Smitty, that'll be my fucking honor."

ALL THE UNDERCOVERS had deep conversations that night. I had mine with Smitty, Timmy got more information from Billy about the weapons cache he'd be guarding, and JJ talked self-defense strategies with the women. Lydia wanted to know if JJ regularly packed. JJ said she did. Lydia said that if things turned sour, their job would be to gather the Old Ladies, get them behind the bar, and take up positions to defend them. She said, "You and me, we'll shoot whoever the fuck comes near us."

As a law-enforcement officer, my first job is to prevent things like this from happening. After the dinner party, the Black Biscuit task force notified the Laughlin and Bullhead police departments to be on the lookout. We hoped a Mongols–Angels confrontation wouldn't even come to pass. But if the Mongols *did* manage to reach the Inferno and things turned bad, then my second job would kick in: protecting myself and my fellow operatives. This wouldn't be all bad: If the Mongols showed and I was forced to protect the Solos and the Angels and lived to tell the tale, then my credibility would be furthered.

JJ was understandably nervous. She didn't carry openly like the rest of us—like Lydia, her pistol was in her purse. She'd never been in a draw-down or fired her weapon in a "live" situation.

So we decided to go over some things.

We'd spent the morning at the Patch, and when we got back to the Verano Circle house we were greeted by a snoring Eric Clauss, who'd crashed out on our couch. We went about our business like he was a part of the family. When he finally woke up he grabbed a beer and walked into the garage. The door was open and the afternoon light streamed in. He took a long swig of beer and scratched his butt.

JJ and I sat on my bike. I had a cigarette in my mouth. I smoked it without the use of my hands, which I kept on the handlebars.

JJ practiced drawing my Glocks from behind me. She reached around my torso and crossed her arms. She pushed her chest into my back. She unsnapped the holsters with her thumbs, then drew the gun on the left with her right hand and vice versa. She uncrossed her arms quickly and came out blazing, a black pistol on both sides at shoulder height, ready to fire. She holstered them and did it again. And again. And again.

And again.

Eric watched and drank his beer. After a while he asked, "You guys are fuckin' serious, huh?"

The guns were holstered. JJ formed her right hand into a pistol, pointed it at Eric, smiled her generous smile, and said, "Yup." I just nodded.

THE PARTY STARTED at one in the afternoon. Timmy and Pops showed up early. JJ and I hung back. We'd be fashionably late.

Timmy called to check in around two. He said, "The guys are on edge, but ready. There's a lot of boozing but not much drugging— except for Vicodin. They're popping them like Pez candies."

I said, "Figures."

"Yeah. They're anxious. There's a lot of shop talk too. Doug and Hank have some shit they wanna sell today. Some other guy wants to sell us a full-auto. Billy told Pops he wants to sell him a couple shotguns, ASAP."

I said, "Jesus, we're like Guns-R-Us."

Timmy laughed and said, "Yep." I told him I'd sign some cash out of our safe before we headed over. He said, "Good. We'll probably need it."

We hung up. I called Slats and let him know the situation. He told me there'd been no reports of Mongol activity in Laughlin.

JJ and I got to the bar around five. The mood was strange. The guys were serious but mellow, zonked by massive quantities of alcohol and painkillers.

JJ broke off to talk to the girls. I went to talk to Timmy, Smitty, and Joby. We said hello and gave each other hugs. Joby, a nondrinker, was not dulled by booze. Smitty was distant but serious looking. This was his party in his town, and he didn't want anything to break bad, but if it did, he'd be ready.

Joby spouted the usual invective against his Mongol enemies. For the time being, they remained imaginary, as did the violence he would unleash upon them. Smitty leaned close and said, "So far, so good."

"That's good news," I said.

Joby closed his eyes and shook his head forcefully. "Fuck that. I want those fuckers to show!" Then he nodded to someone over my shoulder and excused himself. Once he was out of earshot, Smitty asked, "You remember those silencers you showed me?"

"Sure do."

"You change your mind about selling them?"

"They're already sold, Smit. Sorry," I lied.

"Well, you getting more?"

"Not at the moment. What's up?"

"Can you put me in touch with your guy? I'd love to get one of those for my Ruger."

I told Smitty I'd look into it. He said good.

JJ did a few deals, got some Vicodin, and bought a little Baggie of meth from Dolly. JJ told me later that Lydia kept telling her how impressed everyone was with me and the Solos, and how happy she was, personally, that I had such a solid girlfriend in JJ. JJ told me she'd blushed when Lydia told her that, that she was actually flattered. Lydia's words gave JJ confidence, and like a good undercover, JJ flipped that confidence back onto Lydia in the form of credibility.

JJ was getting accepted far more quickly than I could've ever imagined.

JJ became our drug clearinghouse for the evening. They were all small quantities, but she needed to make an evidence drop. It looked unlikely, but we had to assume we'd still have an altercation with the Mongols, which meant we'd be dealing with law enforcement first-responders who wouldn't know about our undercover status. We didn't want to be carrying anything if we got arrested.

I told Doug and Hank to meet us at my place around nine if they wanted to do their gun deal. This was the pretense we used to dip out for a little while.

We went to a Circle K. I stood at the counter and bought a pack of cigarettes while JJ walked down an aisle decorated with shiny bags of snacks. The task force agent Buddha was fingering a bag of Fritos when JJ brushed up against him, pushing a bag of evidence into his back pocket.

We paid and left. Then we drove to Verano Circle, met with Doug and Hank, and did the deal. They were a little unsure of dealing with JJ in the room, but I said if they couldn't deal with her, then they couldn't deal with me. Since they were on the cash end of a decent transaction for three semiauto pistols, they couldn't disagree. They asked for $1,600. I had JJ inspect the weapons, which she did and nodded with the slightest hint of wariness, and I said $1,500, no more. They said that was good too.

I said good news, thanks for keeping the store open. They asked if they could crash at our place that night, and I said by all means, absolutely. I let them know Eric Clauss would be sleeping over again too. They were cool with that. We all went back to the Inferno in the Mercury.

The night dragged on. Some guys started to do meth, others passed out. At one point I asked Smitty why they were letting their guard down. He said, with equal parts of relief and regret, "Those faggots ain't coming."

We left just past midnight. JJ was packed double with me. Doug, Hank, and Eric rode solo. Timmy and Pops drove the Merc. I told them that if we didn't show up at home that night not to come looking for us—we were either out partying or had been arrested.

It was a joke. We all laughed.

On the way home, on a dark side street deliberately taken to avoid a confrontation, we were pulled over for a traffic stop.

The Angels were used to these, and JJ and I pretended to be. They knew what to expect from a cop. In a way, it's a point of honor and pride to be continually jacked by police, even though, to a man, they bitch about it incessantly.

But something strange happened that night. Something none of them had ever seen before.

Typically, when a mixed-club group of bikers is stopped, and Hells Angels are among those present, they get the most thorough attention. Everyone knows the Angels are the ones to be wary of, and that given an inch they *will* take a mile. They must be attended to first.

But they weren't.

The cops yelled and the cherry lights flashed. An officer approached JJ and me from behind. When he got about ten feet from us, he racked a shell into the chamber of his shotgun. JJ's legs pinched me hard.

We didn't move.

I didn't appreciate the sound of that shotgun. Maybe they'd been waiting all night for the Mongols just as we'd been, and since they hadn't come, they took this opportunity to vent some steam.

Over the bullhorn a young, angry voice said, "Bird, do not let go of your handlebars until ordered to do so. Do you understand?" I nodded yes. I held the bars with a death grip. JJ was on me like a backpack.

The Angels were told to remain on their bikes.

I was ordered off the bike by a young, stout officer. JJ and I were separated. They led me behind their vehicles.

Hands on your head.

Lock those fingers.

Cross your ankles.

Sit.

The cuffs went on one wrist at a time.

The young cop said, "You gotta take your jacket off."

I jangled my cuffs. "How'm I supposed to do that?"

He breathed, "Shit."

"Besides, I wouldn't take it off for you even if I could." I knew this was stupid, but I also knew it would play well with the Angels, who were being lined up a few feet away.

The young cop grabbed my arm and hauled me up. "Shut up. We're gonna take your picture."

"Good. I ain't saying cheese."

He tightened my cuffs. They hurt.

He took my guns and handed them off. Another cop started snapping a camera as I got turned around—front, side, back. I was wearing my goatee in two long braids that night, and the cop with the camera said, "You look like a fucking catfish."

As they did this, they positioned JJ so I could see them frisking her. She wasn't wearing a bra and they weren't shy about where they put their hands. They frisked her again. She took it in stride. I was very angry but there was nothing I could do.

When they were done taking pictures, I was led to the curb and told to kneel. I was led at the barrel of a loaded and charged shotgun.

Don't move, we gotta talk to your little girlfriend. We gotta talk to your buddies.

JJ was taken to a marked unit and ducked into the backseat. The guys were cuffed and lined up curbside. No one but me had to kneel. No one but me had a gun drawn on them. The Angels couldn't believe it, but as far as these cops were concerned, I was more dangerous than they were.

A cop came up to JJ and asked her through the rolled-down window of the cruiser what she was doing hanging out with a guy like me. She didn't look at him. She asked, "What, as opposed to a guy like you?" That was the end of that conversation.

She listened to the rap sheets come over the radio. She was clean. I had a few minor, and fabricated, priors. Clauss had some minor stuff too, and Watkins had an outstanding warrant for a traffic violation. That wouldn't wash well with the fact that they'd caught him carrying a concealed bowie knife. He was placed in a marked unit and bound to spend the night in jail. It was Dam's sheet that scared JJ. There was a bunch of drug stuff, including a felony conviction for cocaine trafficking. But the kicker was that he'd been arrested for severely assaulting a police officer. JJ prayed that he wouldn't get motivated to go at it again.

Meanwhile, Officer Shotgun talked to me. He wanted to know where I lived, why was I still in Bullhead, hadn't I heard they'd been looking into me? He said, "You gotta move on, Bird, you gotta get the fuck out of my town."

I said, "You can arrest me or lecture me, but I won't take both, so make up your mind. If you're gonna cut me loose, I'm all ears. But if you're shit-canning me, shut up and take me downtown, 'cause I ain't interested."

He didn't like that. He put his boot in between my shoulder blades and pushed me to the ground. Since I was cuffed I caught the pavement with my cheek. He kneeled, leaned in close, and whispered into my ear: "Motherfucker, if I ever see you in this town again I will fucking bury you in the desert where no one will ever fucking find you."

My recorder was going. I thought, Not good, dude. Not good for you. I knew this guy desperately wanted me out of his town and I knew he wasn't using approved methods. I wanted to tell him what I was, but I couldn't. It would be months until he learned how close he'd come to ruining his career that night.

They took Hank, but they had nothing on us. They cut us loose.

As they wound down their show, puffing out their chests, taking the cuffs off, giving us our guns back, telling us to go home and mind our business, a dark, late-model Mercury Cougar crept by. I saw Pops rubbernecking at us in the passenger window, smiling.

JJ saw him, climbed behind me on my bike, and said quietly, "What a jerk."

23 INHALE . . . EXHALE . . .
INHALE . . . EXHALE . . .

TIMMY, JJ, AND I stayed up late that night, smoking cigs on the back porch while Hank and Eric crashed inside. It had been a hell of a day for all of us, but for JJ especially. She'd learned a lot. Mainly, she'd learned that she'd be keeping any drugs in her boot from then on, since it was the one place the cops didn't bother checking. Timmy laughed at how I'd gotten stomped by the local police, and said he was happy he hadn't missed it. I smiled and told him to go fuck himself in the ear.

The next day, JJ flew home to visit her family for a couple weeks. She'd put in for the time before she'd come over with us, so it was fine, but we were sorry to see her go. I told her we didn't need her around too much because we'd all be away for the holidays soon enough. I told her things would be slow for a while, so take the time to chill. She said she would.

The end of 2002 had delivered Black Biscuit to an operational cross-roads. Most of the hours we logged in December were spent discussing the direction of the case and planning our next steps, not hanging out with the Angels (we explained our absence to them with the white lie that we were traveling on club business, spending time in Mexico and

SoCal, and that my Vegas connection, Big Lou, had invited me out to Miami to lounge around on his yacht and pinch some South Beach ass).

As we took stock of our progress, we drew up a list of case positives and case negatives so we could analyze our positions and objectives.

The main positive was that we'd been hugely successful in a short period of time. We'd gotten in quicker and deeper than we'd thought possible in a mere six months. The downside to this was that things were blurred. We'd moved so quickly from one day to the next—sometimes covering the length of the state in a single day, over three hundred miles, always in role—that it was hard to tell what we were doing. We were drunk on danger and adrenaline.

This led us to the main negative: We were running in place. We didn't need to do any more gun deals with Doug or Hank. We didn't need Bad Bob to broker any more petty drug buys. We didn't need more evidence that Smitty acted like a local gangster, or that Dennis, while no longer cooking, clearly had a fluid and consistent source of meth. I was sick of these minor deals, Slats was sick of processing them and presenting them to the suits. He wanted dealers, not users. The case was supposed to be bigger—it *was* bigger—we just hadn't figured out how to crack it.

Our frustration led to the beginning of a division within the task force. Slats felt that we weren't leaving our comfort zone enough, and I felt that it was too early to branch out. He wanted us to be aggressive with everyone, while I wanted to solidify my positions so I could do exactly that later on. It was nothing major, just a small crack in the wall that began to dribble water. Not surprisingly, I stood tall on one side of the divide, while Slats held firm to the other.

I wanted to pursue the Angels' offers of membership. How often had a group of cops been given this opportunity? Not often at all. I felt we'd never get the true dirt on them as outsiders, that they could profess to trust us as Solos till they were blue in the face, but it would never matter because we weren't Hells Angels. If we wanted to take a swing at these guys—and there was no argument that that was what we all wanted—then this was the only way. My answer to breaking out of the comfort zone was to become a Hells Angel, to give ourselves over to our adversary. I knew I was right.

Slats wanted us to remain Solos. He didn't care about becoming

Hells Angels. If we were to fold into their organization, our operation would become tied to the whims of the club and our sponsors. Instead of buying guns, we'd be pulling guard duty and opening beers. As Solos, we could do whatever we wanted, whenever we wanted, wherever we wanted. He felt that they'd ultimately deal with us out of naked greed. The Solos also provided them with the illusion of a scapegoat: We were a separate party on which blame could conveniently be pinned. Slats's answer to breaking out of the comfort zone was to be brasher, push harder, and ask for bigger deals. Slats is expert in the criminal mindset, and he might have been right, too.

Neither of us budged, though. Our egos were too invested in the work we'd done. He had a grand vision and I wanted to play the hands we undercovers were being dealt. I didn't say as much, but I could feel that another reason Slats didn't want us to try to join the Angels was that he would lose his sense of control—something he'd never, ever willingly relinquish.

There was a third option: One of us could have—maybe even *should* have—suggested that we fold up right then and there. Our case was a good one. We wouldn't have decimated the Hells Angels, but we would've sent serious shockwaves through them. Our message would've been clear and effective: You are not impenetrable, you do not intimidate us, and we will not leave you alone. If we'd ended in December of 2002, we'd have had a respectable case and sustained only a minimum of battle damage.

But no one gave this a single, fleeting thought.

We didn't want a good case.

We wanted a great one.

24 JINGLE BELLS, BATMAN SMELLS, ETC.

JUST BECAUSE DECEMBER was light on contacts, that didn't mean we didn't have any. Things were happening with Rudy that forced us to keep in touch.

On the sixth I got a call from Bad Bob. He was hearing distressing things about Rudy, but he wouldn't discuss anything over the phone. He suggested I come to a Mesa Toy Run—a community outreach event that collects toys for charity—on the fifteenth. I told him I'd like to but I couldn't, since the larger Solo Angeles organization was holding a mandatory Toy Run on the same day in Los Angeles. He said he understood that my first loyalties were to my club, but we still had to get together. He suggested an early dinner on the eleventh. I said I could be in town on that date. It was set.

We'd been hearing the same distressing things about Rudy too. Apparently he'd been very chatty with fellow inmates, dropping Bad Bob's name to gain some prison credibility. Slats went to interview him on the tenth. He found out that Rudy'd been telling people that his crew—that is, us—were running tight with the Angels and that Bob told him we were going to be offered a "patch swap"—a full transfer with no prospecting period. Such a thing is very rare. The Hells Angels don't toss Death Heads out like candy. At the interview, Slats told Rudy in no uncertain terms to shut up. Nothing about the Angels, nothing about the Solos, and most definitely nothing about ATF. One usually doesn't have to remind an incarcerated informer that it would be unhealthy in the extreme for him to admit to working with the law, but given Rudy's track record, Slats wasn't taking any chances.

Rudy promised to keep quiet.

They sent him back to the cages, but had him moved to a single to help him stay quiet.

Jails are like bee colonies. News travels very, very fast. When Rudy was pulled, it didn't take long for the population to hear that ATF had pulled him. And when he was returned in protective custody—"PC'd"—it didn't look all that great. We hoped that by segregating him, experienced prisoners might conclude that he hadn't cooperated and he was being punished. But it could cut the other way too. Some might think he was being isolated for his own protection. Either way, Rudy Kramer got the message. He clammed up.

Bob and I had a lovely dinner at the Baseline and I-10 Waffle House to discuss all this. Waffles for me; cheeseburger, fries, and a vanilla shake for him.

Bob was visibly worried about what Rudy was saying. He didn't think Rudy was going to snitch, he just thought he was being Rudy, but that didn't make things any better. He asked if I'd heard anything about the patch-swap rumor. I told him no, and that I'd never dreamed it was a possibility. He changed the subject, saying he couldn't understand why Rudy, a man who'd been to prison, was so eager to impress people. He said he was not cool with Rudy abusing his "good name." Bob chuckled as he told me that he'd heard all of this secondhand from his longtime brother and friend, Phoenix Angel Howie Weisbrod, who'd gotten it from an inmate who went by the moniker Trashcan. You have to love the self-esteem these guys convey when they're left to pick their nicknames.

"I mean, ain't that ironic?" Bob said, jamming fries into his mouth. "I'm supposed to be Rudy's best influential buddy, and I'm hearing about it through a guy Rudy doesn't even know, just because Howie knows the guy Rudy's mouthing off to. Fucking Rudy, man."

Bob said not to worry, though. He said, "I won't hold the Solos accountable for Rudy's shit, you have my word on that. But you might want to chill out a little. I know you guys been doing a fair amount of business around the state, and that's fine—man's gotta do what a man's gotta do—but take it easy. Rudy's popped, you got that crazy fucking traffic stop. What I'm saying is you're on the radar now, just like us. So take it *easy*. You don't need the attention and we *certainly* don't need the attention." He wedged a quarter of the cheeseburger—which was already half gone—into his mouth. "You gotta meet Howie, anyway. I told him about you, and I also told him not to think about this Rudy guy too much. I told him once he met you he'd understand everything was cool with the Solo Nomads."

I said, "Thanks."

"No problem." He swallowed hard and took a long, silent pull off the milkshake. As he pulled away from his straw, he wiped his mouth with the back of his hand. "Anyway, we both know the patch-swap thing Rudy's bullshitting about is just that—bullshit. But that don't mean we're not interested. I know you've been come at a little." He shoved the remains of the burger into his mouth and licked each fingertip on his right hand. "Well, I'm here to tell you that shit's likely to increase. I'm gonna bring you guys up at the next officers' meeting, ask how everyone feels about the Solos coming in as prospects. Once we come to a consensus I'll tell you how to respond to all the love letters you're gonna get." He smiled at me and slurped the rest of his shake into oblivion.

I finished my waffle, pounded my coffee, and paid the bill. I thanked Bob for everything, once again.

"Don't mention it, Bird. You're my boy." We stood and walked to the door. I held it open for him. "There's one more thing, though. I want you to go talk to Rudy. Go talk to him and tell him to shut the fuck up. 'Cause, you know, sometimes people who can't keep quiet, they get hurt."

I thought, This is probably the kind of conversation Joe Pistone had with his Bonanno associates when he was Donnie Brasco. Bob acted, spoke, and thought like a mobster.

I lit a smoke and said, "Didn't even need to ask, Bob. Consider it taken care of."

Which, in truth, it had been.

POPS AND I went to the Solo Angeles Toy Run in Chula Vista, California, on the fifteenth. It was no big deal. We hung out with Teacher, made sure the local news crew got us on tape, and took some trophy shots with our brothers. We drank some beers and listened to some good Latin music. I was happy for that. If I never heard a Lynyrd Skynyrd song again, it would be too soon.

We had other Solo business on that trip. Our club dues had to be paid in Tijuana. The problem was that Mexico was not in Black Biscuit's jurisdiction. Sovereign nations aren't too keen on having unknown foreign undercover agents poking around in their backyard. Since Pops was our paid informant, he didn't need permission to travel to Mexico in his undercover role. He used to make this trip with Rudy, but since Rudy was indisposed, he'd have to cross the border on his own.

As we got closer to the border, Pops got more and more apprehensive. Within a few miles of the checkpoint he turned to me and said, "Bird, this's got me spooked, man." He didn't want to go into the Solos clubhouse alone, and I couldn't blame him.

What I decided to do I've since regretted—not because I thought it was wrong to help Pops, but because it was a completely rogue action, one that even I, a documented risk-taker, should not have undertaken.

I decided to go with Pops into Mexico to conduct work—without work's permission.

I didn't intend to go to the clubhouse—I just wanted to be in the area should Pops get in trouble. I told him to call me after thirty minutes, and if I hadn't heard from him by then, I'd come rescue him. I wouldn't leave Pops alone, out of his comfort zone, to be eaten by wolves.

We crossed the border and parted ways. I strolled around drinking cola, smoking cigarettes, and turning down offers for everything from sombreros to blow jobs.

Thirty minutes passed. No call.

Forty minutes passed. No call.

Forty-five. No call.

I went to the clubhouse.

Pops was fine. He was better than fine. He told me he'd tried to call, but it kept going straight to voice mail. I looked closely at my phone and realized I had no service in Mexico. Great. Dumb.

Pops said, "Chill out, Bird. These guys love us. C'mon, let's party a little." He was actually eating a taco.

I kept up appearances. I met a bunch of guys, had a beer, and got roped into a game of pool. Between turns, Suzuki, the Tijuana president, approached me and said next time we came he wanted us to bring him a Harley Sportster engine. He also reminded us that we had yet to change our Nomads rockers to the Spanish, *Nomada*. He said, "I don't want none of this gringo bullshit." I gave him a hug and said sure thing, with no intention of complying. I hoped I'd never see him again. When my pool game was over I grabbed Pops and told him we had business in San Diego. He got the message. We left.

We walked through the streets. I told him I felt like an idiot. He told me to relax.

I couldn't. I'd put myself in a completely losing situation. I lost if I allowed Pops to travel alone while he lacked confidence. I lost if I had to attempt an unauthorized undercover rescue. I lost if, after the fact, I told Slats, since this would likely end the case. I lost if I didn't tell Slats, knowing that one day I'd get found out and be held accountable, knowing that my unauthorized action could seriously jeopardize our credibility in a courtroom. I lost because I knew that the longer I kept my trip to Mexico a secret, the worse it would be for me.

But I did it anyway, and I kept it secret for a long time.

We returned to Tucson nervous and unhappy. It was right before Christmas. I dropped Pops off at his house and waved at his wife in the front yard. I told him I'd be back in a couple days to drop off some stuff for the holidays. He said thanks. The words were for the presents I'd be bringing his girls, but the sentiment was for covering him in Mexico, even if he hadn't really needed it.

Then he said, "Sorry."

"Don't sweat it, Pops. *Feliz Navidad,* OK?"

"OK."

I WASN'T THE only one sneaking around that holiday season. Slats had been doing some underhanded stuff himself.

When I got home it was the same—Gwen standing on the porch waiting for me so she could get out of the house to get some shopping done. But this time she was in a good mood. She said, "When I get back you'll help me wrap presents, right?"

"Of course, G."

"Good. I have a surprise for you, too."

I went inside and found our skiing stuff laid out in the dining room.

It turned out that Slats, his wife, and Gwen had planned a trip to Angel Fire Ski Resort in New Mexico, kids and everything.

When I found out I didn't think, Hurray! Family vacation! I thought, This is going to take me out of the game right when I need to be staying close to the guys. The truth was that the Hells Angels were becoming my family, and even though I'd told them I'd be out of town on a collection, a holiday disappearing act could arouse some unneeded suspicion. But the kids were ecstatic that we were going away together, so I told myself to swallow my pride and buck up. If I couldn't have actual fun then I'd pretend to.

We were leaving on the twentieth. We had a few days to get ready.

The Dobyns family ran a clothing and toy drive of its own every Christmas. The kids piled their old clothing on the dining-room table. Then they had to go into their rooms and select no fewer than eight toys for donation. It wasn't a tradition they were too excited about, but it was a good lesson in charity. When everything was together we boxed it up and took it to our church's donation center a few days before Christmas. Every year, I told them, "Don't worry, kiddos, it'll make you feel better when you're all grown up." They trusted me enough to believe this.

I'd asked Pops if he wanted first crack at the goods. He was making decent money, but no one ever got rich as a paid informant, especially not as an ATF paid informant. I told him I didn't want to offend him and he said he wouldn't be offended at all, that he'd do anything to make his daughters happier. I promised I'd bring him some good stuff. Dale helped me out by being kind enough to add two new stuffed animals, some unopened CDs, and some fresh makeup. She even insisted we wrap the nice stuff, which is what we did.

I went over to Pops's alone on the nineteenth. Short visit. We hugged in the driveway. He brought his wife and daughters out. I gave his wife a gentle hug and leaned down to say hi to his two smart, beautiful girls. I knew the girls did well in school, and they were always polite and presentable.

The girls said, "Thanks, Jay," and took the box inside. Pops's wife said, "Merry Christmas," and followed them in. Pops reached inside his windbreaker and pulled out a CD. It wasn't wrapped. He handed it to me. I was a little embarrassed. I hadn't gotten him a present—I hadn't even thought of it.

"Thanks," I said.

"Don't worry about it. Listen to track three. It reminds me of me and you."

We hugged and wished each other Merry Christmas, and I left.

The band's name, 3 Doors Down, was written on the CD in permanent marker. A sheet of paper had the song list. Track three was titled "Be Like That." I put it in the player and hit Play as I pulled onto the freeway.

It was a rock ballad. It started with a guitar riff, the lead singer coming in quietly. It slowly built to a full chorus of drums and thumping bass and crashing cymbals, then went back down for a quiet refrain. It was a good-sounding tune. The singer wanted to know something:

> He spends his nights in California
> Watching the stars on the big screen.
> Then he lies awake and he wonders,
> Why can't that be me?
> Cause in his life he's filled with all these good intentions.
> He's left a lot of things he rather not mention right now.
> But just before he says good night,
> He looks up with a little smile at me and he says
>
> If I could be like that
> I'd give anything
> Just to live one day
> In those shoes
> If I could be like that, what would I do?
> What would I do?

I started to cry.

Damn that Pops.

God bless him, too.

WE CONVOYED TO New Mexico. The Dobynses in one car, the Slatallas in another. It was an eight-hour slog, but with all the driving I'd been doing, it felt like nothing.

Jack sang "Jingle bells, Batman smells, Robin laid an egg," and the rest of it over and over. We sang along with him initially, but after ten repetitions it was just Jack. I told him to zip it, which he did.

We pulled into a truck stop for lunch. Slats's kids jumped out of their car and Dale ran to join them. Jack took his time, walking with the adults. I looked at him. He was uncharacteristically quiet.

Gwen asked him if he was OK. He smiled and said, "Yep."

Not fifteen minutes later Jack walked up to Gwen and tapped her knee. He was as green as seaweed. I stifled a chuckle, Slats grabbed my wrist.

Jack moaned, "Mom, I don't feel so good," grabbed her purse, pulled it open, and barfed directly into it.

I hoped it wasn't an omen for our trip.

We cleaned him up and hit the road again. After puking, Jack managed a PB&J and felt much better. He started singing again. The little guy couldn't wait for Christmas. Dale kept pestering Gwen for details of that year's presents. Gwen said, "I'm not going to tell you, Shoey. And besides, you know Christmas is about more than presents. The presents just remind us that we're luckier than others." Dale whined that she knew all that, Gwen told her to sound more appreciative, and Dale wisely chose to drop it.

I didn't engage in these discussions too much. I checked my phone constantly. I'd missed calls from Smitty and Bad Bob. The missed calls made me anxious. I felt I needed to be with them, massaging their egos and ingratiating myself. I decided to turn off my phone.

Sitting in the car alone with my family for eight hours for the first time in months—maybe even a year—it dawned on me that I'd put myself at complete odds with . . . myself. The part of me known as Jay Dobyns felt guilty, while the part known as Bird was angry at Jay for feeling guilty.

The Slatallas had rented a condo at Angel Fire: four bedrooms, three baths, a nice, small outdoor hot tub. We settled in. Slats and I got lift tickets while the girls and the kids went grocery shopping. On our way to the ticket offices, Slats and I agreed to keep case talk to a minimum.

We both knew that we needed to chill, and that we each needed some exposure to our old, more regular lives. Slats said, "Nighttime only, after everyone's down."

I agreed, "Nighttime only." And added, "At the bar."

"Most definitely at the bar."

Slats made a big breakfast every morning we were there. The first day it was cheese and scallion eggs, toast, bacon, OJ. The next was pancakes. The day after that was French toast; after that poached eggs with homemade hot sauce. He was a regular short-order superstar. I joked that if this federal agent thing didn't work out, he had a future at the Waffle House. He said, "Naw, I'm too good for the House."

We stayed for six nights and seven days. The kids got along great. Dale was the same age as Slats's older son, and Jack was the same as his younger. We'd spend three or four hours a day on the slopes, trying to stay together. I'd constantly challenge Slats to races to the bottom, and he'd constantly refuse them. It didn't matter. I went down hell-bent on shorty skis with no poles. I liked them because I could do anything on them. Their only drawback was that I looked more like a monkey on sticks than like Bode Miller. Each run, I'd be the first to the bottom, where I'd wait impatiently for everyone else. Slats would be last, carving graceful arcs through the powder on parabolic 210s, making sure everyone was down in one piece and not horsing around when they shouldn't be. Then we'd pile onto the lifts and do it all over again.

On Christmas Eve, after the kids went to bed, I snuck out to the back porch and called Smitty's house. I lit a cigarette while the line rang. Lydia answered. She wanted to know what I was up to. I told her Big Lou had sent me on a collection around Santa Fe. She asked what kind of Scrooge works on Christmas Eve? I told her if Big Lou said the word, I'd shoot Santa in the knee and take all the world's playtime swag off the back of his sleigh while he rolled around in the snow. Lydia just said jeez, and told Smitty that Bird was on the phone. We spoke for a few minutes. He said everything was fine, good holiday, I said mine was as good as could be expected. Gwen came outside as we talked. She looked at me, then at the cigarette in my hand, then back at me. I gave her a wild-eyed look. She shook her head and went back inside.

If I'd had a shred of decency I'd have felt ashamed. Instead, I was relieved she was gone.

I hung up, smoked another cigarette, and went back inside, where a game of Scrabble was starting up. With Slats playing, I knew I had no shot at winning. I played anyway.

On Christmas Day the kids were up at the crack of dawn and the coffee was brewing. The sound of three boys tearing into wrapping paper, and one girl carefully pulling apart folds, filled the living room. Their energy was infectious. I started wadding up the wrapping scraps and throwing head shots at the kids, and before I knew it we were in a full-tilt Christmas Day wrapping-paper fight. That wound down and I played hide-and-seek with the younger guys. I was the seeker. Slats made breakfast again and we ate and then we hit the slopes.

That night, after lights-out, Slats and I went to the bar. Since it was Christmas night, there wasn't too much going on—mostly lone-wolf locals and resort workers boozing after another day.

We talked about the case's next step. We agreed that whatever it was, it had to be something that would really knock the Angels' socks off. I suggested we bring them a show of force. We decided to orchestrate a Solo Angeles Nomads run in Arizona, where every Solo who showed was an ATF special agent. We decided to roll hard and deep and show the Angels what we were all about.

This worked into Slats's operational direction of maintaining the Solos, and without conceding anything, I knew it worked to my advantage too. If the Solos came in and proved we were a solid club, then Bird would gain that much more credibility, and I'd become an even more desirable Angels recruit. As far as Slats and I were concerned, this idea was win-win.

We put the case aside for a while and talked about the week. I thanked him for making it happen, saying that if he hadn't, the Dobyns clan would be sitting around our living room staring at the walls. He shrugged, as if to disagree, and changed the subject.

He said, "Earlier today I was thinking about how we ski."

As usual, I'd spent the day racing to the bottom, while he enjoyed the sound of the breeze in his ears and the snow-covered pine trees lining the slopes. Or whatever it was he did. "What about it?"

"Well, you know how you race down and fall and get up and race forward and tumble some more and get up and race forward again?"

"Yeah. If you're not falling you're not skiing hard enough."

"Yeah, well, you know how I cut from side to side and glide and check everything out and make sure everyone gets to the bottom in one piece?"

"Sure. You're slow. I get it."

He let it pass. "I was just thinking we have opposite styles, but in the end we both get to the bottom of the run at about the same time and then we both ride the lift up together. One's really not any better than the other, that's all I'm saying. It's just how we are."

"Yeah, I guess you're right."

We clinked glasses and ordered another round.

25 THE SOLO TEMPORARIES

BEFORE CHRISTMAS I worked fifty to seventy hours a week. After, I knew I'd be facing eighty to a hundred. I threw the switch undaunted—in fact, I was exhilarated.

We busied ourselves setting the thing up in the first half of the month. We called a bunch of ATF agents and ended up securing three for duty: Steve "Gundo" Gunderson, Alan "Footy" Futvoye, and a hot-shot from San Diego, Jesse Summers. Each brought something to the table. Jesse was young and hard—appearing more Latino gangbanger than anything else. Footy was enormous—six-four, 285 pounds—and had an easygoing personality that both frightened and attracted people. Gundo, an academy mate of mine who was ten years older than I, was a crafty old-school UC, a classic, straight-up operator who everyone— good and bad—couldn't help but like.

While Slats, Timmy, and I briefed our peers, JJ and Pops were busy with the minutiae of hosting and outfitting three "new" Solos. They lined up rental bikes, a couple of motel rooms, and, most important, created the cuts and made them look authentic. Our aim was to have the guys up to speed as soon as they hit Arizona, which would be on January 28.

I also equipped the Phoenix undercover house on Romley Road with some new props. My three-foot-long iguana, Spike, hadn't been getting the love he needed from the Dobyns clan, so I'd brought him up from Tucson. Once Spike got to the house, I realized that he should have a friend. For some reason one of the task force agents was selling a nameless eight-foot boa constrictor. I bought him—and his huge glass tank—for a hundred bucks.

We ramped up our contacts after mid-January. Timmy and Pops went out with Bad Bob and the Mesa boys one night. Bob announced there'd be no more drugs in the clubhouse—no selling, no buying, no using. The guys said fine. Bob said there'd been too much of that lately. Then Bob took Timmy and Pops aside and asked, "By the way, you guys got any party favors?" Apparently the rule didn't apply to him. Timmy later told me he had to stifle a chuckle by coughing into his hand, and Pops said he couldn't even believe it.

Not much else happened until the show came to town on the twenty-eighth.

Slats rolled out the equivalent of an undercover red carpet for the temporary Solos: grilled New York strips, ice-cold Cokes, and a makeshift casino in the Patch—craps and blackjack tables and a roulette wheel. I tried to get JJ to dress up like a showgirl, but she told me to fuck off.

We gambled quarters and laughed and ate. Around ten I suggested we go for a ride. Everyone was game.

As we saddled up Slats yelled, "Take it easy tonight. We got a big week."

I said, "Got it."

"No clubhouses. Only soft spots."

"Got it."

"You got no cover."

"Got it."

We left.

I knew these guys were up for anything, so I immediately violated Slats's orders. We headed to the Desert Flame, a strip club owned by a new Mesa prospect named Big Time Mike.

We rolled in seven deep, counting JJ.

Big Time Mike asked, "What's up?"

"Big Time! These are my Solo brothers—Jesse, Footy, and Gundo." Big Time asked us what we'd have, and we told him.

After serving us he said, "You guys should go over to Mesa. Some guys are there, they'd love to see you." Before I could say anything, he called, spoke to them, and hung up. "It's all set. They're expecting you."

"Cool, dude."

I pulled Gundo and Footy aside and asked, "Whaddaya think? We won't go over there if you're not comfortable yet. You heard Slats—he doesn't want us doing anything like this."

Both said, without hesitating, "Hell with that, let's go!"

I asked Jesse and JJ the same, and they were game too. Timmy and Pops were always up to see the boys. I told everyone we wouldn't stay longer than an hour or two. In and out, meet and greet, get the lay of the land, that kind of thing. As we assed-up I looked at my guys. I thought, We don't need a damn cover team. We *are* the cover team. There was no way a roomful of Angels was going to outdo the seven of us. My confidence soared.

Mesa Angel Alex Davies met us at the gate and showed us inside. It was a small group. Nick Nuzzo, Mark Krupa, Casino Cal, Paul Eischeid, and some prospect I'd never seen. Nick stepped behind the bar, poured us all drinks, and toasted the Solo Angeles.

Then he said, "Let's go next door." He meant the members-only section of the house.

For the first time, we went next door. The decor was more of the same, except there was a greater concentration of lounging furniture: a couple of couches, four overstuffed chairs, a low coffee table with nonsense scratched all over it—AFFA, I (HEART) THE HELLS ANGELS; MESA ROCKS; and JAIL, DEATH, AND PUSSY.

Everyone mingled. The new Solos hit the ground running and took over: no fear, no hesitancy. They'd been on the case for twelve hours and they were already performing like A-list actors. For the first time in months I was able to sit back and enjoy myself as my partners worked the room. Nick and Cal started to do bumps of crank off the tip of a Buck knife, openly violating Bob's no-drug rule. Nick must have seen me looking at him, because he sheathed his knife and came over.

He blurted out, "Fuck Bob."

It was the meth talking. I didn't say anything.

He repeated, "Fuck that guy." Cal came over and sat down. Nick sat down. He bounced one of his legs and spoke fast. "Shit ain't right around here, Bird, I'll tell you. Guys are splitting. The guys in this room, we wanna be outlaw. Bob and Whale and Crow, those old fucks, they want us to take it easy." He spit on the floor. "We want to be outlaw—like you guys, you know?" That took me aback. The Mesa Hells Angels wanted to be like us? Like Solos?

Nick sniffed hard. Cal took over talking. "Listen, Bird, we wanna do business with you. But we gotta take it slow 'cause we don't want Bob knowing. He's hoarding you guys. He's paranoid and he's greedy and he's keeping all the good shit to himself."

Nick broke back in, "Shit, you know how many times I seen that fat fuck break his own drug rule? Man, I ain't got enough fingers."

I nodded. They offered JJ and me a bump, and I reminded them I didn't do that anymore. JJ said No thanks, not as long as Bird is my old man.

"Anyway," Nick said, snorting it himself, "not everyone is Bob's boy here anymore. Some shit is fucked up around here lately."

This was good and bad for us: We had the opportunity to exploit some club weaknesses, but we had to keep Bob happy. Under no circumstances could any of us undermine his authority. I told Nick and Cal that we were always interested in business opportunities, but I didn't mention Bob. Nor would I say anything to him. I decided to string them all along and see how everything shook out. I had to do it this way. If I ratted, Bob would know, but he'd also know I was a rat. If he found out later that I knew, then I'd come clean, but I'd add that I didn't want to be the guy to tell him. I'd have to shift the blame onto Nick and Cal for putting me in a bad spot. I knew Bob would understand and respect this reasoning. It was the only honorable course of action.

We left not too long after that. We couldn't stay late. Slats was right, we did have a big week ahead of us.

WE HAD OUR ops planned to the minute. I had these guys for a week and I wanted to get Slats his money's worth.

The twenty-ninth started with some club business that I invited Bob to. It concerned our prospect, Jesse. The Solos huddled around him in the living room of the undercover house, merengue music blaring from some low-rider outside. I waited in the kitchen for my cue, Timmy saying, "What the fuck you looking at, prospect?"

I lit a smoke and sauntered in, my Serial Killer cap pulled low over my eyebrows. Jesse sat in a folding chair in the middle of the room. I paced tightly in front of him, never traveling more than four feet. I stared him down. He swung his knees back and forth. I sucked my smoke. Everyone else was lined up, arms crossed, and bore down on Jesse with scowls.

"I'm not gonna waste your time, prospect. And I sure as shit ain't gonna waste the time of any of my brothers or esteemed guests. You're shit, plain and simple. I hear from your sponsor that you don't do shit, and when you do do shit you don't do it right. I ask your sponsor over there"—I thumbed at Footy—"and he says you can't even open a beer right, let alone do something more complicated like gas up a bike. God forbid he asked you to do something real, something any one of the men in this room could do without thinking. You know what kind of thing I mean?" I stopped. Jesse stared at me like a busted schoolboy.

Gundo said, "Bird asked you a question. Answer."

"Yeah. Yeah, I know what you mean, Bird." His voice didn't waver.

I stepped on his words: "I don't think you do. I don't think you have one single fucking idea what I'm talking about. I'm talking about real shit, man-up shit, shit your momma wouldn't be proud of, you under-stand me, dude?"

"Yeah. Yeah, I do."

"Bullshit!" I barked. He didn't flinch. I pretended not to like that. I leaned in close. I placed my hands on my knees. I spoke quietly. "Bull-shit, prospect. I think you're a pussy. I think you're a spineless, unwor-thy fucking cunt. You ain't no Solo. You wanna ride a bike, I suggest you go home and join a BMX club, you California nobody. You hear me?"

"Yeah." No fear in there.

"All right. Now. Since I'm a decent guy, now's when you talk, if you got something you wanna say."

He respectfully said that he didn't see it my way. He said he'd done everything that had been asked of him and done it as well as he could. He said if it wasn't good enough, then he was sorry. He said, for what it was worth, he still wanted to be a Solo.

I turned my back to him while he spoke, and shook my head. When he was finished I said, "Forget it, man, forget it." I winked at Bob. "Aw, just forget it. Footy, give the man his shit!" And Footy stepped forward and gave Jesse his patch, at which point we all cheered and Jesse let out a big, fake breath. Bob was transfixed. Later he told me it had been the best patch ceremony he'd ever been to. "Except for this one where the new brother accidentally got shot," he added, laughing.

Then came the Solos Angeles barbecue in honor of the Arizona Hells Angels. Around twenty Angels came over to our humble home in the Mexican 'hood. The homeboys next door didn't know what to think when all those bikes roared onto the *calle*. We were good neighbors, we invited them. Some showed up. Crazy scene: Mexican gangsters and Hells Angels commingling like we were in a prison yard in the desert.

Gundo was a piece of work. He'd learned long ago that it was best to just be himself in the undercover world. Along with his cut, he wore light gray corduroys, a white button-down shirt, a plain green baseball cap, and running sneakers. Except for his haircut and his jacket, he looked like an average guy at the mall. The haircut was the kicker. He'd had me shave the sides of his head, leaving a wide mohawk on the top. He called the look "the Seahorse."

I walked through the kitchen at one point during the party to find Gundo nonchalantly holding the clothing of a naked man. A few Angels stood around looking him up and down, their arms crossed. I asked Gundo what was up.

"No one knew this guy," he said. "I wanted to make sure he wasn't miked up."

The guy looked humiliated and frightened. I had no idea who he was. "Well, unless they got mics in dicks these days, I think he's clean. Give him his clothes back, all right?"

Gundo smiled the same smile I'd seen him give his wife a hundred times. "Was just about to do that, Bird."

Bad Bob had witnessed the strip-search and came over to ask what was going on. Gundo explained to him, "Bob, you're our guest at this party. Your safety and the safety of your brothers is my responsibility while you're here. Someone shows up and no one knows him, then he's gonna get shaken down by me until I'm satisfied he's not recording you, not photographing you, and not smuggling in any hardware with bad intentions." Bob beamed and threw one of his massive tree-trunk arms around Gundo's neck, catching him in the crook of his elbow. Bob turned to me and said, "I love this guy." All that was missing was for Bob to give Gundo a noogie on the Seahorse.

I walked through the party shirtless, high on success. I never smiled. I had some drumsticks that I beat on everything—the backs of chairs, the backs of people. I even did a drumroll on Casino Cal's Death Head. I was Bird, full of nervous energy.

JJ started to get tight with Nick's girl, Casey. Casey was the girl covered in tattoos whom Bad Bob occasionally went with. Casey dug JJ, and JJ returned the favor. Casey claimed to be a meth source for a Denver Angel named Nick Pew—as well as for Mesa. She asked JJ if she wanted to do a rail, and JJ said, "I do a rail and Bird finds out, I catch a beating. No way. Thanks, though." Casey said no problem, she understood, boy did she. Casey told her she ran shit to California and back for Nick and his brothers all the time. JJ said she had some friends in Dago who might want some, and Casey told her to let her know how much, that she was her girl. JJ thanked her, said she wouldn't forget. Then Casey told her she'd be willing to drive shit south for us if we needed another driver. JJ said she'd talk to me about it, and when I heard that I laughed.

My new prop, the snake, lived in the living room. The party thumping around me, I took the snake out of the tank and draped it over my shoulders. It was heavy and smooth and cool. It felt powerful.

As I approached Bad Bob, his face went white. He pulled his knife, pointed it at the boa, and yelled, "Bird, you get that fucking thing away from me or it's gonna be cowboy boots!"

I said, "Thanks, Bob." He asked what for. "You just named my snake. 'Boots.'"

The party ended but the ride continued. Nights flowed into days and back into nights.

We roared into Mesa on the thirtieth for the Mesa Run night. Bob, obviously tweaking, cornered me and went off on Rudy. He was worried about him snitching again, saying he knew Rudy had a newborn at home and he'd talked to ATF and maybe Rudy had made a deal to get out while his kid was still young, to spend some time with him and whatnot. I knew Rudy was going away no matter what, that he had nothing left to give us, but I couldn't comfort Bob. All I could say was that Rudy was messed up, but he wasn't an informant. Bob compulsively played with one of the rings on his fat fingers while we spoke. He said he'd hung his ass out for us, that he used to be dead set against other clubs starting up in Arizona, but in us he saw something he liked, something he hadn't seen in a long time. I thanked him for the millionth time. He said as soon as Rudy settled down, things would open up for us.

On the thirty-first we waltzed into the Pioneer Saloon in Cave Creek and got a full introduction over the PA. Gundo was right behind me, and after the announcement ended he leaned into my ear and said quietly, "I don't care who these guys are, but that was fucking cool." I nodded. It was.

Everyone was there, and I mean everyone. Sonny, Johnny Angel, Hoover, Smitty, Joby, Bob, Fang—every guy who had any kind of influence in the state.

Sonny came up and greeted each one of us, and in one of the greatest moments in biker investigator history, we got a group shot with him: just Sonny Barger and Johnny Angel in the middle of a row of Solo Angeles, aka cops, Sonny's arch nemeses. It was a damned coup.

The night of February 1, we went to Cave Creek's clubhouse. Theirs was bigger than Mesa's, on a more open lot in a residential neighborhood. They had a little stage with a stripper pole, and that night the pole had a stripper on it at all times. A blonde with thigh-high red patent leather boots and a dirty brunette in a knit black bikini—or more often out of it—took turns twirling around the stage.

All night Joby bugged me for my silencer source—he must've heard about it from Smitty. At one point Joby pulled me into a side room and said, "I need something that if I was to smoke someone right here, they wouldn't hear it out there." I told him not to worry, I'd talk to my guy, but I had to do it my way. He respected that.

As we left the side room I bumped into a short, roided-out live wire with a shaved head. He looked like my shorter, wider twin. Joby had moved on.

The live wire asked, "What the fuck? You're fucking Bird, aren't you?" He stabbed his finger at me, tapping me hard right where the bullet had come out of my chest.

"Yeah. That's right."

"Shit! I'm fucking Dirty Dan. And I need to talk to you. Come with me." I followed this prison gangster to an empty corner of the clubhouse, preparing to be become a human sacrifice. He turned suddenly, barking, "I heard all about you, Bird. You're some kind of crazy fucking cowboy, ain't you? Shit, brother, I love that."

The veins bulged from his neck and his face turned red. He spat when he talked. I fed off his energy and he fed off mine.

He asked about Mexico. I said I went to Mexico often. He said he'd heard there were Mongols down there. I said there were, but not too many. He said that as soon as his parole was up, he'd like to come with me, see if we could find some. I said great. He said find some and then kill 'em. I said awesome. He said we'd be a two-man massacre crew. I said, "Dirty Dan, you're the kind of Hells Angel I've been waiting to meet." He said that he liked the way I carried myself, that the club needed more guys like me.

I was perversely flattered and thrilled to have stumbled onto what I considered a real-deal Hells Angel. No Toy Runs or public parties for Dirty Dan. Just riding and beating and fucking. Amen, brother.

After several minutes we parted company just as abruptly as we'd come together. We agreed to meet and work out at the gym. He yelled, "All right! Later, Bird."

I yelled, "Later, Dirty Dan."

We'd been in a complete bubble. Hours after that, when we were winding down at the UC house, Gundo told me that when Dan and I started talking, all eyes turned to us. Our body language looked overly confrontational. Gundo said, "Man, I thought you two were gonna hit the deck. I was leaning against the bar with my hand on my gun, getting ready to pull out. I thought we were about to be in the middle of an ass-beating shoot-out."

I laughed and said, "You kidding me? That guy kicked my confidence up about a thousand notches. I fucking loved that guy."

February 2. The Solo Angeles–Hells Angels love-fest had one more engagement: the Florence Prison Run. It was the anniversary of my first run the previous year, when I was a Bullhead nobody riding with Mesa Mike. Oh, how the world had turned.

The main drag in town was choked with bikes. We hung out at Yolanda's bar, drinking light beer and bullshitting. A band played. Ghost took the stage and sang a song. He was pretty good. Everyone was happy to be there. In spite of all the rival clubs in attendance, the mood was easy and there weren't any beefs.

We rolled into the desert. All two thousand plus of us. The cops could do nothing but watch, and it was glorious.

No longer relegated to the back of the line, we were fully integrated

into the Hells Angels' thundering column. We rumbled through the
dust, all the colors of all the clubs flying. We were surrounded by our
Red and White brothers, the Eight-Ones. All the Arizona Hells Angels
charters were there: Nomads, Cave Creek, Mesa, Tucson, Phoenix, Skull
Valley. Beyond them were all the states and many of the countries with
Hells Angels charters. We banked wide around a turn and passed the
yard. JJ casually slung her arms around my waist and I gunned forward,
the orange jumpsuits standing at attention while we yipped and yelped
like pound dogs. Timmy, Pops, JJ, and I all had orange bandannas
wrapped around our heads. They were the same color as the jumpsuits.
I screamed as loud as I could: "Orange Crush!! Orange Crush!! Orange
Crush!!" Timmy joined in. It was for the guys locked up, but really it
was for us, our little inside joke. We were the Solo Angeles Nomads,
our colors were black and orange, and we were the Orange Crush.

No one heard us, though. The bikes were too loud, and we were
rolling too strong.

This undercover scam had become my life. An ex-partner of mine
used a baseball analogy to explain successful undercover work. In baseball, if you hit .250 you're an everyday player. You hit .300 and you're
an all-star. Approach .400—just for one season—and you're a lock for
the Hall of Fame. The same percentages gauge a UC's success—one
that goes out and gets good intelligence 30 or 40 percent of the time is
a rock star.

I was batting 1,000 percent with the Angels.

And I was being corrupted by success.

26   WILL YOU BE MINE?

WE DEBRIEFED ON the third and took a big exhale. We drove Footy and Gundo to the airport, gave them loud, back-slapping hugs, and thanked them over and over. None of us could believe how successful the week-long ruse had been.

JJ drove back to San Diego with Jesse. She'd be off for a couple of weeks and then return to work full-time. Her value was immeasurable, even Slats couldn't disagree with that. He'd held several conference calls with her superiors during the Solo week and persuaded them to let her go until the case came to an end. She was thrilled.

After the guys left we got our house in order. We cleaned up the Patch, tuned up the bikes, and took a good look at our suspect matrix. Slats and I decided that with Mesa feeling split and unpredictable, and with Bad Bob concerned about Rudy, we should shift our focus. We decided our next best opportunity was to see what Joby Walters could add. We moved him to the active area of the board. We'd go to work on him as soon as we got back from a couple of days at home.

That other house of mine—the one I was ostensibly in charge of, the one that contained Gwen and Dale and Jack—was not in order. Not at all.

I got home late on Friday night. No one was home. I knew they'd be gone. Gwen had told me earlier that they'd be spending the weekend camping in the mountains. She said I still needed to come home, though, to take care of the yard and fix part of the overhang on the back porch. For some reason it was leaking.

I got up early on Saturday, checked out the overhang, and made a trip to Home Depot. Some animal had peeled away a few of the composite roof shingles. I tore the old ones up, put down a patch of tar paper, and covered that with new shingles. I swung down from the roof, had a beer by the pool, fixed myself a tuna sandwich, and mowed the lawn and trimmed the plants around the edges.

I watched TV that night and put calls in to Smitty and Bad Bob from the comfort of my own couch. They didn't answer. I left them messages. "Hey, it's Bird, just checking in," that kind of thing. Smitty and I had a gun deal in the works and Bob, well, I just wanted to hear his voice to make sure he wasn't flipping out over Rudy.

I was glad the house was empty. Even the dog was gone. There was no pressure to change, no need to become someone I wasn't. I could remain Bird, a visitor in my own home. I didn't have to fake being Jay. That was the worst thing about coming home: There was no reprieve. The Angels knew only what I told and showed them, but Gwen had known me for eighteen years. I couldn't hide anything from her or game her into thinking something that wasn't so. Coming home was becoming more difficult than hanging out with the Hells Angels. This didn't make me sad, it made me angry. Angry because I was beginning to feel that I shouldn't have to change, that I should be able to simply decide that I was just going to stay in role. Gwen wouldn't let that happen and she was right not to, but I couldn't see it her way at the time. All I could see was that the house was empty—even with me in it—and I was relieved that I didn't feel guilty for not being my old self.

I called Gwen on her cell on Sunday morning and told her everything was taken care of. She said they'd be back in the afternoon. I told her I had to go back to work early, there was a meeting first thing the next morning and I needed to get some paperwork done. She said the kids missed me and I said I missed them, too. I hadn't given them much concrete thought over that weekend—they existed in my thoughts as abstractions belonging to Jay Dobyns. But as I said the words I realized it was true. I did miss them. In fact, I missed them so much it hurt. Even so, I told Gwen I wouldn't be around and to tell them I loved them. She said of course she would, and hung up.

I drove back to Phoenix at noon on Sunday. That night, after an hour or two of writing reports, I put on my Solo cut, hopped on my bike, and hung out at Sugar Daddy's in Scottsdale—a place I knew the Angels went to from time to time. I drank beer and played pool and made appearances.

No one showed up.

AS THE WEEK started, Pops told me he'd been getting calls from Joby about that thing he'd asked me about—the silencers.

We discussed this problem at Monday's debrief. There was no way I could hook Joby up with my old Bullhead silencer source from Operation Riverside, the machinist Tim Holt. We decided to walk a very thin line. I knew Holt was still making the tubes, and I knew Smitty was aware of it. I called Joby and told him that Smitty was going to have to hook him up because I wouldn't be in Bullhead anytime soon. He said fine. And that was that.

My ethics prevented me from brokering a direct silencer deal for Joby, but I also knew there was nothing I could do to stop it from happening. The simple truth is that cops cannot prevent criminals from making illegal purchases. If we could do this, the world would be a much different place. For example, I could choose not to sell a machine gun to suspect X, but I couldn't prevent him from buying a different machine gun from a different seller. I could arrest him for completing such a transaction, or I could buy that machine gun from him and use the purchase against him later, but I couldn't prevent a third-party deal. That was the principle we were operating under with Joby and the silencers, except that we stretched our limits by referring him to Smitty, who we assumed would refer him to Holt.

We sunk ourselves back into work that week. Timmy bought a 9 mm Ruger from Cal that Bob didn't know about, Pops and I bought more tiny bags of meth from a Phoenix Angel named Aldo Murphy. He lived near our Romley Road house with his wife and their ten-year-old daughter, a perennially dirty, undernourished girl with the unfortunate name of Harley Angel.

We'd bring the bags to the Patch for field-testing, and Slats would bark at us, "What, another half-a-half-a-half a teener? I'm sick of this shit." We said we were sick of it too. He implored, "Get me dealers, not users." We reminded Slats of the Casey woman, Mesa's meth hookup, and he waved his hand like he was brushing a cobweb from his face. He said, "Fine. When JJ gets back I'll put her on the tattooed wonder." I was convinced we weren't finding any mega-scale drug trafficking because we weren't fully trusted. Everything we knew told us that the Hells Angels moved volumes of drugs, and it was embarrassing to me and frustrating to Slats that we weren't getting them. He thought we had to push harder, I thought we had to gain even more credibility.

I hoped to do just that when Joby invited us to a Valentine's Day party in Prescott. He said some guys would be there whom we had to meet. I asked if I should bring flowers. He laughed and said, "Naw, Bird. Just you."

Prescott is in a central valley between Flagstaff and Phoenix. People who haven't been to Arizona tend to think of the state as one big desert, but places like Prescott dispel that image pretty quickly. It's beautiful. Pastureland, swaying blue grass, horse farms. Mountains to the east and north, desert encroaching from the west. It's lush and cool—often cold—and it gets a fair amount of annual precipitation. It's a college town with libraries and sports facilities and bars. It's got a Starbucks—a fact I never miss. I often thought I'd retire to Prescott. But it's a small town, and since I now know a few guys there, I don't think that would go over too well.

But I didn't know them then. Pops had rolled up ahead of Timmy and me. He'd called us on Joby's behalf and told us to meet them at the Desperadoes Bar, the only joint in town that allowed bikers. He said it was right on Main Street.

When Timmy and I walked through the door, Joby floated over to us like he was the host of some high-class cocktail party. He carried a club soda. He patted us on the shoulders and led us to the bar. I felt like we were the guests of honor.

Pops sat at the bar with five or six Hells Angels. Surrounding them was an assortment of other club members. There were Vagos, Vietnam Vets, Americans, Desert Road Riders, and Red Devils. They orbited the Angels like subservient moons around a dense planet. Timmy and I were brought to the center.

I didn't think it was possible, but Joby introduced us to four Arizona

Angels we'd never seen before. They were Teddy Toth, Bobby Reinstra, Joey Richardson, and Rudy Jaime. He also reintroduced us to Robert McKay, the Tucson Angel and tattoo artist who'd recently had his non-association clause lifted.

The four unknown men belonged to the Skull Valley charter of the Hells Angels. Teddy Toth was the president. I'd heard about him. He was a former East Coast Angel from New York City. He'd transferred out west when his health started to fail. We knew a little about him from Slats's intelligence. Teddy was an old-school, thirty-year member—an Angel power broker, on a par with guys like Bad Bob, Hoover, Johnny Angel, and even Sonny Barger himself. He took no shit and operated by the outlaw book.

In spite of this stature, my first impression of him was that he could die any minute. He carried haggard sacks underneath his eyes, and a pair of tubes were stuffed up his nose. The tubes led to a wheeled oxygen tank that leaned against the bar. He was fat and slow. I knew, however, that I couldn't trust appearances. Teddy was dangerous. Just like an old mobster who no longer needed his health to rule the family, Teddy was a man to be reckoned with.

I didn't know anything about the other guys. Bobby Reinstra, another East Coast guy from Boston, was Skull Valley's vice president. He was younger and physically stronger. He had as much expression as a log. He didn't smile when we met. I didn't either. I'd call us kindred spirits, except that Bobby was quiet when he spoke and careful of what he said. He was the proverbial strong, silent type, which in a Hells Angel can be pretty terrifying. Rudy Jaime, on the contrary, was all smiles and energy. He was the junior member and had piercings all over his head. Joey Richardson, the last member, looked like your standard muscled-up, middle-aged weightlifter. They called him Egghead.

I walked up to Teddy holding a support card with $100. He took it and I gave him a hug. As we pulled apart, Teddy wheezed, "I like you, walking in here all dick-out cocky. Just like a New Yorker would."

I said, "Just paying my respects."

Teddy said, "Good, good."

We shook everyone's hands. Rudy asked Pops if he wanted to get high. Pops shrugged and disappeared with Rudy to the far end of the bar.

We drank. Joby played host. He'd recently transferred to Skull Valley as their sergeant-at-arms. The guys didn't loosen up, but as we spent the next hour talking, I got the feeling they never loosened up. Teddy and

Bobby were old-school bad boys who impressed people with their lack of humor. They were the kind of guys who spent every waking minute waiting for a reason to pull out a lead pipe and put it to use on the backs of someone's knees.

I could deal with that.

After a while Joby asked me to step outside and we excused ourselves. We stood on the sidewalk while laughing college kids in baseball hats and sorority sweatshirts drifted by. I lit a cigarette and we stood shoulder to shoulder. We spoke out of the sides of our mouths.

"Whaddaya think, Bird?"

"Of what, dude?"

"The guys."

"They seem like good guys."

He nodded and I took a deep drag. "Listen. First off, thanks for putting me with Smitty on the carburetor hookup." That was slang for silencer.

"You got what you need?"

"Yeah, think so. The guy's working on it."

"Cool. Make sure you field-test them. Sometimes they come up loud."

"Will do. Thanks."

"No prob."

"Look. I know you've been hearing shit about coming over, and I got a proposition for you."

"OK."

"I want you guys to come up under me, here at Skull Valley."

"Really? I mean, don't get me wrong, Joby, I'm flattered." I waved my hand at the town in front of us. "But why here, dude? It's pretty and all, but this place looks about as exciting as paint."

"It is. That's my point. I know Bob wants you, and between you and me, Tucson wants you too. I think that's why Mac's here, actually. I know Smitty already voted to bring you on with the Nomads in Flagstaff. Shit, you even got Dirty Dan sniffing on you for Cave Creek. Here's the deal. You go up at Mesa and you gotta get twenty guys to give you the stamp of approval." Prospects had to be voted in with mandatory counts. "You piss off one guy, or get sideways with some political bullshit down there, and you're a prospect forever, dig?"

"Yeah. Yeah, I do."

"Tucson, they're small but fucked up. Smitty's Nomads are good too, and I love them, but they're kind of the black sheep. But here—you come up here, it's nice and quiet and we got no competition. There are five guys in Skull Valley. You've already got my vote, so that means you gotta make four guys happy. Four versus twenty. Shit, Bird, whaddaya say?"

"Joby, you trying to get in my pants, dude?"

He laughed. "Fuck yeah, I am. You gotta come up here, man. It's the easy way in. After, you can transfer with me to that Mohave Valley charter Smitty's setting up in Bullhead. I'll be an officer there, Smitty'll be the damned P. You'll come in big."

"What about Timmy and Pops? What about Bad Bob? I got obligations to other people, you know? Big Lou, my down-south pistoleros, the Solo Nomad brothers you met last week . . ."

"Bob—I'm working this all out with him, don't worry. The other Solos—naturally Timmy and Pops are part of the deal. We love them too. When you guys are in, then you can prospect your out-of-town boys to your heart's delight."

I paused to stomp out a cigarette and lit another. I asked, "What about prospecting, Joby? You know me. I can't spend a year being someone's step-and-fetch bitch."

He shook his head. "Don't worry. I'm talking to people, Sonny's helping me out. You guys are gonna be fast-patched. We don't have to teach you guys shit, you know the drill up, down, and inside out. Two-day hangarounds, ninety-day prospects. You'll have club duties, but they'll be light. No questions about business—we understand you guys travel a lot to make your living and that's fine by us. Telling you, Bird, one day you'll just wake up and you'll be Eighty-Oned."

"It sounds real good, Joby." It really did. "Thank you for thinking of us, dude, it means a lot."

"So that's a yes?"

"That's a strong maybe. I'm sorry, I can't just say yes. I been a Solo for a long time and I gotta talk to my boys before I say anything either way."

"I understand."

"I won't string you along, all right? You got my word."

"All right."

I thought it was a great pitch and one hell of an earnest Valentine. I finished smoking in silence, thinking this must be what a popular freshman feels like during rush week. I went back inside. Joby had a high bounce in his step, like there was a pebble in his boot. He nodded at Teddy as he walked up to the bar. Teddy didn't move. He just wheezed.

27 "9-1-1! 9-1-1!
GET OUT OF THE HOUSE!"

LATE FEBRUARY 2003

ON FEBRUARY TWENTY-EIGHTH my cell rang. Timmy, JJ, Pops, and I were hanging out at the Phoenix UC house on Romley Road.

"Yeah, Bird."

"Get the fuck out of the house right now!" It was Slats. He sounded scared.

Slats never sounded scared.

I twirled my finger through the air like a little tornado. Everyone got up, grabbed their weapons, and ran outside. I followed, pressing the phone to my ear.

"What's up?"

"Don't have time. Get to the Patch right now. Watch your asses."

"We're already out the door. We'll see you in fifteen."

We piled into the Cougar. I turned the engine on and peeled out.

We drove in circles a little to make sure we weren't being followed. We pulled into the Patch's office park and went around back. The bay doors were open and we pulled in. They closed behind us.

Slats paced. He spat into a can. I lit a smoke. Slats said, "C'mon."

As we made our way to the conference room he told us what was going on.

"DEA's got a snitch associated with the Phoenix charter. His handler called up half an hour ago and told me that Chico put together a hit squad and they were on the way to Romley to smoke you guys." He was talking about Robert "Chico" Mora, the Phoenix Angel that Mesa Mike had warned me of over a year ago.

I asked, "Why the fuck's Chico wanna smoke us?"

"That asshole in Tijuana—Alberto?—apparently he's been talking about you." I'd heard a little bit of this. Our receptions in Mexico had been generally warm and easygoing, but there were always guys who rocked the boat. This Alberto was the Solos' vice president. He'd always given us the cold shoulder. I assumed he'd had some bad blood with Rudy that went back years, and was never going to give us the benefit of the doubt. We chose to ignore it, hoping it would stay in Mexico.

It hadn't.

Slats said Alberto was complaining that we'd muscled our way into the club, had never prospected, and weren't legit. He spoke the truth. Somehow this had gotten back to Chico.

We didn't know what to do. SOP in a situation like that was to pull the operatives. Mortal and imminent danger was not tolerated or risked. If there was a slight but verifiable chance any of us would be killed, then that was that. Cricket and Slats thought the case was dead. They started to discuss whom they could arrest with what we had.

But I wasn't so sure we couldn't get out of it. We had plenty of evidence that corroborated our Solo Angeles backstory, it was just a matter of getting it to the right guy as soon as possible.

That's when my phone rang again.

"Yeah, Bird." Everyone in the room was stone silent.

"Bird. It's Bob." His voice sounded deeper, more serious.

"What's up, Bob?"

"We need to talk."

"What about?"

He cut to it. "You're a real Solo, right?"

"What the fuck you talking about, Bob?"

"I know you're really a Solo." He sounded convinced in an unconvincing way.

"Fucking right I am. What's going on?"

"We need to talk. It is *very* urgent."

"OK."

"Be alone."

"OK."

We agreed to meet at a sports bar on Baseline, a place we'd never been to.

In one hour.

THE ENTIRE TEAM stuffed up with armor and grabbed their long guns. An advance team got to the bar quickly. They took their places and waited. Sat at the bar and did crosswords, feigned watching games on the TVs.

Timmy and Pops were in the surveillance van. Timmy was armed to the teeth. If things broke bad with Bob, I'd likely be fine.

Still, I didn't have a good feeling about the meeting.

Before leaving the Patch, Slats helped me put together an impromptu package of Solo credentials. Photos and video news footage from the December Toy Run, dues receipts, photos of Pops and Rudy in the Tijuana clubhouse, random flash we'd picked up. We talked dialogue, Slats role-playing Bob, me in role. We'd sell our case to Bob like we'd sell a crime to a prosecutor: physical evidence, historical evidence, and an argument for our position. Breaking character, I asked Slats if he thought Bob was try-ing to prove to his brothers where his real loyalties lay, if he thought Bob might be taking this opportunity to take me out. We all knew that as I went, so the Solos went. Slats said he wasn't sure, and if I didn't want to meet with Bob I didn't have to. That meant the end of the case. I said fuck that. He said OK then, let's get out of here.

I drove the Cougar and consumed half a pack of cigarettes. I was openly scared and not proud of it. I called my old buddy Chris Bayless. He talked me down and gave me the old "Jesus Hates a Pussy" speech, finishing just as I pulled into the parking lot.

I went in and walked to the bar. Five minutes later a haggard Bad Bob loped through the door. He looked around as he approached me. He said gravely, "Let's get a booth."

We made our way to a quiet corner of the bar and sat down. I put my hands on the table and laced my fingers together. My rings, my rings. They meant something to me. In an instant they reflected all that I'd lied about, all that I'd come to personify, all that I'd risked.

I decided to ignore them, but not before I asked them to protect me.

Bob talked about what was going on. I acted shocked. I didn't deny the charges that we'd muscled our way in, but I insisted we were legit.

"Your guy's got it wrong, Bob, I don't know how else to say it."

"You understand what you're saying?"

"Yeah. I don't mean any disrespect, and I'm not calling them liars, it's just that they got bad info. We're legit Solos, Bob. We've been doing everything right by you guys—you think it'd be any different with my own damn club?"

"I don't know shit about your club, Bird—other than you guys."

"Well, we're real, man. Believe it, we're real. Look." I showed him the photos, I gave him the videotape of the news shows and told him to watch it. I showed him the dues receipts and the flash we'd picked up in Tijuana over the months—T-shirts, stickers, patches. I wrote down Teacher's number and told him to call him and ask him if we were for real.

"Look, Bird. I want to believe you." He paused. "I *do* believe you. But I'm in a bad spot. I gotta call Joanie"—John Kallstedt, the Phoenix charter P—"I gotta call Joanie and tell him you're all right—a guy none of us have known longer than a year—and Chico's wrong—a guy I've known over two decades. How you think that looks?"

I agreed that it didn't look good, but I insisted, with expletives, that I was telling him the truth.

He said, "Let's go outside and have a smoke."

I said, "Yeah, let's." My confidence rose a little.

The bar had a big back porch. No one was out there. Bob got out a pack of cigarettes and fumbled with it while pulling out a smoke. When he went to put the pack away, he couldn't figure out which pocket to put it in—first the outside left breast, then the right, then finally the inside left. I flipped open my Zippo and offered it to him. The tip of his cigarette was shaking as it glowed orange.

Bad Bob was nervous. My confidence went back in the tank.

Fear fell on me like a ten-foot wave. I hadn't been so scared in years.

Bob stepped to the edge of the porch and ushered me to the corner. I was completely exposed in three directions.

"I hate these kinds of situations, Bird, hate them."

I fought back a shaking voice and answered hard: "I don't like them either."

"These are the kinds of situations where people get hurt. Bad. You know?"

"I know. But listen—"

He waved his hand through the air. I shut up. I thought that he'd just green-lighted some sniper to remove my head or hollow out my chest. I thought, Jay, you're dead.

"No. Listen, Bird. I know you're used to fighting for your life—"

"That's all I do." He didn't know how true that statement was.

"I know. That's all men like us ever do. But what I'm saying is you ain't never had to fight *us*. Am I right?"

"Yeah. Yeah, you're right."

He smoked deeply. He turned and walked to the other end of the porch.

This was it.

Head explodes.

Chest caves in.

Air sucks away.

He walked back.

"I'ma call Joanie. I'ma call Joanie and tell him you're good."

Exhale. "Good. Thanks."

"I'm not doing you any favors, understand?"

"Of course."

"I'm doing this 'cause I know you ain't shitting me."

"I know. I ain't."

"But you need to do a couple things for me."

"Anything."

"No colors till I say. Your Arizona privileges are hereby revoked."

I wasn't happy about that, but I said OK.

"You need to clear this shit up, Bird. Motherfuckers cannot be talking shit about their own like this. Fuck, we take better care of you than your own damn club!"

It was true. I said, "Don't worry. It'll go away. And I know you look out for us, Bob. I can't thank you enough."

He mumbled, "Fuckin' motherfuckers." Bob was insulted that the Solos had insulted me. I was too.

He dialed Joanie and told him to back off. He said he'd bring over the stuff I'd given him—the photos, the tape, everything—and that they'd talk to this Teacher motherfucker.

We went back inside. I paid the tab. We walked to the exit. We shook hands solemnly and parted.

I knew I'd just saved the case. I'd pulled a rabbit and a goose and a snake out of my hat, then fed the rabbit to the snake and watched as the

NO ANGEL   207

goose laid a golden egg. I'd snowed one of the most influential Hells
Angels in the state of Arizona, and it was exhilarating.

I suddenly wasn't scared. I'd lost all my insecurity.

I was invincible.

I DEBRIEFED WITH Slats in his car outside the Patch. It was just the two of
us. He handed me a beer, opened one for himself, downed it, and
opened another.

"That sucked," he said.

"No shit."

"No, I mean it wasn't that good. You sold it better at the Patch."

I couldn't believe it. I said, "Frankly, Joe, I couldn't remember what
we said at the Patch. But it worked, didn't it?"

"We'll see. You put a Band-Aid on this fucker, we'll see if it heals."

"It will. You know Bob'll make it happen."

"I fucking hope so."

"It will."

He drank half of his beer in two gulps.

"But shit's gotta be better going forward, Jay. I can't take this fly-by-
night stress anymore. You gotta stay on the program."

"When the fuck did I go off it, Joe?"

"You go off it every fucking day, Jay. Every damn night we say,
'Tonight's the night Dobyns goes off the rez and we end up doing a rescue mission.' We're taking fucking bets on it, Jay."

That was news to me. "The fuck, Joe. One day it's 'Get me more,'
the next it's 'Ease up'? Which way you want me to go? I'm giving everything I got, Joe, I can't think of how to give you more. This is the way I
operate! You knew that going in! It's why you hired me!"

"Listen, Jay. I know you're under a lot of stress, but it's nothing compared to what I deal with. I hired you, but I can pink-slip you too."

"Excuse me?"

He took a deep breath. "The fact is you're ten percent of this picture.
You and JJ and Timmy and Pops. A crucial ten percent, but *only* ten
percent. I have to deal with all of your shit, plus all of the evidence, all
of the surveillance, all of the tech issues, all of the money, all of the
approvals, all of the protocols, and all of the personalities. I have to
massage everyone's balls above me and rub everyone's backs below me.

You may feel like you're the one at the middle of this thing, but you're wrong."

I couldn't believe what I was hearing. I lit a cigarette. It was like Slats had intercepted a pass intended for me, and now I was playing defense. "Joe, you may be dealing with a hundred percent of this, but you're not working any harder than I am. You're not fricking redlining any more than I am. And you get to go home at night and sleep in a bed with your wife, and your kids are sleeping down the hall! You have any idea the last time I spent every night of the week with Gwen and the kids? I can't count that fucking high! No. Instead, I get to sleep in a shithole undercover house and half the time our marks are crashing in the living room! While you're sitting there counting money and typing reports, I'm sitting face to face with a guy who, if he finds out who I am, I'm going to get smoked! So I don't want to hear how fucking hard it is for you."

I opened the door, got out, and slammed it shut. I threw my empty beer can as far as I could.

I couldn't figure out what had gotten into Slats. So I'd gone off script—I was having a fucking conversation, for crying out loud. You can never predict what the other guy will say or do—I had to react on the fly. That was my damn job!

It took a long time for me to cool off. I had a hard time understanding where Slats was coming from. I eventually concluded it was all about control. He felt that if I kept increasing my unpredictability, the reins of Black Biscuit would be taken from him.

I didn't care about that. It was *my* case, and as far as I was concerned, he could go to hell.

28 THE IRON SKILLET

I TOLD TIMMY and Pops about my argument with Slats. They couldn't believe it. Timmy was especially mad, since, like me, this was his career, not just something he did for money like Pops. Timmy asked, "Why should we hang our ass out so much for someone who doesn't think we're doing a good job?"

I shrugged. "You know—do something right and no one remembers, do something wrong and no one forgets."

Timmy nodded and said, "Damn straight."

The truth was that Slats *was* under more pressure than we were, but neither Timmy nor I was about to admit it. We could only feel our own suffering. We'd each sold our empathy up the river. All that was left was pride, determination, and loyalty.

It was around this time that I started to pop Hydroxycut.

Hydroxycut—a weight-loss pill that suppresses appetite and injects a burst of energy—helped me to focus on whatever was directly in front of me. It was convenient: I could bump the pills anytime and they were readily available—any Walgreen's carried them. The recommended dosage was no more than six pills in a twenty-four-hour period. That's where I started.

I needed the energy because I was running ragged. The life of an undercover cop is not one of leisure. I was up every morning at seven, going over notes from the night before or transcribing audio from one of my recorders. The notes couldn't be half-assed or glossed over, they had to be dead-nuts on. Then I'd do my expenditures, and those had to be to the penny. I kept track of everything—drinks, gas, cigarettes, coffee, food, drugs, guns, tribute payments—everything. Then I'd contact the suspects—some of whom were occasionally crashed out in the living room while I did reports behind my bedroom's locked door—and set up meetings and deals for the day or week. Then I'd call Slats and go over everything with him. Then I'd meet a task force agent to exchange notes and evidence. Then I'd start making my runs, seeing the boys, hitting the spots—just being seen is a job in itself. Then I'd make my scheduled meetings, do the buys I'd set up, hit the clubhouses, and have conversations. Some days I'd ride from Phoenix to Bullhead and back, others I'd put a hundred and fifty miles on my bike just riding around the Interstate loop in Phoenix. All along I checked in not only with Slats but also with Bad Bob, Smitty, Joby, or whoever else was featured at any given time in the case. While bullshitting with the boys, my mind constantly turned, thinking up new schemes, new ways to build credibility. The sun would set, the heat would dissipate, and the nights would begin. I'd go out and, despite drinking, would try to stay lucid enough to be able to defend myself, JJ, Timmy, or Pops if any of us got made. The stress of being in near-constant mortal danger is what we were trained to endure, but undertaking it day after day is enough to fry anyone. I'd get home, cross myself, smoke cigarettes, down coffee, jot down notes and reminders, and then try to get a few hours sleep before doing it all over again the next day.

It was no coincidence that I started with the Hydroxycut after my argument with Slats. I was drawn too thin but had to keep going—my commitment, ego, and drive wouldn't allow me to quit. My family was beginning to hate me—if they didn't already—Slats was up my ass, the HA were getting farther up my ass, I was responsible for the safety of my crew. It was like the movie *Groundhog Day*, where the guy lived the same day over and over, except that if I got found out I'd get killed—and that would be that. Hydroxycut gave me an energy boost that went beyond the three Starbucks Venti lattes, two-packs of Marlboro Lights, and half-dozen Red Bulls I consumed on a daily basis. I knew the pills weren't good for me—nothing I did then was good for me—and I knew they'd make me look like a junkie, but I simply didn't care.

I also started to take them in March because of our up-in-the-air status. Bad Bob's suspending our right to wear our cuts made me uneasy. I needed to do something that would make me feel rooted to who I claimed to be, so I decided to get sleeved with tattoos. It was something I'd wanted to do for a long time, and I knew it would also boost my credibility, since most cops won't submit to getting inked-out prison-style.

I'd been checking out Robert "Mac" McKay's work at his Tucson tattoo parlor, the Black Rose, for a few months. Mac was very talented, and I knew he'd do a great job on my arms. We'd started discussing my getting sleeved when I'd met the Skull Valley guys in Prescott. He said he'd be happy to hook me up and give me a good deal. I didn't tell him how good a deal it would be—since it could be tagged as an operational expense, ATF would pick up the tab. I told him I wanted my arms to depict good and evil, since I was neither. He liked that.

I had plenty of tats by then—the Saint Michael on one shoulder, four intertwined strands of barbed wire, which paid tribute to the four ATF agents lost at the Branch Davidian compound in Waco, over the other. Spanning my shoulder blades like a bridge was the word JAYBIRD. These tats were bold but pretty benign.

Getting a tattoo is funny. It always depicts something contemporary about you—a friend dies, a child is born, an epiphany is had—and you get inked. When you get one you think you're marking something about you that will never change. You think, I'll always be young, I'll always put my children above everything else, I'll always honor the dead. The reality is that while the tattoo remains, the person it's etched onto changes.

For instance, I had the dates of the deaths of the ATF agents killed at Waco inked onto me along with the strand of barbed wire. But I had to have them covered because I was afraid that someone—specifically, Scott Varvil from the Riverside case—would put two and two together and want to know why I was commemorating an infamous date in ATF's history. Before I got those dates covered, I asked one of the agents who'd fought at Waco what he thought I should do, and he told me that if they were hindering my ability to work confidently, the guys who'd been killed would absolutely want them blacked out.

I blacked them out, something that for me bordered on sacrilege.

I didn't think about it too much when I told Mac I wanted my sleeves to depict good and evil. I knew that deep down I was good, but I also knew that in order to survive and do my job well, I had to appear evil. What I didn't admit was that I was in the process of giving in to my darker tendencies. I'd been tamping down the good in me for months. Ironically, I accepted evil in the service of defeating it.

I was Bird. I was Jay Dobyns. I was good. I was evil. I was all and none of the above.

So. Both arms got skulls and flames and demons mixed with flowers and clouds and angels. Like the rings I wore on each finger, the earrings I had in each ear, and the bracelets I wore on each wrist, these talismans balanced each other out. I was the scale, and they were the weights and counterweights. I thought by evening these things out on my body I would remain balanced in my mind. This was just lip service, though. I couldn't have been more out of whack.

But Mac *was* good. We would do an hour on one arm, an hour on the other. JJ would sit in the dark room and make phone calls. She'd talk business with Casey, Pops, or Timmy. Sometimes Lydia would call to see what was going on. Slats and I had numerous coded conversations while Mac's needles buzzed away under a bright desk lamp.

Mac asked a lot of questions about my collections business. I told him it was pretty easy money. He wanted to know if I beat a lot of people up. I told him the near-truth—that I rarely beat anyone up (or never, since I never did any actual collections). I said it was usually enough to just show up with a baseball bat and a couple guns and my SERIAL KILLER cap. He wanted to know how much I made. I told him it depended, but usually ten percent. I told him the most I ever made was fifty grand. He asked, no shit? I said no shit, and, travel time aside, it never took longer than twenty minutes.

Mac said he'd like to get in on it with me, if I ever needed the help. I told him I'd keep him in mind, but that with Timmy and Pops I was pretty well covered.

Mac also wanted to know what the story was with the Solos. The fact that Bad Bob had pulled our colors was a hot topic. It was also unpleasant. The control the Angels exerted on us by pulling our vests was good for the case—it would bolster the RICO charges—but it felt awful to be twisting in the wind.

And it was a noisy wind that snuck through all the cracks. All through March we fielded constant calls from Smitty, Dennis, Joby, Doug Dam, Casino Cal, Dan Danza, and a host of others wondering what was up with us and our club. The guys' questions were more curious than accusatory. They wanted to know why the Mexican Solos were kneecapping us. We told them the truth: We didn't know and were taking care of it. Mainly, though, we kept our fingers crossed. We weren't sure whether Bad Bob would be satisfied with the evidence I'd given him, but based on the calls he'd put in to Joanie, the Phoenix charter P, it looked encouraging. However, if Bad Bob or Joanie wasn't satisfied, then the case could easily have folded. In the event that this happened, several task force agents were in the preliminary stages of drafting search-warrant affidavits.

Despite our concerns, the case continued. In the wake of the Chico threat, we shut down the Romley Road house and got a four-bedroom on Carroll street—a pool and everything—in a quiet neighborhood on the edge of the Cave Creek charter's territory. It felt good to be back in a middle-class, suburban neighborhood. Jay Dobyns still lived some-where inside me.

I spoke with Bob on March 6. He said he'd gone over everything with Joanie and that they were convinced. I asked him if we could suit up again and he said, "You guys are good, Bird. Put your cuts back on. But I ain't happy with these Solos. I'm getting fed up with taking care of your shit. I didn't vouch for you so I could be your babysitter. This isn't over." He didn't elaborate, but I guessed what was coming.

We were about to get pushed.

On the morning of the seventh we met Joby at the Iron Skillet Truck Stop in Kingman to further discuss our Angelic future.

We sat in a window booth, the powerful semis outside growling and idling. It was before noon, but the sun was strong and soaked the thin veneer of clouds with a blinding white sheen. Timmy and I sat across from Joby, JJ was wedged between Joby and Pops. Joby ordered eggs, sausage, dry wheat toast, and coffee. The rest of us ordered waffles. Joby wanted to know what was with us and waffles. JJ asked him what was wrong with waffles? We all laughed.

Our coffee came. Joby spoke quickly. He ranged over topics like a crop duster over pest-stricken fields. Laughlin: He was afraid he'd soon be arrested; he'd stabbed guys there; he'd given CPR to a fallen Angel named Fester, whom he couldn't revive, and under whose body he'd hidden a firearm; he might go to Mexico if it didn't look good with the law; he'd expected to die the night of the riot. "I didn't think we'd make out the way we did. I think that's why we won. We went in there knowing we were outnumbered four or five to one, knowing we were dead. So we weren't afraid, you know?" He stopped there. He shook his head.

Our food came and we dug in. Joby moved on to the Solos. He repeated everything he'd told me at the Valentine's Day party, how we had to come up to Skull Valley, how we'd be given freedom to conduct business, how we were ready. He said he was planning on giving us a formal recruitment offer when he got back from the fifty-five-year anniversary party in Berdoo the following week. This was nothing new. What *was* new was that he said our membership was essential to consolidating Angel power in the area between Bullhead, Vegas, and San Bernardino, California. Joby let on that we were *needed*. This sent me flying. I could use it to bargain not only with Joby and the Hells Angels, but with Slats and our superiors.

Breakfast was over. I tried to pick up the tab, but Joby insisted. We were on a frigging date.

Joby and I walked side by side through the parking lot. He asked me if I had any support stickers. I thought he was asking if I had any Red and White stickers. I began to remind him that I didn't wear those things, when he interrupted me. "No. Not those. Do you have any for the Solos?"

I said, "Pops has some."

He asked Pops. When we got to our bikes, Pops dug through his saddlebag and came up with three or four that read SUPPORT YOUR LOCAL SOLO ANGELES. Joby took one and walked over to his bike, peeling the backing off the sticker. He laid his hand over his oil bag and smoothed it into place. He turned and looked at us. JJ leaned on my hip, I had an arm around her shoulders. Timmy and Pops straddled their bikes. We must have looked like Stallone's gang in *The Lords of Flatbush*. We couldn't believe what we were looking at. It was possible that this was the first time a Hells Angel had placed another club's flash on his bike, ever. And that club was ours.

Joby knew what he was doing. "I don't care, Bird. Timmy, Pops, JJ." He looked each of us in the eye as he said our names. The semi trucks rumbled. "I don't care. You guys are right by me, and I support you."

I walked away from JJ and gave Joby a hearty hug. I said, "Thanks," into his ear.

He barely shook his head. "No need. You guys are my brothers. I'll talk to you when I get back from the fifty-five party."

29 "LOOK, LADY, IT'S NOT LIKE I DON'T GIVE A FUCK WHAT YOU'RE SAYING, BUT I DON'T GIVE A FUCK WHAT YOU'RE SAYING."

IT DIDN'T STOP. Alberto, the trash-talking Solo, had the ear of Guy Castiglione, the Dago P, who was under DEA surveillance. (The evidence
gathered against Castiglione led to a guilty plea on his own RICO
charges.) Alberto continued ranting that we weren't legit, that we didn't
come to Tijuana often enough, that we were impostors, that Rudy
Kramer was a piece of shit, and that we'd never brought Suzuki his
Harley Evolution Sportster. Guy passed this to Bob, Joby, and Smitty at
the fifty-five party, and they barked back that we were the real deal, that
our club was abandoning us and the Solo Angeles organization was
worthless. Joby also caught all kinds of grief about the Solos support
sticker he'd pasted to his bike, but he took it in stride and didn't back
down. He told them to wait, as soon as they met us they'd understand.

I saw Bad Bob again toward the end of March, in the middle of a
three-day meth bender. He looked like a wet paper bag that had been
shot through with electric current. Barry Gibb was dead. Bob said all
the Solo Angeles drama had ruined the Hells Angels fifty-fifth anniversary party for him. He was fed up. He said, "I should just go down to
Tijuana and beat this Alberto fuck into the Pacific."

He told me solemnly that we were through. As of April 21, 2003, no Solo would be allowed in the state of Arizona. "Not even to pass through," growled Bob. Then he said, "Bird, you gotta quit fucking around and state your intentions," like I was marrying his dearest daughter.

Which in a sense, I was.

Oddly, the anger and confusion that Bob and Joby and the rest of them felt toward the Solo Angeles in Tijuana never transferred to us. The worries revolving around our legitimacy put any lingering concerns about our cover story to bed for good. The Hells Angels had been given the perfect opportunity to question us, to take a good look and ask if we were what we claimed to be. They'd been told the truth about us and they'd dismissed it as jealous lies and slander. They felt they'd done their due diligence—we knew at that point that they'd conducted at least three independent background checks on us—and they felt they knew us. As Bob said to me, "I back you to my fullest, but I'm tired of this shit."

But the fact that we were set did not put our anxiety at ease. If anything, March was the most anxious month on the case since August. It came down to continuing on an uncharted path or shutting the whole thing down before it had run its course.

We made an unspoken decision to ride it out. We had too much invested to end it because the Hells Angels were forcing our hand. I wouldn't shut down because the opportunity to join the Angels was too important. Slats wouldn't stop because he refused to be swayed by the biker rumor mill.

We continued with the game.

Mac finished my sleeves. One morning in the middle of March, as Mac was putting the finishing touches on me, JJ called. She said she was with a guy at a local diner, having breakfast. I told her to keep him there, I was on my way. I flipped shut and asked Mac, "You wanna make a few bucks? JJ's pinned down a guy I been trying to collect."

He put down his needle and gauze and said, "Hell yes."

Mac took off his cut, knowing he couldn't wear it on a collection without club sanction. We left and Mac locked up the shop.

As we climbed onto our bikes I looked at my arms. They were dark with ink, red around the areas he'd been needling. They glistened with a thin coat of Vaseline. My arms looked great. They belonged to me.

They belonged to me more than they had before they were covered in ink.

We went to the Grant Road Waffle House. We parked our bikes and stalked toward the entrance. Mac asked what he should do, how he should act, what if we had to beat on the guy? I told him to stay quiet, follow my lead, and simply support me. He said he could do that.

JJ sat next to a twentysomething white guy in a window booth. She wore a black tank top and jeans, and the guy wore a white Roca Wear track suit with green piping and amber-tinted sunglasses. We walked up and stood over them, our arms crossed. I said, "Move over there, sweetie," indicating the other side of the booth. The guy just said, "Shit."

I sat next to the guy. Mac sat next to JJ. Mac eye-fucked the guy hard. JJ stared at the table, playing the part of the dumb girl in the wrong place at the wrong time.

I pointed at the guy's food and asked, "You eating that?" taking the fork out of his hand.

He said, "I was."

"Not anymore." I pushed the food around his plate and reached across him and grabbed his coffee and downed it in one gulp. "You know who I am?"

"I have a pretty good idea."

"Good. I just wanna let you know today's your lucky day." He harrumphed. "See, they could have sent someone else, someone who introduces himself by putting a pipe on the back of your knee." I stuck my chin at Mac. He nodded slowly. "But you got me."

"Great."

"Don't show no lip." I took a mouthful of hash browns and mumbled, "Listen, don't talk. Dig?"

"Yeah."

"Good. We're getting along great. Now. I need that fucking money."

I'd told Mac that the guy owed Big Lou twenty-one large. The guy said he didn't have that kind of money on him. I said that I hoped he didn't—it wouldn't be too smart to walk around with a wad like that. I asked if he had a checking account. He said he did. Then that means you have a checkbook? Yes. How much you got in that account? I reminded him not to lie. He said he thought he had about seventeen. I slid his plate over so it was in front of me and said that was a good start, we were getting places. I told him to start by writing out a check for seventeen, to sign it but leave the pay-to line blank. He said OK and fumbled in his pocket. I told him not to move too quickly. He didn't. He pulled out his checkbook. The checks had whales on them. A conservationist. As he made it out, I asked what else he had. He said about three hundred cash and a gun—a Sig 9 mm. I said I'd take both. I asked him to keep his hands on the table and asked him where the gun was. He said in the back of his waistband. I asked him if he had a concealed-carry permit. He said Uh, no. I told him to take it easy, what did he think I was, a cop? He laughed nervously. I removed the pistol and slipped it into my jacket. I reminded him of the cash. He took out his wallet and handed over a small wad. I counted it quickly—$314. I put a twenty on the table for the food, nodded at Mac, and got up. He got up too. JJ and the guy stayed in the booth. I said, "You guys too. C'mon." They got up. We went outside.

The guy thought JJ was going to go with him, but as we walked through the parking lot, JJ looped her arms through one of mine. When the guy saw this he stopped short. Mac and I climbed onto our bikes, JJ climbed on behind me and hugged tight. She said to the guy, "See you later, sweet pea." We peeled out, leaving the guy to think it over.

Back at the Black Rose, I gave Mac $200. I said, "See? Ten minutes, two hundred bucks. That's how easy it is to make money with me."

He smiled, shook his head, and said, "Thanks."

"No problem. Thank you. I'll see you soon."

"Sounds good."

JJ and I pulled out and headed to Phoenix.

THE COLLECTION VICTIM had been ATF Special Agent Eric "Otter" Rutland. He'd played the part perfectly.

JJ AND I spent the night in Phoenix. It was an off night. Timmy and Pops were at their real homes. She asked if I wanted to go drinking.

"I'm sick of bars."

"Yeah, me too."

"Well, let's do *some*thing."

We tried to think of the last place a Hells Angel would show up, but our imaginations were dead. I didn't feel like going to a movie, JJ didn't want to go out for dinner—we needed to blow off steam, not go on a bullshit date at the end of which nothing would happen. Finally, I asked if she played golf.

"Couple times. Not really."

"Wanna go hit balls?"

"Sure. Yes."

We went to a driving range in Scottsdale. She'd lied—she had a great swing. We each hit around a hundred balls, drank beers, and had a good time.

Gwen called midway through the fun and wanted to know when I'd be home. I said tomorrow. She reminded me that we had a barbecue to go to. It was at the house of some old friends. I said I hadn't forgotten and that I'd make it.

I'd forgotten.

I hung up. JJ leaned on a seven-iron, drinking beer from a brown bottle. She looked right at me.

"That Gwen?"

"Yeah."

"She all right?"

"Doubt it. She's sick of me not being around." I teed up another ball. Why should I have to explain the broken state of my marriage to the woman I was pretending to sleep with? I owed JJ loyalty, guidance, friendship, and protection—not explanations.

"Off to Tucson tomorrow, then?"

"Yeah." I hit the ball with my driver. It hit the ground just shy of the 250-yard marker and rolled past it, stopping around 270.

"Cool. I'm gonna hang around here. Maybe see if Timmy wants to hit a movie or something." He'd probably do that. Timmy had also developed a mentor-like friendship with JJ, and I knew they did things on their own, too.

She put her beer on the floor, teed a ball, and smacked it. With the seven-iron, JJ could drive the ball 120, 130 yards. This one went straight down and rolled past 150.

She laughed. "Oh man, Jay. Wait'll Gwen gets a load of those arms."

OUR FRIENDS KNEW I was the police, but none of them knew what kind. Most thought I worked long hours as a city narc or on a homicide task force. I can't think of one who knew that I'd done deep cover work for over fifteen years. This created some familial tension. Both Gwen and I would deflect questions about my job with half-truths and allusions. I was researching a drug ring, I was chasing down illegal firearms, I was backing up investigators looking at an interstate trafficking consortium. I was busy. No specifics. No talking about how I'd been shot, nothing about the guys I investigated, no mention that I'd had guns pointed in my face dozens of times. The pride I took in these events was private—or at least limited to the company of my peers.

This reticence wasn't such a big deal for me—I lived in a world of cops. I could stand around the water cooler and talk about my experiences till the cows came home. I had regular mental-health checks from ATF shrinks and old friends and partners like Chris Bayless. I had outlets.

Gwen bore more of this burden than I did. In a sense, she had to live an undercover life too. She couldn't let on that she was the wife of a UC for the simple reason that doing so could compromise me or my partners and associates. She'd learned a long time ago to keep the things she said about my job to a minimum. Our close friends got used to not hearing much about me. That was the way it had to be, and it was the way I liked it.

Usually it was easiest if I didn't put her in the position of having to lie. As the years passed I'd grown accustomed to telling her less and less about my work. There were things she'd never know or need to know. I felt there was nothing to be gained from letting her in on the intricacies of my life. Of course, that wasn't true. While I hadn't yet lost her trust, I'd lost a closeness we'd once had. Telling her more about my work might not have made her feel better or ease her worries, but it might have prevented her from feeling so alienated.

As for the tattoos, I'd spoken to Gwen for years about getting sleeved—a long time ago she'd even drawn the flowers Mac had put on my upper arms. She liked what my tattoos said about me—that I wasn't the usual suburban husband. But while she understood that I wanted to get sleeved, she couldn't understand why I wanted to look like a gangster. I said it wouldn't look too badass if I got covered with Yosemite Sams, Tazmanian Devils, and bunny rabbits. I knew that wasn't what she meant, but it's the way I thought about it. I liked the prison-ink look. I guess in regard to tattoos I wasn't too different from the people I strove to take down.

Gwen wasn't surprised when I showed up with my arms done, but she was a little disappointed.

"I guess you're just a biker now, huh?" We were in our bedroom, getting ready to go to the barbecue. I was tired but rallying, sucking down a Red Bull.

I poked her in the ribs. "Are you kidding me? You know I don't like riding bikes."

"That's not funny."

"I think it is."

She didn't say anything. She went into the bathroom. I sat on the bed jonesing for a smoke. When she came out she looked great. She pointed at my tattoos and asked, "What's she think of them? I bet she loves them, huh?"

"'She' who?"

"That woman you're working with. Jenna."

"I'm not even gonna—"

"I know what's going on, Jay."

"G, nothing's going on. Even if I wanted to, and I don't, I wouldn't have the fucking energy."

"No, you wouldn't have the 'fucking' energy, would you?" I sighed and maybe rolled my eyes more than I should have. Gwen repeated, "No, you wouldn't," and walked back into the bathroom

This wasn't new. Gwen had been dropping hints for a few weeks. I hadn't dignified them with a response. Guys on the task force had also started to point at JJ and me and rib me when she wasn't around. I told them the truth, that I was maxed-out enough as it was. I'd say, "Dude, even if I could get it up, which I can't"—probably thanks to my Hydroxycut problem—"I wouldn't have the energy to put it to use."

However, this was the first time Gwen had come out and said it. I tried to let it go. When she reemerged from the bathroom I said, "Look, if it makes you any happier I'll wear a long-sleeved shirt, OK?"

"Whatever, Jay."

Yeah, whatever.

I went into the bathroom and took four Hydroxycuts out of a pair of jeans slung over the towel rack. I gulped them down with the Red Bull.

The party was at a house not far from ours. The family who lived there had a son who was Jack's age and played on Jack's Little League team. The father owned a construction company and the wife was a pharmaceutical rep. They had another boy who was a couple of years older than Jack. Whenever we made it to church, we'd see them there. They were a good family.

We got in the car. Gwen drove. We didn't speak. I wasn't in the mood to go to a non-biker party. I didn't want to talk about sports or mortgages or home extensions or kids or vacation plans, of which I had zero. I didn't want to calm down or chill out. I wanted to keep my pot boiling. As we drove through a gorgeous Tucson evening, the sky streaked with pinks, purples, blues, and greens, I got more and more tense. My knees twitched. I wanted a cigarette, but I knew I couldn't smoke around Gwen. I didn't have my release—a business-casual cocktail party in the 'burbs did not compare to a Hells Angels clubhouse. My mind moved back to the place I'd been trying to force it to vacate.

The case was all-consuming. I thought of what I'd say to Slats, how I'd have to pitch him, thinking about how some of the task force agents had taken me aside to say they thought pursuing membership was a good idea. They made me angry when they did that. I'd say, "Hey, that's great, but I don't need you to tell me in private. I *know* it's a good idea. I need you to step up and tell Slats."

Gwen interrupted my thoughts with a harmless question. "They'll want to know what you think about the boys' team this season."

"What? What team?"

"The baseball team?"

"Oh. That. All right."

"Just try, OK?"

"All right. I will."

We arrived and walked in. I might as well have been at a cocktail party on the moon. Some guy handed me a drink and I drank it quickly. Tasted like a no-salt margarita, but I couldn't be sure. Gwen and I separated and I found the beer. I decided to go with that. Before the case I'd been a lousy drinker, but by then I was in tip-top shape. I could guzzle with the best of them, and even though I wanted to get fall-down drunk, I knew I shouldn't. I took it slow.

I horsed around with some of the kids. That was easy. They were playing in the pool and they kept begging me to throw them in. It didn't take long before I did. I put my beer down and rolled up my sleeves a little and started chucking them into the deep end. They loved it. I did too.

The woman throwing the party approached me holding two drinks, one full and one half empty. She held out the full one. She wore pink cotton pants cropped below the knees, a fuzzy, light green sweater, and dangly turquoise earrings. Her smile screamed *hostess*. I took the drink she offered and downed half of it. She looked at my arms and I self-consciously pulled the cuffs down to my wrists. I hadn't felt so exposed in months.

She didn't say anything about the tattoos, but I could tell she wanted to. She asked how I was doing and whether I thought the boys would have a good team that year. She talked about how hard my job must have been lately, since she hardly ever saw me. I didn't ask, but she said Gwen seemed to be holding up well. My end of that conversation was minimal. If I could have gotten away with grunts, I would have.

She was neither cruel nor ignorant, but she pressed on. She was probably just curious. I must have looked like a circus attraction at that party. I was strung out, and fresh tattoos peeked out from the edges of my clothing. I was also the only guest with a twisted five-inch corkscrew goatee, that's for sure.

All I could think was that I'd rather be hanging out with my guys. Not just Timmy, Pops, and JJ, but Smitty, Dennis, Bob, Joby—any of them. I didn't like them more, but I didn't feel so weird around them.

I wanted to say to this decent suburban mom, "Look, lady, it's not like I don't give a fuck what you're saying, but I don't give a fuck what you're saying. I'll see you later."

Instead I stood there and watched her earrings and took my medicine. It was bitter.

30   HOOVER'S HIT

ON MARCH 29 we had a funeral to go to. Daniel "Hoover" Seybert had been shot through the forehead on March 22.

He'd been killed in the parking lot of Bridgette's Last Laugh, a Phoenix bar, surrounded by his brothers, who conveniently—and ludicrously—didn't see a thing. According to the Hells Angels witnesses, Hoover had just started his bike when he suddenly slumped over the bars. There was no exit wound. They didn't hear a discharge. Some claimed that until they saw the wound in his forehead they thought he'd had a heart attack. Some said that he'd been hit by a sniper firing a large-caliber rifle—and they were all convinced that the shooter must have been a Mongol.

We weren't so sure. The medical examiner concluded that the wound was from a small-caliber, close-range shot. We later heard that Sonny postulated his beloved club would have been better off if he'd been the one in the casket. Hoover was revered and respected nationally and internationally by friends and foes—he'd been groomed as Sonny's replacement and was a perfect fit. His death devastated the club and drove their paranoia to new heights.

Hoover's murder remains unsolved. The wound and the Angels' reactions—and the lack of a spent shell casing in the parking lot—all pointed to an inside job. There was plenty of internal tension among the Angels in those days, centering on which way the club was headed, what they'd symbolize as they continued their wild ride through American cultural history. The dispute between Bad Bob and Cal Schaefer concerning drug use and the amount of partying the Angels allowed their members to engage in offered a good snapshot of what the club was faced with on a broader scale. Generally, younger members felt as though they'd joined the Hells Angels to raise hell, to do what they wanted to, when they wanted to, and not be told otherwise. Older members—members, it should be said, who'd lived this freer, hell-raising lifestyle in decades past—preferred to rest on their laurels, doing whatever they could not to attract attention from the law. These Angels were content with being old-time kings of the hill and selling T-shirts at motorcycle rallies. Ironically, the old-school mentality was embodied in the aging Sonny Barger, historically one of the hardest, no-shit-taking-est Angels to ever walk the earth.

Our theory was that the assassination of Hoover was designed as a message to those in the club who'd have them take the easier road. Hoover, after all, was a dear friend of Sonny's. The two men co-owned Sonny Barger's Motorcycle Shop and had great respect for each other. Officially, Sonny was nothing more than a rank-and-file member, but his word was still bond, and Hoover, it seemed, always deferred to Sonny's judgments and opinions.

I have a slightly different theory. Whenever I think of Hoover's death, I think of all those silencers the guys had been asking me about. I can't speculate who actually pulled the trigger, but I think the evidence strongly points to an inside job by someone in Arizona, maybe even by someone I knew. Maybe the man who'd done it wasn't satisfied with the Hells Angels' lack of action against the Mongols. Maybe he thought there should have been a top-down effort to eradicate the Mongols from the face of the earth, and he was deeply disappointed that there wasn't. Maybe he felt that the men hindering this explosion of Hells Angels vengeance were the same ones preventing some of the younger members from raising hell and living free.

Maybe.

This is all unsubstantiated conjecture based on very circumstantial evidence and my own gut feelings, and I wouldn't confidently be able to point at any one person, but I think it's a reasonable theory, if not a likely one.

Whatever the real reasons, there was no doubt the club was divided, and I believe my Solo Angeles Nomads bridged that divide. I may be flattering myself, but it's my belief that we were highly regarded by both factions. The older guys liked us because we were buttoned-up, respectful, and consistent. The younger guys liked us because we didn't take any shit and were into doing business. They all liked us because they believed we were connected enforcers, earners, and killers. I truly believe that the Angels saw in us a standard they could respect and even aspire to.

I hoped to find out. And I hoped I wouldn't have to wait too long.

TWO DAYS AFTER the shooting, Timmy, Pops, and I met Joby at the Cave Creek clubhouse. Hoover's murder, whoever had committed it, had spooked the Angels, and the place was on lockdown. Full-time armed guards secured a perimeter around the wide, two-story house. No one was in a good mood.

Joby asked us upstairs. We were joined by Cave Creek Angel David Shell.

Joby went over the same stuff I'd been getting from him and Bob and Smitty for the past couple of weeks. Our time had come, we had to join. We didn't say anything. We weren't yet fully approved to accept an offer. Honestly, I wasn't sure how to proceed. I assumed we'd have to wait a few more weeks, or at least until Hoover was in the ground.

Not so.

Joby paced as Shell rolled a joint and lit it. After complaining about having "to deal with all this Hoover bullshit," Joby got to the interesting part. "Anyway, it's set, Bird. You're coming up with us in Skull Valley. I worked it all out with Bob and Smitty. Smitty's been cool with it all along—he knows you'll be with us in Mohave Valley once that's up and running. Bob was a harder sell. He was pretty sure the only place for you was Mesa. I convinced him otherwise."

I said, "Great. Thanks for pushing for us, Joby, it's a real honor."

He said, "Yeah, well, you know how I feel about you guys." Shell had taken a deep pull and now tumbled into a hoarse coughing fit. I thought it was pretty funny, like he was choking right when it sounded like Joby was about to profess his love for me and the Solos.

"So what's all this mean? Practically speaking?" asked Timmy.

"Practically, it means you gotta come to Skull Valley's next church meeting. All of you. You're gonna be under Joey, Pops will be under me, and Bird will be under Bobby." Bobby was Bobby Reinstra, the muscled-up Boston bricklayer. "It also means you gotta get a place in Prescott." A Hells Angel had to maintain a residence near his charter. "And it means you gotta hang up your Solo cuts." He kicked a dust bunny on the floor for emphasis.

I said, "OK, but I need to deal with the rest of this Solo shit." I paused and added, "Again, this is a real honor, Joby. Thanks." Shell asked if we smoked weed. I lied and said yeah. He said good, the club needs more smokers. Then, as the stuff hit him hard, his eyes rolled blissfully into the back of his head.

Business done, we left. We had to talk to Slats.

WHICH WASN'T SO easy. Slats and I had been on very touchy terms since our fight after the Chico threat. In fact, we hadn't spoken at length in weeks.

Dan Machonis, our respected Phoenix Field Office supervisory special agent, had noticed and asked me to meet him at a sports bar near the Patch. He said we had to discuss some operational issues. It was a setup. When I showed, Slats was there, under the impression that he too was having a one-on-one with Dan. We met at the bar, Dan paid for a pitcher of beer, grabbed three mugs, and directed us to a horseshoe booth near the pool table.

Dan sat between us. Filling the mugs with beer, he asked, "You guys ready to sort some stuff out?" Without looking at him or at each other, we both said no. "Great." When he was done pouring the beer, Dan said, "Here's the deal. We're gonna sit here and drink this beer—and if we drink all this beer I'll get more beer—until you put aside your bullshit and start talking." He picked up his mug, held it over the middle of the table for a second, brought it to his lips, and downed half of it. Neither Slats nor I moved. Dan put down his mug, wiped away a frothy mustache with the back of his hand, and said, "Drink. That's an order."

We waited a couple more minutes. I think I moved first. Maybe it was Slats. The other followed almost immediately. We picked up our beers and each downed them in a few gulps. Dan poured out the next round.

Midway through the third pitcher we started to talk.

I said, "I know you're under a lot of pressure."

Slats said, "Damn right. And I know you are too."

We didn't need to say much more before the floodgates opened. By the time Dan was coming back with the fourth pitcher, Slats and I were bitching about everything we'd had to deal with over the past months.

We started to play pool. I beat Slats the first three games as we talked about how to move forward.

I said, "We have to accept the offer they're giving us. It doesn't make sense not to."

"They're gonna run you all over. The freedom tour'll be done."

"That's fine. It's what you're supposed to do when you're prospecting. I can handle it."

"What about Timmy and Pops?"

"They're in. You know they are. Timmy talked to you, right?"

"Yeah." He leaned over the table, lined up a short bank shot.

"They can handle it. No sweat."

"JJ?"

"She's fine. She's ready."

Slats said, "Hnh." He made the bank. He stood up and watched the cue ball move into position for the next shot.

He didn't appear to be convinced about JJ. I said, "She's strong."

"I know that, but this is still her first assignment."

"I'll protect her, you know I will." I would have taken a bullet for her or any of them.

He made a straight shot up the side rail. "No, *I'll* do that."

I let him have that one. "OK."

He sank two more balls and missed a thin cut. I moved to take my turn.

I continued my pitch as I shot. "We have to go over. We shut down now, and what do we have? You know as well as I do that if we allow them to force us over, then it's good for the RICO. Coercion, intimidation, all that. If we don't go through with it, all we can say to the judge is, 'They wanted us to come over with them but we didn't.' We do it and we can say, 'They made us go over to them.'"

He didn't say anything. That was good.

I continued, "I'm not taking anything away from the Solos, you know that. It was a hell of an idea and it's worked. Shit, your idea's been *too* good. Neither of us thought the Angels would press us like this. No one could've predicted what we're dealing with."

I sank three balls and missed an easy shot into the corner. Slats had two balls and then the eight. He didn't say anything. Dan, content that he'd done his duty, sat in the booth nursing a beer and doing the *USA Today* crossword. Slats made a tight shot, squeezing his ball between a rail and one of my balls. The cue ball moved directly in line for his next shot, a gimme into one of the side pockets. The eight was frozen on one of the short rails between the corner pockets. Slats cheated his last ball into the side pocket with a lot of draw. After contact, the cue ball curved slightly and ran right up the table, stopping five inches from the eight ball for an easy shot into the corner.

"Corner pocket." He pointed the tip of his cue at the target. He leaned over, took a few practice swings, and shot. He hit it too hard. The eight rattled in the jaws and stopped, hanging over the lip. "Fuck."

As I sank the rest of my balls, Slats said, "OK. We'll try it out. You know I know all about the prosecutorial benefits of letting it play." Of course I knew. This was a guy who, during a lull in his career, had taken the LSAT on a lark—no studying, no guides—and scored in the ninety-sixth percentile. He was like Rain Man with a gun. He could cite incidents, addresses, suspects, and statutes off the cuff—and they were always right. I'd seen him play five hands of craps at once, win, and then correct the dealer on payout mistakes. Even when we were at odds I trusted his knowledge and intelligence.

He continued, "But if I get a feeling or something smells bad, that's it. If you do something too crazy, that's it. If they want you to do something too crazy, that's it. If I wake up one morning and my back hurts and my feet are screaming at me and the Pepto ain't doing its job—that's it. Got it?"

"Got it." Slats was still in control. I sank the hanging eight with authority, just to tick him off.

"Good." He yelled over to Dan to get us another pitcher, our fifth. Dan looked up from his paper, nodded, and climbed out of the booth.

Slats turned to me and said, "Let's play some more. See if you can win just one more game."

We played for two more pitchers.

Win? We were pretty drunk, but I don't recall even shooting at another eight ball all night long.

31 NO MORE SOLOS

CHURCH CONVENED ON April 3 at a Super 8 motel in Prescott. Skull Valley had a clubhouse, but for some unknown reason we couldn't use it. We met Joby first, drove to the motel, parked, and went inside.

We went up to the second floor and walked to the room. That day's *Arizona Republic* lay on the threshold in a plastic bag.

Joby knocked on the door three times, paused, then knocked once. The chain came off and the locks turned. The door swung into the room. Rudy Jaime, the short, pierced meth head, stood in the dark hall wearing a half-smile. He nodded and told Joby to come on in.

Joby turned and gave us a deep nod. He went inside. The door closed, the locks tumbled, the chain slid back into place.

Timmy, Pops, and I stood in a tight circle looking at each other. Pops made a little frown and shrugged. Timmy and I were motionless. Rudy was probably watching us through the peephole.

Twenty minutes in a motel hallway. An eternity. We couldn't go anywhere, we couldn't smoke, we couldn't talk. The ceilings were low, the hall smelled like Febreze. We lined up against the opposite wall and three cleaning ladies walked by. They were from south of the border. Pops said *Hola* as they passed. They giggled and mumbled *Hola* back.

We didn't know it at the time, but this was the first course of our prospecting phase. It was a small, uninspiring appetizer, but it was pretty indicative of what we'd be going through in the coming months: a lot of standing around and waiting for nothing to happen.

The door made its unlocking sounds. It swung open. Rudy again. He pointed at me and said, "No phones." I handed my cell to Timmy and went in. Rudy closed and locked the door behind me.

I moved through the hall, past the bathroom and closet. It was a standard room. Rudy squeezed by me and sat on the edge of the king-sized bed. I stood at the threshold of the room, the large dormant TV to my left. Joby and Rudy were joined by Bobby Reinstra and Joey Richardson. Joby explained that Teddy couldn't be there because his emphysema was acting up. I said I hoped it wasn't serious. Joey said he'd fight through it, just like always. Then we got down to business.

Bobby asked the questions. What's your name? Jay "Bird" Davis. Why are you here? To announce my intention to become a Hells Angel. Why do you want to become a Hells Angel? Because I'm tired of playing in the minor leagues. Do you understand what being a Hells Angel means? I understand that I will have to make sacrifices. Do you know how hard it can be to become a Hells Angel? I don't care how hard it is or how long it takes. I am loyal, I am dedicated, and I am a warrior. All I want is a chance to earn the privilege of being a Hells Angel.

They liked that. It wasn't mockery. I was sincere and I was serious.

They asked me questions they knew the answers to. Questions about how I made money, about where I came from, about the people I knew. They asked me what I thought about the Solos' association with the Mongols. I told them I didn't like it, and that, in part, their relationship was one of the things that had compelled me to seek membership with the Angels, the Mongols' sworn enemy.

They liked that, too. I was excused.

Then Timmy, then Pops.

They spent about fifteen minutes with each of us. Then we waited in the hall for another thirty minutes. Then we were called back in, together.

The room was tight with all of us in there. Joey and Rudy smoked. I asked if Pops and I could smoke too. Joby said sure. Bobby went over some club rules. He said that Skull Valley was a no-dope-dealing outfit. We were ordered not to bring any more drugs back with us from Mexico. We said that wouldn't be a problem. He said personal use was tolerated. Joby nudged Rudy and said, "Like this tweaker motherfucker." Rudy chuckled.

Bobby didn't smile. I'd never seen him smile. "The last thing is this," he said. "You gotta clear up your Solo status. Take care of it in person, get rid of those cuts. Don't fuck around. As far as we're concerned there's no such thing as a Solo Angel in the state of Arizona. You no longer exist."

Joby said, "We're gonna kick those motherfuckers outta the whole U.S. of A."

Bobby didn't move.

We said that wouldn't be a problem.

Bobby said, "OK, then that's it," and we shuffled into the hall.

I was excited about coming in under Bobby. He was a perfect Hells Angel role model, someone I could learn a lot from. I knew he'd die for the club or his patch, and I knew he didn't take shit from anyone. Whether I agreed with him or not didn't matter. We may have been dedicated to different things, but it was the dedication itself that mattered most.

As we walked down the stairway Bobby asked, "Bird, you ever get any steroids?"

"I don't use them, but I might be able to help you out."

"Really? You look juiced." The Hydroxycut had taken what little fat I had and obliterated it. All that was left was muscle, bone, and nervous energy.

"Just genes and hard work."

"All right. Well, I'm looking for tes, D-bol, and Anavar. You come on any, let me know. I'll pay for 'em."

"Will do."

I know it's a technicality, but I thought: So much for not dealing drugs and the no-needle rule.

ANOTHER ANGEL WENT down in early April: Bobby Perez. Perez was a guy who'd cheated death for far too long. He'd walked out of several shoot-outs without so much as a bruise, Laughlin included, while his adversaries hadn't been so lucky. Once, in San Diego, he'd singlehandedly taken on three Mongols, killing one and getting stabbed in the fight. The surviving Mongols ran off, and he became the West Coast HA prom king. Nothing so dramatic caused his death: He'd been arguing with his neighbor and his neighbor had had enough and gunned him down. For some, karma's a bitch.

His funeral service would be in Dago, and we were instructed to ride with Skull Valley.

We decided to take advantage of the fact that we'd be on the coast: Before hitting the road I called Teacher, got Alberto's number, and called Alberto.

"Hello?"

"This Alberto?"

"Yeh." That's how he said it. *Yeh.*

"This is Bird. You know who I mean, right?"

"Oh. Yeh."

"Me and my guys are gonna be in Dago in a couple days. We wanna meet. We got some things we need to say to you."

"OK," he droned. I was hoping he'd sound scared, but he didn't.

"Bring whoever it is over there's been talking shit about us. We need to clear this up for good. All of us. OK?"

"Yeh, OK, Bird."

He said we could meet at the Chula Vista Denny's on April 12. I told him we'd be there.

We rode out to California through the high desert, nothing but sand, dirt, scrub, and blue sky as far as the eye could see.

Neither I, Timmy, nor Pops wore cuts. We were in biker limbo.

We took the Alberto meeting seriously. If he showed up with a bunch of guys, we intended to state our problems, say we were done with the Solos, and not back down. If he came with even numbers, then we were intent on showing him up, maybe even smacking him around a little. The Angels knew we were going to talk with him and what we were going to tell him, and we had to guard against the possibility that they'd tail us to see how we handled ourselves.

We got to the Denny's first. No Alberto. We crammed into a booth. Pops and I gruffly ordered coffee, Timmy politely asked the waitress for a Diet Coke with lemon. She was unfazed. She was a fortysomething waitress at a California Denny's, she'd seen everything guys like us had to offer and more.

I was riding high on six Hydroxys and two Red Bulls. The piss-weak Denny's coffee barely ticked my caffeine receptors. Pops was quiet except that when his coffee came he poured in a couple ounces of sugar and stirred it for about five minutes. *Ring-a-ding-a-ding-a-ring. Ring-a-ding-a-ding-a-ring.* Timmy sat there calmly, reading a paper that had been left on his side of the booth by the previous customer.

Alberto came in. Timmy said, "Yo. He's here." Pops and I turned to look.

We weren't prepared for what we saw.

He was alone.

"Timmy, tell him we'll meet outside, behind the kitchen." Timmy got up. I rummaged in my pocket and pulled out seven or eight bucks and put them on the table.

The waitress saw it and came over and asked, "You boys done, then?"

"Uh-huh," said Pops. We waited for the receipt.

We got up and went out back. Timmy stood facing Alberto. He was a short, sturdy guy pushing fifty who wore a drooping mustache and a pair of aviator sunglasses. Timmy wasn't talking to him. He pinned Alberto down with a hard stare and crossed arms, under one of which was tucked his neatly folded Solo cut.

I looked at Pops as we approached. He lit a cigarette and offered me one. I waved it off. He put the pack in his breast pocket, leaving it sticking out a little. He looked calm.

I walked up to Alberto and asked, "Where the fuck is everybody?"

"Yeh. They ain't coming."

"Just you, then, huh?"

"Yeh. Yeh, just, uh, just me." His voice shook. This was going to be easy.

"All righty, then. Here's how it is. We're leaving the Solos, effective immediately."

"Why—why you wanna do that?"

"Why? We thought you'd be happy, all the shit you talk about us."

He shrugged and pushed his glasses up his nose. "Still gotta ask. You got a cigarette?" he asked Pops.

Pops shook his head slowly.

I looked Alberto up and down. There was nothing to the guy. "We're leaving because the Solos are a chickenshit outfit with no balls. And since you showed up here alone, I'll add that you're stupid too." He didn't say anything, just stared at us through those aviators. I asked, "Why'd you talk so much shit about us?"

He gathered himself and said, "I wasn't telling no lies, man."

"Yes you were. We were legit and we are legit. Just because we're not in Mexico doesn't mean you get to run your mouth. You had a problem with me or us, you should've called, taken care of it man-to-man like we're doing now."

"Yeh. Well. I guess I didn't do that."

I stepped a little closer to him. "No shit, Two Dogs. Look, I don't want an apology, I could care less. I just want you to know our relationship with your club is over." I turned to Pops and signaled for a smoke. He handed me one. I held it, unlit, in between my fingertips.

Alberto asked, "That's it, then?"

"Yeah, that's it, Al." I lit up.

"Well, I'll need to have your cuts, then."

I couldn't believe him. "Really? Maybe you do have some balls." I looked at Timmy. The muscles of his face moved in increments. His eyelids were sleepy, his smile was slight and amused. I looked back at Alberto. "No dice, *cabrón*. We keep the cuts. Payment for our inconveniences."

"Can't do that. You know it's a club rule."

I took a hard drag off the cig. "Well, tell you what. Pops and I don't have ours on us. But if you want Timmy's, feel free to go and take it from him, if you think you can. You get his cut, we'll mail you ours." I took a beat and said, "Besides, we're not in your club, so fuck your rules."

Alberto looked at Timmy and actually moved backward half an inch. Timmy huffed a near-silent laugh.

"Right. Listen, Al, you ever want our cuts, then you can get a crew together, come to Arizona, and take them from us. Won't have a problem finding us—just ask the first Hells Angel you see. Otherwise, it's been real."

He shrugged so slightly a fly wouldn't have been scared off his shoulder. Other than that, none of us moved. Alberto was wedged between us and a filthy, dark green Dumpster. I stepped to the side and said, "You can leave now."

He scampered off, not saying anything.

I imagined the guys in the cover van were laughing their asses off.

We got on our bikes and went straight to Dumont's, Pete Eunice's bar in El Cajon. Bobby and Joby greeted us as we walked in. I said it was done. Joby asked how they took the news. Timmy said the guy pussied-out and he didn't take it one way or another. Bobby patted me on the back and said, "Good. We got some stuff for you guys."

We walked through the bar. Hells Angels from all over the West milled around. I nodded to Pete, who was behind the bar fiddling with the TV remote, and a few other guys I recognized. They all knew who we were, they all nodded back.

Joby opened the back door and we moved onto a patio.

No one spoke as Bobby and Joby grabbed three vests off a folding table. Joby held two, Bobby one. Bobby said humorlessly, "You guys done good so far—"

"—Congrats. You're official hangarounds," Joby twanged, chasing Bobby's words like they were his own.

Bobby spoke in the same continuum: "—You now represent the Hells Angels. Anything and everything you say and do is a direct reflection on the club—"

"—walk strong and—"

"—Take Care of Business."

Joby amended, "Take Care of *fucking* Business."

Joby handed Pops and Timmy their new cuts. Bobby held mine up for me to put my arms through. I did and turned to face them. We each jostled our shoulders and smoothed the cuts over our chests. They felt good. They were black leather, brand-new, and completely free of any flash. Bobby reached in his back pocket and pulled out three tabs and handed them out. They were white with a red border. In simple red block letters the words SKULL VALLEY were stitched into them.

Bobby said, "They fit. Don't fuck up."

32 BIG LOU AND GAYLAND HAMMACK RUN SOME GAME

ON THE EIGHTEENTH of April, Bobby, Joby, Timmy, Pops, and I, along with JJ, Bobby's girlfriend, Staci, and Joby's girlfriend, Caroline, mustered up to ride to Las Vegas for an HA poker run in support of the Sin City charter. The poker run was a fund-raising event that lasted a couple days and moved from one place to another. We wanted to go up, have some fun, and represent Skull Valley. I also think that Bobby and Joby wanted to show everyone where the former Solos had signed up for HA service.

They wanted to brag on us. We were happy to oblige.

Hells Angels can be very forward-thinking when it comes to scheduling and attending runs, but they very often neglect basic things—like reserving rooms. Availability of hotel rooms just doesn't register for a Hells Angel: It's a square-world concern. This was the price—or reward, depending on one's perspective—of living free in the biker mold. As we were getting ready to leave, Timmy asked where we were staying. No one said anything. Bobby said he didn't know. I said that I thought I might be able to get us rooms.

Joby asked, "What, at like a motel?"

"Naw, Job, at a place on the strip. The *new* strip."

"Bullshit," whined Joby. "We're sleeping in the dirt."

Timmy said, smiling, "I always wanted to try the Debbie Reynolds Hotel, what about that?" I laughed but no one else got it.

Bobby surprised me. Ignoring Joby he said, "Don't bother, Bird. Staci called ten places last night: Venetian; New York, New York; the Luxor. You know. Some convention's there, there ain't shit for beds. We'll just have to improvise."

"Let me see what I can do. I'll call Big Lou and see if he can work some of that Vegas magic."

I called Gayland Hammack, the Vegas Metro sergeant in charge of the local undercover crews. I told him the situation, pretending he was Big Lou.

He sighed, "Well, it's tight in town this week."

"All the same, me and my brothers would appreciate your help, sir."

"You're with those crackerjacks right now, huh?"

"Yes, sir."

He was silent for a second, no doubt filing through hotels in his mind. "OK. Shit, Jay, what kind of Vegas cop would I be if I couldn't snag rooms on short notice? I'll call you right back."

"Thanks." I flipped shut. I turned and looked at the guys. They stared at me like I'd turned green. They'd never heard me talk like that to anyone.

Joby said, "Nothing, right? I'm telling you—tonight?—we're sleeping in the dirt."

I walked toward Joby and lit a cigarette. "I doubt it. Big Lou's no joke. A moneymaker, and you know what that means in Vegas. He doesn't fuck around with dead-end deals. He does game machines, hot minks, bookmaking, jewels—top-end shit. He's got the strings, he'll find something." Joby shook his head and went into the clubhouse to get his bag. My phone rang. I flipped open. "Yeah, Bird."

"Hey. It's on. Three suites at the Hard Rock, two standard queens at the MGM. All comped, too."

"You're a lifesaver, sir. Maybe I'll see you around this weekend."

"I doubt it, Mister Hells Angel Wannabe."

"I'll talk to you later, sir."

"Tell Slats he owes me a lap dance."

I flipped shut.

Bobby stared at me. "Well? What's up?"

"Nothing much. Just comped suites at the Hard Rock and a couple rooms at MGM for Timmy and Pops." I drew hard on my smoke and threw it down. Timmy looked at me and smiled. Bobby looked at me and smiled. It was the first time I'd seen him do that. Joby came out of the house with a small duffel over his shoulder.

"Well?"

Bobby chuckled at Joby. "You can sleep in the dirt if it makes you feel better. But I'll be hanging in my suite with my old lady, thank you very much." Joby said no shit and Bobby, patting me on the back, said no fucking shit, Joby.

I popped a few Hydroxycuts while we finished getting ready. I needed the pills for the ride—a long, boring 235 miles through some of the most barren land you've ever seen.

We cruised through Chino Valley—the area north of Prescott where the Skull Valley clubhouse stood—under a wide blue sky raked by lines of puffy clouds. Joby and Bobby were up front—Joby packed double with his girlfriend, Caroline—and Timmy, Pops, and I fell in behind our Angels superiors. JJ and Staci orbited us in the truck, sometimes passing, sometimes falling back. We rode fast.

Through the rain, as it turned out. The good weather didn't last. An hour out, the sky turned black and churned in front of us. We rode into the teeth of an Old Testament rainstorm at eighty miles an hour. Normal bikers on a weekend ride might stop, if they didn't like getting wet, or if they had a cautious bone in their body. But rain was another of those things that wasn't worth considering in the Hells Angels' world.

We sliced through Kingman, rounding the Purple Heart Trail, and turned north onto 93. We picked up a Nomad hangaround named Elton Rodman at a gas pump in Grasshopper Junction, a few miles outside of Kingman. He rode in the back with us. The Martian landscape of northwestern Arizona, soaked with rain, took on rust- and purple-colored hues. The ground around the road ran thick with Sedona red mud.

The skies dried as we crossed the state line at the Hoover Dam. We rumbled over its tall, arcing road, the white towers at either end watching over us and a few undaunted, ponchoed tourists. The deep blue of Lake Mead peeked around the corner of the barren hills to the north and east. Ten minutes after we crossed, the rain started again. Bobby and Joby didn't slow down. We kept the throttle at eighty-five, ninety miles per hour. I couldn't help but think of JJ in the truck, warm and dry and no doubt amused. I also feared that I might be hydroplaning and was seconds away from slamming into a guardrail at a very unhealthy velocity.

The cover team followed us at a distance of thirty or forty miles. When they got to Vegas they'd hook up with Gayland, whom I thought about as we made our way to Vegas. Something I'd said to him—the thing about seeing him later—replayed in my mind. It struck me around Henderson, right outside of Vegas proper: If Bobby was interested, we might be able to throw together a show for him. Gayland could get one of the metro cops I knew to play the part of Big Lou. I'd have to get Slats to sign off, but as we sloshed through the desert I felt like I deserved the chance to make an impromptu play. I'd call them as soon as we checked in.

We roared onto the strip around six, and made our way to the Hard Rock. We pulled in looking like a pack of drowned rats. The valets tried not to stare at us as they attended to the normal procession of cars containing tourists and minor television stars. Two security guards approached as we unassed. They were big guys in nylon jackets with earpieces.

"Excuse us, gentlemen."

Bobby said, "Hey, how ya doing?"

"You're staying with us at the Hard Rock Hotel?"

Bobby faced them. We gathered behind him. The guards weren't scared. "That's right," Bobby said. "We got suites, actually."

"That's great. But it's our policy here that you will not be allowed to wear your jackets inside the hotel."

Joby spat. Bobby said, "Fuck you."

A guard asked, "Excuse me?"

"Fuck you. I wouldn't take my vest off to shit in this place even if a greasy turd was running down the back of my leg."

I dialed my cell as I put a hand on Bobby's shoulder. Joby repeated something about sleeping in the dirt as Gayland came on the other end.

"Sir, we're by the valets, getting jacked by security. They say we can't come in with our cuts on. We ain't taking them off."

Gayland chuckled. "No problem. Give me a minute." He hung up.

I told Bobby it was being taken care of. He didn't believe me—he was climbing back onto his bike. One of the guards put a finger on his earpiece so he could hear better. He grasped the lapel of his jacket and said ten-four. Then he said, "I'm sorry, gentlemen. There was a misunderstanding and we apologize for the mistake. Please go in whenever you're ready. Welcome to Las Vegas. Welcome to the Hard Rock."

Bobby smiled again. This was possibly the first time ever Bobby had smiled twice in one day. He got off his bike and gave me a hard slap on the back. "'Gentlemen.' You hear that shit? Fuckin' A, Bird, when we get settled, call my room."

I asked, "What's up?"

He yelled, "Just call my fucking room after you take a shower!"

Fine.

We checked in. Each couple got a room. JJ and I took turns in the shower. It felt good to wash off the road. When I called Bobby, he asked if I was planning to see Lou while we were in Vegas, and if I was, could he meet him?

"So you want me to set something up?"

"Fuck, yes, Bird, that's what I'm trying to tell you!"

"Big Lou isn't too into meeting new people, but I'll see what I can do. Give me a few minutes." We hung up. I called Slats. He conferenced in Gayland. We thought it sounded good. We could intro him and talk around a gun deal we could complete the next day. I asked if we could get a load of prop guns to make it look like a big haul. Slats said no problem. I reminded Gayland that whoever he got to play Big Lou, the guy had to come on hard, like a real-deal crime boss. He said it wouldn't be a problem. They said they needed half an hour to throw some things together. They'd call me back.

I went into the suite's living room. JJ watched *Jeopardy*. I heard her say, "What's a terrapin?"

I joked, "I'll take assholes for one hundred, Alex."

She perked up, remembering where we were. "What's up?"

"What's up is that you, me, and Bobby are going to go meet Big Lou."

"Really? Why do I have to go?"

"'Cause Big Lou wants to see you too, sweetheart."

She rolled her eyes and climbed out of the couch, sighing about me making her work too hard.

Slats called to tell me when and where. I hung up and called Bobby. "It's on."

He whispered with excitement. "Really? What should I wear?"

I said incredulously, "What you always do, Bobby."

"He really wants to see me?"

"No, Bobby, he wants to see me and you just happen to be coming along. Who he *really* wants to see is JJ." I changed the subject. "How's the room?"

"Great. Staci won't shut up about how great it is, anyway. But five bucks for a bag of M&M's is fucking nuts, isn't it?"

"Yeah, these places get you coming and going."

"You got that right," he agreed.

"Look, JJ and me'll meet you in the lobby at ten. No Staci."

"Are you kidding? I couldn't get her out of the room if I laid down a trail of speed to the slots. I'll see you then."

"Cool. See you then."

WE GOT IN the truck and made our way to PT's Pub. Halfway there my phone rang.

"Yeah, Bird."

"It's Slats. Listen—Gayland couldn't get any of the guys you know to play Lou."

"Are you shitting me?"

"No. But don't panic. The show's still on. Gayland's got a guy he says'll be terrific. Says you won't have any problem figuring out who he is."

"Fuck me. OK. We'll be there soon."

"Bobby with you?"

"Yeah."

He chuckled, saying, "Tell Reinstra I told him to go fuck himself." He hung up.

Bobby asked if everything was OK. I told him everything was better than OK, Big Lou just won fifty grand beating the spread on the Mets game. Bobby raised his eyebrows and nodded, impressed. I had to cover myself and hoped he wouldn't bring it up at the meeting.

We pulled into the parking lot and got out. I didn't like going into this kind of situation blind. All of a sudden I didn't know anything about a guy I'd supposedly known for years.

The bar was open and dark, with a low ceiling. Red neon lights framed the booths, flat-panel screens above the bar showed baseball games and horse races. There was a Keno game tucked into a far corner. I saw Slats and Gayland. They glanced at us and then turned their attention back to a game. It was casual and well played. If they hadn't checked us out—like every citizen in the bar was doing—it would've been as suspicious as staring us down.

I looked for my guy in Vegas.

I didn't have to look for long.

From the back of the bar a short, wide, balding guy, whose remaining hair was slicked back in shiny streaks, walked toward us with open arms. He had on large, square eyeglasses with an amber tint in the top half of the lens. He was about sixty. He wore a dark suit—it was hard to tell the exact color in that light—with a chalk-line pinstripe, a checkered blue shirt, and a solid red tie. He had a pinkie ring and a brass tie clip. His black tasseled loafers were glossed to a high shine. Two very large guys—one fat, one just cranked with muscles—moved slowly behind him. They wore matching track suits.

I thought it was just too much. Cookie-cutter wiseguys.

And then he started to talk.

"Jaybird! My guy! JJ! Come over here wheres I can see you." He dipped his head and shook his fingers in the air, beckoning us closer. I went to him. He reached up, grabbed my neck, pulled me down, and planted a loud kiss on each cheek. When he was close to the ear farthest from Bobby, he whispered, "Don't worry. We're good."

He pushed me back and looked me over. I held him by the shoulders. Locked together, I said, "Mister Lou. It's been too long since we've seen each other in the flesh."

"You ain't fuckin' kiddin'. And look at this"—Lou was a "dis" and "dat" guy—"JJ. What's it been—a year? More?"

"Yeah. More than that, Lou," said JJ, tossing it out like Lou was her favorite uncle. "I can barely remember."

"But I'll never forget you. Never, my darling." He moved toward her, took her right hand, and actually kissed it.

I thought we were done. The guy was too much. I wanted to look at Bobby or Slats or Gayland—anyone whose face would tell me if it was working—but I knew I couldn't.

Lou graciously directed JJ to a reserved booth and snapped for a waitress. He told JJ we had business to discuss and suggested she take it easy. She sat down. I said, "Lou, this is that guy I was telling you about."

Lou looked at Bobby as if for the first time. He squinted and said, "Yeah, all right," like Bobby had asked him a question.

Bobby held out his hand and introduced himself. Lou took it and gave it a cursory shake. "How ya doin'." Lou looked at me and gave me a small shrug. Then he let go of Bobby's hand and stared him dead in the eye. "You said Bobby, right?"

"Yeah."

"Good, good. Now listen here, Hells Angel Bobby, sit the fuck down!" The goons stepped forward menacingly. Bobby was so shocked he promptly sat. He must've been battling some strong urges to pound the old guy into the carpet—no one talks to a Hells Angel like that and gets away with it.

Lou stabbed a thick index finger at the air in front of Bobby and said, "Now listen good, Bobby, 'cause I only say things once. I don't give a midnight fuck about the Hells Angels. I care about you as much as I care about fucking pussycats. You do what you do, I do what I do. Thing is, my gang is bigger than yours, badder than yours, and meaner than yours. And sure as shit, my gang is smarter than yours, 'cause we don't walk around town with no fucking logo on our back that says 'Wiseguy.' You, I can see you coming a mile down the street. Me, you don't know if I'm standing next to you at Mickey D's. You capeesh?" He pointed at me. "Anything happens to this guy here while he's doing this Hells Angel thing, you answer to me. He makes money for me. He carries money for me. I trust him to take more money across the country than you'll see in ten years. He wants to ride bikes, do this motorcycle club *bull*shit, that's his thing. But if that shit overlaps with *my* life, fucks me outta so much as a quarter—if he gets hurt or can't come to work for me when I call, well . . . the Hells Angels are gonna be disappointed, I'll tell you what. I'll start burning down houses with the doors locked from the *out*side. Or maybe I go easy on your guys and one day they find you lying on the floor, all blue and gray, having had a little accident with a dry-cleaning bag. I'm sayin' it to *you*, all right? Now, you're a smart man, Hells Angel Bobby. Give me a minute with Jay." He took me by the arm and led me to the back of the room, one of the bodyguards staying by Bobby and JJ, the other trailing us at a respectful distance.

I would've given every penny I had to see Bobby's face. But we all had a part to play, and I played mine.

When we were out of earshot, I told the guy it was nice to meet him. He said the same, but that I was smaller than he'd imagined. He said he thought all bikers were built like linemen. I said not all. He asked me how we were doing. I said we were doing good, but maybe it was a little over the top? He held up his hand. "I know how a crime boss thinks. Made guys really *don't* give a midnight fuck about Hells Angels or whatever they are. Wiseguys were making money before there was even such a thing as a motorcycle, and they'll be making money when those guys are gone. Trust me, Jay, we're doing good."

"All right, dude, keep going. No point in changing course now."

"That's the spirit. Now go bring that guy over here, we'll straighten him out."

"OK." I went and got Bobby. We went back to Lou. I could hear Slats and Gayland laughing their asses off, just two guys in a bar having a good time.

Lou said, "Sorry about that, Bobby, we just gotta understand each other."

Bobby said, "Yes, sir."

Slats and Gayland laughed again.

Lou said, "Jay tells me you might like to do some work for me."

"Yes, sir."

"Good." He pulled a long Cohiba from inside his jacket and held it in his fist. "I like you, Hells Angel Bobby. You know when to talk and when to shut the fuck up. I'll let Jay know when we can use you. And when we do use you, don't fuck up."

"Yes, sir."

"Good." He turned to me. "Jay, I got a mess of guns coming through tomorrow. You know me and guns—I won't keep 'em around. I wanted you to have first crack at them. You want 'em, great, no, that's no shakes either. I'll give you a call."

"Thanks, Lou."

"No problemo. Well, that's it, boys. Drinks and dinner are on me tonight. I gotta make a date." He moved past us and walked up to JJ. "JJ, as always, I'm enchanted. I don't know why you hang out with this guy, but he's lucky for it. Take care of him." And with that he left, his bodyguards silently drifting behind him.

I sat down next to JJ, Bobby sat across from us. He was entranced.

I asked, "Well, whaddaya think?"

Bobby took a breath. "I think that guy's just like the guys back East. I hadn't seen one in so long I'd forgot."

"Forgot what?" JJ asked.

"Those kinda guys are real fucking badasses. Yeah, I think it's good. I hope when my time comes I can prove myself, make Lou proud."

I lit a cigarette. "I'm sure you will, Bobby, I'm sure you will."

I CALLED GAYLAND later on, after I'd seen Bobby to his room.

Gayland asked, "So, how was our guy?"

"He was good. Almost too good. Bobby bought the whole thing, though, said Lou was a real-deal gangster. I don't know where you got him, last minute, but he was good."

"He better've been good. He's New Jersey mob. He came out here and fucked up. We caught him and got him to flip. He wasn't faking it, Jay. Unlike you, he *is* the real deal."

33

"GET ME THAT BROWN MUSTARD, NOT THAT YELLOW SHIT."

APRIL–MAY 2003

BOBBY ACCOMPANIED ME on the completion of the ruse gun deal the next day. It was a nice little haul: an Uzi, two Mac-10s, a silencer, and two AK-47s, both of which were full autos. JJ paid our contact—the task force agent Buddha—five grand in cash and we went our separate ways. For his trouble, I gave Bobby a hundred bucks. I said, "Not bad for five minutes' work, huh?"

"Naw. Not at all."

I repeated what I'd told Mac: "That's how easy it is to make money with me, dude."

He was impressed.

Our last night in Vegas we decided to take the girls out to dinner at New York, New York. We hung around the casino floor while Staci and JJ decided where they wanted to eat. Bobby looked uneasy and asked me to take a walk. We strolled outside and stopped on the corner of Las Vegas and Flamingo Boulevards, surrounded by tourists, traffic, and a roller coaster. A blind hot dog vendor stood in front of his cart yelling, "Red hots, getchya red hots here!" It looked like Bobby wanted to get something off his chest but couldn't find the words, or didn't want his words overheard. I lit a cigarette and offered one to Bobby, lighting his. "Hey, Bobby, want a dog?"

"Yeah, sure."

I ordered and gave Bobby his pre-dinner snack. He still wasn't speaking. I tried to break the ice. "Bobby, you ever think about where you're gonna be in a year, five years?"

He looked at me like I'd insulted his mother. "How the fuck do I know? Shit, maybe I'll take a pencil and poke my eyes out and sell hot dogs."

I paid for the dogs and we sauntered away. My icebreaker worked. He said that he'd felt a little awkward around Big Lou because he didn't know how to tell him that he'd "done work" before—as he said those words he mimed firing a pistol. I was a little surprised. This was the first time Bobby had opened up regarding the alleged murder he'd committed for the club. I nodded gravely and didn't interrupt. He said he'd gained the reputation of a rat-hunter—a guy who killed snitches or informants—and that "three can keep a secret if two are dead." Normally this kind of talk is idle bullshit, but I believed Bobby. He was calm, matter-of-fact, and not boastful. He assumed I was in a similar position, an assumption I didn't deny. He said that "some call it stupidity, but it takes balls to walk up and shoot someone between the eyes." He said some other guys couldn't live with themselves after the fact, which was a problem he didn't have. "Me? I take care of business. Anyone crosses me, I'll get payback. It may take me four or five years, but I'll get it. I'll be the guy standing by your pillow at three a.m. holding a two-by-four, waiting for your eyes to pop open." The words weren't hypothetical. They were meant for me. He said, "Remember that. You're in and you're with me, so don't fuck up. Blood in, blood out."

The next day, after I'd downed a handful of Hydroxys, we rode back to Arizona. Timmy and Pops had gone home the night before to see their families, so it was just me and Bobby. Right after crossing the dam, Bobby's bike broke down and we loaded both bikes into the trailer. JJ and Staci got in the back and I drove. The road hypnotized me. I tried to picture the day Bobby would find out I was a cop, tried to guess what his expression would be. I wanted to gauge his level of shock, because I didn't have any problem imagining what he'd look like standing over my bed at 3:00 a.m., grasping a rough-hewn two-by-four.

. . .

SLATS LIKED THE Big Lou ruse. He wasn't sure what it gained us, but he had a good time watching it go down. Still, it made him nervous. He said our plays were getting too intricate and too risky. "Tone it down. Play it out with these guys, don't play it up." He reminded me that he could pull the plug whenever he wanted. He said, "You guys get too close to the fire and I *will* stamp it out."

"All right, fine." Slats wanted to hear the words, so I said them.

I knew I was lying, though. Being HA hangarounds—and soon-to-be prospects—was not easy. I thought March had seen the worst, that my days and nights had reached their saturation points. I was wrong. Since we'd become hangarounds, each day's obligations had mushroomed. If it wasn't Slats, it was the Hells Angels. If it wasn't either of them, it was my family. If it wasn't my family, it was me. I couldn't shut down.

Every morning started with my Hydroxys. I swallowed them down with coffee or Red Bull and took more in the afternoon, and if I was out with anyone at night, more after dark. I drank alcohol while on them; worked out on them, wrote reports on them. My spelling suffered, my bike riding actually got better. My ability to gab endlessly also improved—something I thought impossible. I felt edgy and my stomach shook all the time. When the pills wore off, I plunged into a deep chemical—or lack-of-chemical—depression. Most nights, after scribbling reports and hiding them in the safe under my mattress, I'd lie down and pray for sleep that seldom came. It was not uncommon in those days for me to cry while trying to get a few hours of physical rest. The tears were born of exhaustion and the stress of leading a double life. Anyone looking at me would always see the same Bird: Bird the debt collector; Bird the cop; Bird the bullshitting-a-mile-a-minute hustler. On the inside, I thought I was something else, something I'd never been before. I sometimes swung completely, and quickly, from confidence to doubt, from righteousness to guilt. If I'd had the capacity for self-reflection I might have noticed the changes being wrought on me, but I had none. All I could do in those days was feel and react and think about ways to succeed with the Angels.

I'd look in the mirror, shaving my gaunt cheeks with a straight razor, and the only things that stared back at me were the cold blue eyes of Jay "Bird" Davis.

Anyway, we got a residence in Prescott. We got our hands on a single-wide trailer and put it in the corner of a trailer park, aspen trees and a patch of grass out back, a picnic table by the steps. It was way too small and anything but homey.

I hated to give it to him, but Slats was dead-on about one thing: We weren't freelancers anymore. We had new responsibilities to our brothers, responsibilities that required a lot of hanging out with Angels. What was even worse was that, given our desire to gain real membership, we actually *wanted* to hang out with the guys. Time bled into a continuum of pills, bikes, riding, guns, guard duty, lectures on rules, and general monotony. Rarely did one day seem much different from another. The only way I could remember anything was by listening to recordings and reading and writing daily reports.

April 24, church at the clubhouse. The Skull Valley house was on a nice country road surrounded by farms and crop fields. Bobby and Staci lived in a first-floor apartment, Teddy lived upstairs. Joby had turned a large closet into a bedroom to crash out in. The main room was a storage facility.

Before church convened I asked Joby what we should do if any of us came across a Mongol. "Kill or otherwise fuck that bitch up. Ask Teddy." I did. He said, "Yeah, it's your duty to kill him and not get caught."

Bobby announced that church that day was members only. We were ordered outside to secure the perimeter. It was cold—around forty degrees—and we were underdressed. We blew on our hands and stamped our feet. Pops and I crossed paths every ten or fifteen minutes. The moon was up, invisible things scurried through the grass. At one point Pops asked, "Who are we guarding these guys from?"

"Bunny rabbits, dude. They're full of rabies around here."

Pops laughed. "Maybe we should fire off a round, just to scare them." I wasn't sure whether he meant the rabid rabbits, the Hells Angels, or both. It didn't matter. I laughed too. The boys finally had some hangarounds to pull guard duty, just like the other charters. I laughed some more. It felt like a big joke. The boys were probably in the clubhouse laughing too, knowing no one was going to interrupt church at Skull Valley.

After an hour they whistled from the house. We trudged up in the moonlight and went inside. There was an empty bucket of fried chicken on the table, and dirty plates strewn with bones. There were three unopened containers of coleslaw. They asked if we'd had any recent run-ins with the law, when they knew we hadn't. Asked if we were wearing wires. We lied. We said fuck no, thinking, What are we supposed to say if we are? Yes? They lectured us again on being hangarounds and prospects, though we were reminded that we weren't prospects yet. They said for the time being we were basically body-guards for full members, and that each member had his own way of dealing with guys in our position and that whatever that was, we had to respect it. They said no drinking, no drugs, no fucking around unless given permission. We said we understood. They dismissed us back to the cold and continued with their heavy "members only" shit.

We went up to Bullhead at the end of the month to check on Smitty and Lydia. Smitty invited us to their place. It was nice to see them, nice to see Lydia's glass-strewn yard. There was a hominess there that all of us had been missing. Not long after we got in, Lydia microwaved us a meal of beef stew—the kind with the creamy gravy, potatoes, and car-rots. I thought, Wow, this is how real people live. I'd gotten so used to the Waffle House, I'd forgotten what a real meal was like, even one that came from a can. After she fed us she said she was going to bed. It wasn't late, Lydia was turning in at a decent hour—something I hadn't done in months. Smitty lit up a Red, I lit up a Newport—I'd recently switched to menthols for no reason—and he proceeded to bitch and moan about his problems. He was having trouble getting backing for the Mohave Valley charter he was trying to set up. He felt like guys in his own charter—the Angels Nomads—were pulling their support and he couldn't understand why. Compounding these troubles were the persistent rumors of Mongols over the hill in Kingman, guys who'd miraculously avoided detection for months. He told me he was looking for untraceable guns so he could pop some of those guys off.

On May 1, I sailed back into Prescott on warm spring winds and the chemical loft of weight-loss energy pills. JJ and I met the boys at the broke-dick strip club they owned, the Pinion Pines. Teddy sat in a booth with his tanks of oxygen and his girlfriend, Devon, who was tak-ing a break from pole-dancing. She sat on his knee, her perfect ass con-cealing his thigh in mounds of bikinied flesh. Bobby lounged across from them smoking a Marlboro Light. JJ slid in and I sat next to her. They wanted to know how Bullhead was and, again, if we'd had any trouble with the law. I said no, not this time, but JJ and I told them the story of our traffic stop back in November. They said they'd heard something about that. Teddy wheezed, "I keep my eye on them, ya know? We're trying to get started up here and we don't want no fucking trouble but we want respect too, ya know?"

Bobby said, "Anyway, Bird, you let us know if anything happens to you with them, even a ticket. I mean, a cop so much as says hello to you, tell us." I said OK.

I told them Smitty was having problems starting the Mohave Valley charter and that I wanted to talk to Joby about it. Bobby said, "Don't concern yourself with that shit. It's nice Smitty's opening up to you and all, but that's none of your business." I said OK.

Teddy said through a smile, "Everyone's green, I'm tellin' ya." I asked him what he meant. "I mean they're jealous we're the ones that got ya."

Bobby said, "That's right. But don't talk to anyone about it, all right?" Once again, I said OK.

Next day was church, again for members only. Timmy, Pops, and I arrived early and I walked up to Teddy holding an envelope containing $500. Before I got close enough to hand it to him, he barked, "What the fuck with those?" He pointed at my feet.

I was wearing flip-flops.

"I got stinky toes, Teddy, I like to air them out."

"Fuck that. Whaddaya think this is, a fucking hobby? Something you do for fun? Naw. Get rid of those fucking things. I catch you wearing those again, I'll run you on errands for tampons and Barbie dolls. I mean really, Bird, *flip-flops*?" I considered the complaint and decided I'd wear boots more often, if for no other reason than not to have to hear it.

I handed him the envelope, hoping it would change his mood.

He took it, holding it like a dirty piece of toilet paper. "I'll accept this, Bird, but ya can't buy yer way into the club."

"I know that, Teddy, I'm just doing what I think is right. We made a lot of money off Big Lou's guns. I thought you'd appreciate it."

"I do, I do. Thanks."

"'Sides, Teddy, I wouldn't want to be a member if I *could* buy my way in."

Timmy and Pops seconded that, and Teddy said OK.

Bobby then told us we had to go get them sandwiches from Subway. Teddy stuffed the envelope in his back pocket and growled, "Right.

I'm hungry. Subway sounds good. I wanna hot cappy sandwich, pro-volone, lettuce—and tomatoes if they're red. They got any white or green in them, or they look mealy, forget the tomatoes. And get me that brown mustard, not that yellow shit. No fucking mayo." Bobby said he changed his mind and felt like a burger and a black-and-white milk-shake. He said we'd have to get that somewhere else, maybe TGI Fri-days. Joey wasn't there yet, but they told us to get him a small salad, no dressing, since he was on a "bullshit health kick." As we were leaving, Teddy yelled, "And get a variety of beverages!"

We filled their order and came back. As Teddy chewed his sandwich he said, "Good job on the mustard."

Bobby slurped his milkshake and said, "Yeah, yeah. That's good shit, hangarounds. You just earned yourself some beers." We got some cold ones. Joey showed up, they gave him his salad, which was also from Subway, and laughed at him. He ignored them and told them it was actually what he wanted. He went to the fridge and drenched it in ranch. He didn't thank us. We were told to go outside and secure the perimeter.

We walked the fence again. While outside, Pops told us he'd wiped all of their straws with his dick. We tried not to laugh too hard.

We went down to Phoenix on May 3 and spent the next couple days catching up on paperwork. Gwen called and asked me to cut the grass. Things hadn't been going well with us—I looked more and more like a biker, and even though I insisted she was making things up, she refused to believe I wasn't having an affair with JJ. I told her I needed to avoid the kids because I didn't want them to see me in my current condition. She said they planned to be busy on the sixth, to come by then. OK. I'd make it a quick trip.

I got to my place, hopped off my bike, and went out back.

The yard needed a serious trim. I fired up the mower, took my shirt off, and started pushing. I couldn't have cared less about that lawn, but I wouldn't give Gwen any additional ammo to use against me—I wouldn't do it unevenly or leave any mohawks. In times past, my green-thumb perfection had come from a place that would only accept the best—now it came from hatred. I'd built that house with my own hands, planted the yard with my own hands. I used to love both, but now I hated them. I cut the lawn short and neat.

Halfway through, my mom and dad showed up. I hadn't seen either of them in months. They must've heard the mower because they came around back and watched me. I didn't see them. They didn't call to me, or if they did, I didn't hear. I turned. I killed the motor. My mom was crying.

"Hey guys, what's wrong?"

"What's wrong?" my dad asked.

"Yeah, why's Mom crying?" I could tell my dad knew, almost telepathically, exactly why it was his wife was crying.

She wiped her tears with her arm and pointed at me. "What did you do to your arms?"

My tattoos. She hadn't seen them. My parents had gotten used to my other tattoos, but each time I added one, I think they prayed that would be it. At least I think my *mom* prayed for that.

I sighed and said, "You have no idea what I'm going through. I'm doing what I have to do. Let me finish this and we can talk." I fired the mower back up. I didn't care about my mom's tears. They went inside, but when I was done they were long gone.

TIME PASSED IN a blur. Back in Phoenix, on the eighth, I worked out with Dan Danza, the crazy musclehead Angel I'd met when our Solo Angeles crew came to town back in January. He pumped his iron, veins in his neck bulging, and waxed hopeful about the end of his parole—thirty-one days out. JJ and I went with Bobby on the ninth to set up a T-shirt booth at a run. He intimidated the guy in charge into giving us free passes and the best booth location. Bobby said he was going to run the Americans Motorcycle Club out of there if he saw them. He and Teddy bitched about how they hadn't been giving the Angels their due respect, and that they were going to force the Americans out of the area, maybe even the state. As Bobby had said, "Our sandbox is full of cat turds. We gotta sift it clean." Rudy brought his infant daughter to the run. She wore a tiny black SUPPORT YOUR LOCAL HELLS ANGELS shirt. No one paid her any mind. She cried in the heat. I picked her up and rocked her. She didn't stop crying. I changed her diaper right there—it looked like she'd been wearing it for a couple days. I rocked her some more and she calmed down. JJ sold T-shirts, Timmy and Pops and I took turns bodyguarding the guys and standing in the T-shirt booth as tough-guy advertising, arms crossed, scaring and inspiring people into buying shirts and stickers. I was back with Danza on the twelfth. More pills, more weights. I worked on my legs. I still liked Danza's intensity, he still liked mine. He asked again about Mongols in Mexico. I confirmed that there were some down there, and told him that if I saw any, I was going to kill them. He said that when his parole was up he was going to come with me. We'd get our kill on.

More time flew. I consumed Hydroxys like they were sugar pills. I thought of Bobby and his two-by-four. I thought of two Bobbies and their two-by-fours. I thought of four of them, surrounding my bed at 3:00 a.m. I saw Teddy with a pair of pliers one day, working a section of fence near the clubhouse, and the image stuck. More and more I zoned out on rides, my waistband stuffed with the reassuring feel of loaded guns. I never got stopped, I couldn't figure out why. The cops should've been knocking a guy like me down out of simple curiosity. I was in Tucson on the thirteenth, visiting Mac's shop. Mac wanted to collect for me, beat for me, work for me. Do more for me. He said I should start using a cattle prod for my collections. Later that week, JJ and I house-sat for Joby while he was out working some state fair with his mechanical bull. He lived in a Quonset hut in Kingman and he had a nice arsenal. JJ and I field-tested all the guns into water-filled buckets, capturing slugs for ballistics, hoping to find the gun that did Hoover or anyone else. We didn't. Pills, beer, pills. Time moved so quickly it became meaningless. On the fifteenth I went to Steve Helland's house, also in Kingman. He was the guy who'd offered me his eighteen-year-old daughter, April, at a run back in October. His son had been killed in a drug deal, and he believed he'd found out who'd done it. Steve said he wanted to torture the guy with a blowtorch and dismember him. He asked me to consider doing the job for him—not the torture but the killing, which was what he really wanted. I felt sorry for him. I said OK, if you really want it, but let me do it my way. I would string this murder-for-hire along and never do anything.

Standing in Steve's living room, talking about killing someone for a Hells Angel, I heard the distant rumble of a Harley. I thought of Kingman's phantom Mongols.

It was then that I started to get an idea.

PART IV

THE END, AGAIN

34 HYDROXYCUT HIGHWAY

ON THE SIXTEENTH, Pops and I sat in the trailer watching the Discovery Channel—a show about the African savannah. The English-accented narrator spoke about wild dogs, the lowest predators on the food chain, calling them the "low-ranking snouts." Pops observed that lately, with all our glorious hangaround duties, that was us. "We're the low-ranking snouts."

I called him a lame gazelle and Bobby a lion, and Pops didn't laugh. He was getting tired of the whole show. It wasn't worth $500 a week any longer. I put my hand on his shoulder—Pops was still a good friend—and told him to hang in there. He just pointed his bottle at the TV and repeated, "Low-ranking snouts."

My phone rang. It was Chris Bayless, my old partner and friend, checking in on me. He asked jokingly, "You fall in love with your sponsor yet?"

"Fuck, no. One, he's a murderer. Two, he loves mafiosi. Three, he lectures me on how to be a badass. Four, he—"

"All right, got it. How's your head?"

"Screwed on sideways and halfway up my asshole."

"Sounds about right."

"Yeah, it's great."

"What're you looking forward to?"

"Me? I think I got a plan. I'll run it by you soon. Have to sleep on it. Other than that, putting these psycho loner clowns in jail."

"That sounds about right too. Give Slats my love."

"Will do."

Since April, when the Solos got dissolved, I'd been getting more head checks from Chris, from my psych officer, Paul Hagerty, and, since our weekend in Vegas, from Gayland. They were making sure I wasn't cracking, that I hadn't decided I liked the bad guys more than the good guys, especially since they all knew how much of a pain in the ass the good guys could be.

I wasn't sure why they were so worried. Maybe it was my appearance, or how much time I was spending with the Angels, but I didn't like the bad guys more, not at all. I was more concentrated on Black Biscuit than on any case I'd ever been involved in. It was, in every sense, my life.

I told them I was fine.

We came up for more guard duty on the twenty-first in Berdoo. Rode out with Joey and stood around the clubhouse in the blazing sun. At one point I was relieved and told to go inside. Timmy and Pops had been sent on separate errands. We were split in three directions, making it nearly impossible for our cover team to protect us. I was sure Slats was sick of it and thinking of calling the whole thing off. Joey saw me and told me I could have a beer. I said thanks and asked him if I could smoke. It was a facetious question, but it went over his head. In front of the other Angels he had to act tough. He told me no, only when I was off duty. I said OK, thinking, fuck that motherfucker. Walking to the bar I accidentally bumped a full patch, a sandy-haired California dude I'd never seen. He growled at me and said, "Outside. Now."

I said, "Hey, dude, I didn't mean anything. It was an accident."

"Fuck that."

"I didn't see you, that's all."

"You didn't fucking *see* me? Motherfucker, you *always* see me. That's your fucking job. Outside. NOW!"

Bobby had lectured me on this too. The rules of fighting for a Hells

Angel were simple. A non-Angel picks a fight with an Angel, all Angels come to his aid. This situation will not be fair, but as far as the Angels are concerned it will be just. On the contrary, when an Angel picks a fight with an Angel—or an official hangaround or a prospect—it will go down one-on-one. Angels have the privilege of settling scores among themselves. He told me that if I was ever challenged, the only admirable thing to do was fight.

I didn't disagree.

I said, "All right, let's go." I followed the guy. He wore tight Levi's and shit-brown riding boots. He was bigger than me—not taller, just broader across the shoulders and thicker around the arms. His legs were skinny.

As I walked through the clubhouse I started to take the rings from my fingers, stuffing them in my pockets. I was prepared to take a beating, but I wouldn't go down easy. We got outside and he turned. Ten or twelve guys stood around, waiting. We were underneath a twenty-foot-high pole in the middle of the compound. On top of the pole was a disk—it looked like a gas station sign—with a huge Death Head on it.

The guy sized me up in the shadow of the disk. Joey Richardson stood behind him, looking like he'd decided to back his patched brother and not me. I thought maybe Joey had put him up to it to mud-check me. The Angel watched me struggle with a ring I hadn't removed in over five years.

He asked me if I was Bird. I said I was. He asked what I was doing. I said, "I'm taking my rings off so when I start to beat on your face it doesn't get too fucked up." He smiled slowly.

Joey laughed out loud. "Shit, here comes Skull Valley."

The smile on the Angel's face faded. He shrugged and said, "Aw, fuck it. What were you drinking?" I looked him in the eye and told him.

Mud-check passed. I put my rings back on.

Four days later we pulled more guard duty at Cave Creek. There was no shade to be had there, either. It was a big party, guys were coming and going from all over. A guy from England, the London P named Marcus, was there. Bad Bob, Smitty, Joby, Dennis, Mac, Pete Eunice, Sonny Barger, a whole mess of West Coast Angels—everyone. We'd met so many guys by then that Timmy, Pops, and I were introducing Hells Angels to one another. I'd been asked, at various times through the day, for beer, a bottle opener, cigarettes, a condom, a pen, five dollars, my phone number, ketchup, help pushing a dead bike, and a sewing kit. I had everything but the sewing kit. Timmy offered that guy safety pins. He took them.

Around six, the party humming, the same classic rockabilly tunes swirling around the clubhouse, mixed in now and then with Metallica, Korn, and Iron Maiden, a car started to drive back and forth in front of the house. A California prospect—he said to call him Pit—didn't like it. The guys in the car looked lost, and they looked Mexican. They must've been ignorant of bikers because they showed no trepidation in repeatedly, and slowly, cruising past the clubhouse. As they approached the fourth time I said, "Hey, Pit, let's scare these guys outta here."

"Sounds like a fucking plan."

We stepped into the street, and Timmy took a position by the gate. We stood in the middle of the road and waved at the car—an early-nineties Toyota hatchback with a lot of miles on it. It stopped. Pit asked who they were.

The guy held up a crumpled piece of paper and pointed at it. He didn't speak English. He looked like an itinerant looking for a relative's house. Pit didn't look at the paper. He asked, "It look like I speak Spic?" The guy didn't understand Pit or his insults, but he and his buddy understood the guns. He started to repeat OK, OK, OK, holding his open hands in the air. I could see his buddy tapping him on the shoulder like they had to leave.

Pit was not happy with them. "Listen close, hombre. You're in Hells Angels territory. Cruising by too many times and too slow will get your ass shot." He held up his pistol, a small-caliber, blue-steel semiauto, and shook it for emphasis. "Get it? Bang, bang?"

"OK, OK, OK." The driver put it in reverse and slowly backed away. We didn't see them again.

Pit and I went back to the front yard. "Those wetback motherfuckers were Mongols! I fucking know it, Bird. They come back here and I will slit their throats and give them Colombian fucking neckties. I will cut off their dicks and stuff them in their mouths. Can you believe the balls on those motherfuckers? Mongols coming around here, Cave Creek, Hoover's backyard?"

I told him to calm down, they were probably just poor sap nobodies who'd gotten lost. Pit wasn't having it. Timmy whispered in my ear, "We bring any tranquilizer darts?" I chuckled.

As if on cue, the guy started to beat the air. At first I thought he was acting out what he'd do to them. He was high-kicking and punching and doing little spins. Some guys wandered out to watch him. His words were unintelligible. His head started to go this way, then that; he looked at the air around him with wild eyes, like he was all of a sudden losing his imaginary fight, fists coming from everywhere. Someone stood next to me. It was Mac.

"What's with that guy?"

"Don't know, dude. Looks like he's about to have a seizure."

That's when we started to understand what he was saying. "A fucking bee! I'm fucking allergic! Get this fucking bee away from me!"

I started howling. Mac had to hold me up.

"I'll fucking die, man, I ain't got my EpiPen!"

Marcus marched out from a side entrance, collared Pit, and yanked him inside. He was an embarrassment.

I laughed harder than I'd laughed in weeks, maybe months. Tears fell from my eyes. When I could talk again, I told Mac about the Mexicans. "I mean, this guy goes from Billy Badass to mortal combat with a honeybee inside of five minutes. That guy's a punk."

Bobby heard that. He came up and told me I was right, but I shouldn't say it. He said the guy was just a prospect, but that I was just a hangaround. I said I was sorry. Mac said I was right anyway, the guy was a punk, at least he thought so. Bobby told me to stop goofing off and get to work, and to bring him a beer. I asked Mac if he wanted one, and he shook his head. I got Bobby a beer from a cooler by the front door, walked back, and fought the urge to open it for him and spit in it, knowing I'd be seen. When I got back they were talking about guns.

Bobby said, "Yeah, I got my old lady a little twenty-two. A nice hit piece. One behind the ear, gets in there and scrambles everything up. Like on *The Sopranos*, you know?" He turned to me and reached for the beer. "You know, right, Bird?"

"You know I do, Bobby. Anything else? I gotta secure the perimeter." I lit a cigarette.

"Naw. That's good." Then he said wait, held up his beer bottle, and told me to open it for him. The guy had an opener right on one of his belt loops, but didn't even move for it. I took his bottle, opened it, handed it back, and walked off.

I HAD A hard time falling asleep that night. I'd taken four or five Hydroxys late in the day and they were still working their magic. When I was idle, not working or riding or talking or writing, the pills caused my mind to switch and flicker. That night, trying to sleep, I saw Bobby ordering me around, I saw the outlines of my developing plan, I saw Dale asking for her new guitar, I saw the spiderweb tattoo on my elbow, I saw Slats trying to rein me in, Teddy with the pliers, Joby when he drew down on the tweaker so many months back. I saw Bad Bob that first night at Mesa when he reminded me of Barry Gibb. I saw my mom's tears, heard Gwen's accusations, held Jack's rocks. He'd never neglected to put one in my hand as I left the house, or if he wasn't there, leave one for me on the kitchen counter. I had more Jackrocks than I could count. I passed them out, and guys at the Patch had started to keep them for themselves. I could only vaguely remember the way Jack looked as he rounded the bases in Little League. I thought, Jackrocks are a shit substitute for Jack.

That night, exhausted and overrun, I cried myself into an uneasy sleep.

I was met, at some point in the middle of the night, by Bobby standing over my bed with a two-by-four. He wore his shades. He was harshly backlit, as if he'd driven his motorcycle into my bedroom and left its headlight on. He pursed his lips and raised the piece of wood, bringing the butt-end of it down on my face. I saw the splinters as it came down. It didn't hurt. The next thing I knew, I was in the Skull Valley Clubhouse. Teddy was there, holding his pliers and a bloody Chucky doll that he kept in a corner of the living room, the centerpiece of a caricatured shrine to death. He shook the doll at me, and drops of blood spattered off it. Teddy said something I didn't understand in a bad, high-pitched impersonation of the murderous toy. I looked around. We were all of a sudden behind the clubhouse by the wire fence. Teddy pulled his oxygen tubes from his nose, inhaled loudly, gathering phlegm, and spat on me. He was powerful, no longer sick, possessed of all the menacing vigor of his youth. He click-clicked the jaws of the pliers. They were rusty. Chucky was gone, and in his place were a pair of silver Vise-Grips. Bobby still clutched the two-by-four. They said I was a rat. I couldn't speak. Maybe my face was too bashed in. They must have understood, though, since they insisted I was a rat. I spat some blood and managed some words, saying, "No, I'm something worse." I thought, Rats don't have partners. Rats don't have backup.

But backup never came.

Bobby wedged my mouth open with a pair of wooden blocks. Using a nylon compression strap, he secured my head to a fencepost. I couldn't turn away. Teddy came toward me. He stuck the pliers in my mouth. They tasted like a penny. I could tell because they latched onto my tongue. He pulled. Through it all I remembered the taste. He pulled and pulled and pulled and when my tongue was far enough out of my mouth, Bobby raised a serrated Buck knife and—

I woke in a cold sweat, my heart racing. I stood up and fell down with dizziness almost immediately. I crawled to the doorway and pulled myself up. My left arm began to hurt. I slapped myself a few times and tried walking again, touching my face, making sure it was still there. It was. I made it to the kitchen. I grabbed my car keys. I went outside, fell into the Cougar. No one else was home. Timmy and Pops were with their families, JJ was off for the weekend. I sat there and clutched my chest, short of breath. There was a hospital close by. I turned over the engine and put it in gear and drove.

I drove to the emergency room, but when I pulled up I stayed in the car. My chest still hurt, but I wasn't so woozy. I looked at the light of the hospital and knew if I admitted myself and Slats or anyone else found out, the case would be over. I took ten deep breaths. I told myself I was fine, that I'd had worse from hits on the football field back in my playing days. I remembered one time when I'd gotten laid out so badly I didn't know left from right. Never one to let a defensive player gloat over my sprawled-out body, I popped up and returned to the huddle. Someone tapped me on the shoulder, pointed across the field, and said, "Dobyns, you're in the wrong huddle, man." It was the guy who'd hit me, the middle linebacker. I was standing with the defense, not the offense. He laughed his ass off. I gave him a starry-eyed look and ran to the sidelines for some smelling salts.

Thinking back to those days calmed me down. I laughed at myself. I knew what had messed me up. The pills. My heart stopped racing. I took another ten breaths. I rolled down the window and took ten more. I put the car in gear and drove back to the undercover house, concluding I'd suffered a panic attack. When I got there I went into the bathroom, filled the sink with cold water, and dunked my head in it. Then I emptied the Hydroxycuts into the toilet and flushed them away. I'd never take them again.

35   BOTTOM ROCKERS ARE US

FROM THEN ON, Starbucks, Red Bulls, and smokes would have to do.

Without the pills my everyday particulars became less exacting. I couldn't recognize it when I was popping them, but they'd given me a kind of tunnel vision. In most instances this is a good, if not necessary, thing for an undercover agent, but in my case it was no longer a necessity. I didn't have to fool anyone anymore. It wasn't just that I *felt* invincible, I *was* invincible. Truth was, the deeper I got with the club, the safer I got. The guys at the Patch couldn't understand it, but the more I was trusted by the Angels, the more I was protected. I didn't need the cover team because the Hells Angels were looking out for me. This became crystal clear when I flushed the Hydroxycuts. The vibrating edge brought on by the pills evaporated quickly, and in its place was something I hadn't felt in months: focus.

Everyday things still happened, but after the panic attack my ultimate goal crystallized: I'd do everything I could to become a Hells Angel.

Quickly.

The idea that had taken root in my pilled-up mind took on definition. It was simple, and it hinged on one simple fact: that for the

Hells Angels, violence is power. I decided that to prove my ultimate worth, I'd play by their rules.

I'd become violent.

I DIDN'T TELL anyone about my panic attack. No one could think I might be breaking down.

But we were all breaking down.

JJ, an athletic seven-year ex-smoker when she came onto the case, was back to a pack or more a day, and she'd gained thirty pounds. Timmy spent every free minute at home, recharging his batteries with family. Pops was gaunt, bent over, and showing his fifty hard-lived years. The task force agents were tired of covering us. I didn't care. In those days I'd just call Slats and tell him where I was and not to worry. He didn't like it—he knew he was losing control. He needed several drinks every night just to grab a little shut-eye.

Because Slats could see things I couldn't, and probably knew more about my physical and emotional degradation than he let on, he ordered me home for Father's Day. He said that we were all too vested, and that a little rest and relaxation wouldn't hurt anyone.

Rest, anyway.

I went home and gave the outward impression of relaxing—lying around on my couch, twisting my straggly goatee, catching up on *SportsCenter*—but true relaxation was impossible. I stared out the sliding doors of my living room at a stand of blooming saguaros and, beyond them, an electric-green golf course. I thought of something task force agent Sean "Spider-Man" Hoover had told me: "Man, this is such a joke. These guys look at you as some hard-luck hit man, and you live in a fucking mansion on a golf course." My place wasn't a mansion, but it *was* nice, and I do play golf. He was right. I tried to picture any of the Hells Angels I knew swinging a seven iron, digging through weeds for a lost ball, or trying to read a green. These were ludicrous images, ones that perfectly reflected how disconnected my life had become.

Gwen floated around me that weekend, keeping her distance, sometimes bringing me snacks I barely touched. We'd drifted far from each other. Maybe "drifted" isn't right: She'd stayed put while I'd run away at a dead sprint. She seemed resigned to facts. She'd told me she wouldn't give up on us—Gwen can be just as stubborn as I can—but it was evident she wasn't happy about our situation. Only because of Gwen's will have we stayed together. She didn't say much to me that weekend, but I remember her asking why I had to do everything to the limit. I didn't say anything. There was no answer; it was the way God made me.

Jack drew me a Father's Day card and handed it to me when I was zoning out on the couch. I opened it. On the left was a gun with a tracking line drawn from the barrel and through the chest of a figure—me—on the right. Below that was another picture of me, lying on a hospital gurney. There was a splatter of red ink where the bullet hit me, and above that the word "ding!" The caption at the bottom read HAPPY FATHER'S DAY, I HOPE THIS NEVER HAPPENS TO YOU AGAIN. LOVE, JACK.

The card broke my heart. I rubbed his head. I told him that Slats had a whole team of guys who always looked out for me. I said they wouldn't let anything bad happen. I told him if he didn't believe me, he could ask his mother and she'd tell him it was the truth.

He ran along and my mind turned back to work.

My professional situation was untenable and I knew it. It wasn't just that prospecting was going to be unbearable. It was also going to be a hard sell in terms of operational viability. The bosses would be resistant to funding our adventures as would-be bikers, especially since I knew Slats wasn't behind the effort 100 percent. I was fighting a two-front battle, one I thought I could win, on both sides, with the implementation of my simple idea.

My mind was tuned to blood, and the particulars of shedding it.

A few days before I went back to Phoenix, my best friends from high school came by—John Williams and Scott Hite. They thought they'd surprise me. They didn't. I could smell them coming. Only a downwind cougar could've snuck up on me. I smiled at the window as they walked up. They were dressed in khakis and golf shirts—one white, one light blue. They had on gold watches and golf spikes. One wore a black Titleist hat. They were members of Jay Dobyns's suburban life, not cops. They were fathers and husbands—mysteries. Here were two men I'd known for almost thirty years, and only by force of will could I remember what either of them did for a living.

They knocked on the glass. I didn't get up. I swiped my hand through the air. Scott slid the door open.

"Hey, man."

"What's up, dudes?"

"Not much."

They stared at me like I was a captive animal in a life-size diorama—The Federal Agent at Home.

John finally said, "Jeez, Jay, you look like a fucking junkie, you know that?"

I tried to laugh. "Yeah. Thanks a lot."

Scott asked, "Wanna come out for a round?"

I dug myself into the couch a little more. "Naw, I'm busy."

They shrugged, we bullshitted a little more, and they wandered off.

I turned off the TV. I watched the golf course. Unlike me, it never changed.

GWEN ASKED ME to go with Dale one Sunday morning to pick up her new guitar. I said I didn't know if I could, but when I saw how excited Dale was, I realized I'd be happy to do it. Gwen gave me the address. The shop was a few blocks from Mac's Black Rose tattoo parlor.

It was before noon on a Sunday, and I wasn't too worried that we'd run into Mac or anyone else. Nevertheless, the kids and I had established a few simple gestures that would indicate to them, should the need ever arise, that we were about to be approached by one of my "bad guys."

We went to the store. The clerk brought out a full-sized Fender Sonoran acoustic, a new case, and a cloth rainbow strap. Dale held it in front of her and strummed it, felt its weight and twirled it around. She smiled and nodded. I paid the balance and we walked out.

The bell on the door rang as it shut. I held Dale's hand. I looked up from her and standing in front of us stood Robert "Mac" McKay.

I gave Dale a squeeze. She squeezed back.

I let go of her hand and shook Mac's. Gave him a hug. I said, "This is my kid."

He leaned in close to her and said, "Pleasure to meet you, little lady. You got one hell of a dad here."

Dale was as cool as could be. She said thanks without a trace of nervousness.

He asked what we were up to, and I told him that I'd been promising Dale a new guitar for months. She held it up. There was no reason for me to lie. Mac was in good spirits, but before we parted he pulled me aside and said intensely, "Where the fuck is your cut, Bird? Represent!" Then he turned to Dale and, in a honey-dipped voice, repeated that he was pleased to meet her.

After we got into the car, Dale asked, with all the innocence of youth, "That was a Hells Angel?"

"Yup."

"He didn't seem like such a bad guy. He was pretty nice, I thought."

"He was on his best behavior. Don't be fooled—that guy is bad news. You ever see him again, walk the other way."

"OK."

"Promise me."

"OK! I promise."

I put my hand on her knee and pulled out of the parking spot.

ON THE THIRTIETH I got a call from Bobby, who wanted me to call Timmy to tell him he needed to call Bobby. I asked him why he didn't just call Timmy himself, and he bellowed, "Because I'm calling you, mother-fucker!"

I called Timmy. Timmy called Bobby. Then Timmy called me back. He said Bobby had ordered him to pick up a package at Cave Creek from Spa Bob, the Cave Creek P who'd succeeded Hoover, and bring it to Skull Valley the next morning. He said Bobby had told him not even to think of opening it.

After getting it, Timmy called and said, "I couldn't open this thing if I wanted to, not without them knowing. It's a shoebox wrapped in about ten layers of duct tape."

"So, what're you doing?"

"I talked to Slats. We're going to X-ray it."

"Awesome. Let me know. Me, Pops, and JJ'll be at Casa Trailer by midnight."

He called me later and told me the package, which was very light, appeared to contain three strips of cloth. Our bottom rockers.

The next day was church. There were some guests of honor at the clubhouse—Bad Bob, Pete Eunice, and Marcus, the London P. When we walked in they didn't look happy. Joey shuffled around the entrance, his head hung in what looked like a mix of shame and anger. Joby stood next to him, his arms crossed. Bobby tapped a wooden ax handle on the palm of his right hand. Pete spun the cylinder of a .38 revolver, snapped it out, snapped it back into place, spun it again. When we all got inside, Joby suddenly turned to Joey, who had moved into the open doorway, and shoved him in the chest. Bobby crept behind him, arms crossed, sunglasses down. Joby yelled, "Get the fuck out of here!" to Joey, who backpedaled, his face still hung low. I looked to Bobby for a clue to what was going on. He didn't have time for me. Joby repeated, "Get the fuck out of here!" and Joey turned and slunk away. Rudy got up, grabbed Timmy by the arm, and told him to come with him. They left.

In addition to whatever was going on with Joey—I later found out he'd screwed around with another member's old lady without his permission—Bobby was pissed about dinner. He'd sent Staci out to get it—we knew JJ had met her while she was out—and now they were late. "Those bitches better be here soon with our fucking grub or it's lights out." I nodded. Teddy told Pops to wait outside and keep an eye on the grounds. Pops left.

Everyone turned to me. Pete, still holding his revolver, placed it in the front of his waistband, resting his hand on the rubber butt. Bobby tapped the ax handle. Joby closed the door and leaned against it next to Marcus. They stood shoulder to shoulder, staring at me. Bad Bob was in the back of the room, smoothing his hair.

Teddy removed the tubes from his nose and started to talk. He growled, "Ya gonna have to leave too, Bird." I didn't say anything. Teddy was legitimately terrifying. He wielded his infirmity like a blunt weapon. He continued, "I know ya've been doing ya best, but it ain't good enough. Y'ain't got what it takes to be a Hells Angel."

"Get the fuck out." It was Bobby.

I took a deep breath. "No fucking way. You can kick me out, but I ain't walking out. I got too much in this." As I said the words it occurred to me that they were monumentally true. "You want me gone, you're gonna have to lift me up and throw me out."

I was pretty sure it was bullshit, but witnessing Joey's ouster gave me some lingering doubts. Maybe they were cleaning house? If they'd boot Joey, they'd boot anyone. Still, Teddy's words were familiar. I'd run the same game for Jesse when we patched him Solo, as Bad Bob had witnessed. I knew they had our bottom rockers. In addition, I knew I was

the best damn prospect they'd seen in years. I had the drive, the toughness, and the arrogance that Hells Angels love. This was my life and
they knew it. I was going to be a Hells Angel, and I was going to be one
of the best.

Teddy smiled. "OK. If that's the way you feel, I guess I'm going to
have to give you a second chance." He reached behind him and stood
up in one motion. When he turned to face me, he was holding an Arizona bottom rocker. Bobby told me to stand up. Everyone smiled.
Bobby and Joby patted me on the back. I took the rocker. Teddy gave
me a bear hug. The old guy could still muster a lot of strength when he
wanted to.

As we separated, Teddy said, "We're doing ya partners next. Ya keep
quiet and pretend like we just stole ya lunch money."

I said all right. An hour later the three of us were official Hells Angels
prospects. We pinned our rockers on with the safety pins Timmy carried with him. Bad Bob pointed at the pins and said, "Damn, you guys
really got it covered." I smiled at him. He told me he was proud of
me—of us—and that he knew we'd get patched quickly.

I hoped so, but I just said, "As long as it takes."

Bobby said, "That's my boy."

My phone rang.

"Yeah, Bird."

"Hey, Daddy." It was Dale. She sounded happy. The volume on my
phone was up, and Dale's little-girl voice could be heard before I could
click it down.

"Hey. What's up?" The guys listened to me.

"Nothing much. Just calling to say hi, that I like my guitar."

"That's great, but I'm pretty busy right now. You got something you
need, or are you just bothering me?"

"Daddy, what's wrong?"

"Nothing's wrong. I just don't have the time to deal with you right
now unless you have some kind of emergency." Silence. "I guess not.
Look, I'll call you later. Bye."

"Bye—" I flipped shut.

Bobby asked who that was. I said, "It's one of Big Lou's guys." He
laughed. Joby smiled. Teddy too. They knew I was lying.

I looked at Timmy and Pops. They knew I never talked to one of
"Big Lou's guys," I only ever talked to Big Lou. They correctly assumed

it was Gwen, Dale, or Jack, and they both had looks on their faces like I was the biggest prick in the world.

I was, but I truly didn't care. I'd just gotten my bottom rocker, and I wasn't going to spoil it by taking the time to have a chat with my little girl. I was so upside-down with who I'd become that I'd been willing to lose my daughter's and my own respect in the service of a case. I was consumed with a mixture of exultation, indifference, and hate. I could only make real-time decisions, and invariably I made those with the lone goal of maintaining my credibility in the eyes of the Hells Angels, my new brothers.

I knew they knew I'd just hung up on my daughter, and I knew they approved.

As if reading my mind, Bobby approached, nodding gravely. He said quietly, "That's right, Bird. You have to give up everything—your family, your life, your woman, your job, your money, your car, your dog—to be a fucking Hells Angel. We did, and you will too." His hand held my shoulder firmly.

Then Teddy announced, "Boys, as Hells Angels I can promise you three things: violence, jail, and death."

If I'd been in a more sober frame of mind I might have burst out laughing, yelling, "That's your fucking sales pitch?" But as it was, I just nodded. They told the truth. I was prepared to play along precisely because I believed *I* was the one who would send them to jail.

It was right after this that Staci and JJ arrived with the food. As we heard the gravel of the driveway under the tires, Bobby said, "That better be them," and when he confirmed it was, he added, "She better have gotten in a bad fucking accident, she's so late," and when he found out she hadn't, and was completely drunk, he growled, "That's it. She's catching one tonight." I quickly went up to JJ and told her to stay in the car, hand me the food, and drive away. I couldn't be put in the position of being ordered to beat JJ. She said OK, Staci got out, and then she left.

Bobby took Staci roughly by the arm, the food she was carrying falling onto the ground in a pile of take-out boxes. He dragged her yelling into their apartment on the ground floor of the clubhouse. We brought the food inside. Teddy ordered us to secure the perimeter while they ate and talked club business. We went outside. Bobby emerged from his apartment fifteen minutes later. I was too far away to see how he looked. There was no sign of Staci.

Later on, out in the fields down from the clubhouse, Timmy asked, "Was that Dale on the phone in there?"

"Yeah. It was."

"You have some fucking nerve."

"What was I supposed to do? Go lovey-dovey on her right after getting mud-checked? I don't think so. Those guys like shit like that, you know that."

"I don't give a fuck what they like. Call her back."

"I'll talk to her later."

"I'm not asking you. Call her back."

I knew he was right. I also knew he could kick my ass in about two seconds. I said, "OK, OK."

I called. Dale was still crying. I apologized and tried to explain my situation. Gwen grabbed the phone and laid into me. "Jay, do not ever, ever speak to our children like that again! They're not props. Do you understand?" I told her I did, though I didn't believe it. Fuck her, she had no idea what I was into. She asked me again if I understood. I said I did. Why Gwen didn't say she was leaving me right then, I don't know. I asked to speak with Dale. I suddenly realized what I'd done. For a moment I reverted to Jay Dobyns. I told her the guy who said those things wasn't me, he was someone else, I didn't mean those things, I loved her so much, I was glad she liked the guitar. She settled down but was still upset. I promised her I'd make it up to her. I asked her if she could forgive me. She was a child, what was she supposed to say other than yes?

I hung up. Anger bubbled inside me, but I didn't know where to direct it. I hated the Angels, I hated ATF, I hated Timmy for making me apologize, I hated my wife, I hated my family, I hated myself, then I hated the Angels again and repeated the cycle. I tamped my hatred down and tried to stay cool. I told Timmy that Dale was all right. I sounded convincing, he believed me. Or pretended to. I apologized to Timmy and he said it was OK, we were all under a lot of stress. I wanted someone to blame for what I'd become and every person I knew raced through my brain, but it was me. I was to blame.

The truth, however, was that I'd been all too willing to sell my family down the river if I thought it would curry some favor with the Hells Angels. I thought, perhaps foolishly, that my family would ultimately understand, that if given an inch it was OK, even expected, for me to take a mile. The truth was that by then I wouldn't have hesitated in doing what I did to Dale again. Bobby's words came back to me: "You have to give up everything to become a Hells Angel." His words had sounded ridiculous to me, but suddenly they made a grotesque kind of sense. I felt pathetic. No. I *was* pathetic.

I was more Bird than Jay Dobyns. My transformation was almost complete.

When we were called back to the house, Bobby wanted to know who I was talking to on the phone. I told him I was lining up a big deal in Culiacán, Mexico, for later that week. I said we'd have to be out of town for a little while, but that we'd be back for the next church meeting on June 6. Bobby said OK, they'd known what they were getting into when they brought us up, and they'd promised us our freedom when it came to business. I said thanks. Joby told me to be on the lookout for thirty or so handguns he could distribute to the San Francisco charter so they could arm local and sympathetic street gangs. I told him I would. The following day, June 1, we left Prescott for a breather.

Slats was not at all enthused with the bottom rockers, but I could've given a fuck. If I was prepared to write off my family, I wouldn't bat an eye doing the same to a co-worker, even one of Slats's stature. This was a golden opportunity I had worked too hard to accomplish. There was nothing Slats could do to stop me. I'd developed a hero syndrome: I was bound and determined to save the day, no matter the cost and against all odds. I felt like it was up to me and only me to make all of it work.

By then, the task force was solidly split into two groups, one headed by Slats and the other by Timmy and me. For Slats's group the bottom rockers represented a new, exhausting phase in the investigation. They meant months—maybe years—of additional work. They meant that the pace we'd been running at over the past several weeks would continue and, in all likelihood, intensify. My group believed that once we got patched, the evidence would get better; we'd be brought into the Hells Angels' inner circle. Joby's request for thirty firearms was a good indication of this belief. If we could do a sale of that size—across state lines, no less—then we'd have a nice addition to the RICO. I knew it was just the tip of the iceberg. Timmy was becoming more demonstrative with Slats. He lobbied passionately to see this through to its utmost ending. The Black Biscuit pot hadn't boiled over, but it was foaming and bouncing on the burner.

Timmy and I met with the task force on the fourth, back at the Patch. I told them not to worry, that I had a plan to get us in quick. I said it was risky and that we might not pull it off, but that if we did, it would ensure our position. Naturally, they wanted to know what it was. I told them I couldn't go into details yet, but that I'd do so the following week—that was a promise.

After the meeting I headed out to the Dumpsters for a cigarette. There was no moon, no clouds, nothing to reflect the night lights of Phoenix. The sky was a limitless pool of ink suspended overhead. Slats wandered out. He spat a wad of chaw. It exploded on the pavement. He opened a beer and handed it to me. He had another one for himself. He asked me what I was thinking of doing.

I drank a few sips of beer and said, "That's simple, Joe. We're going to kill a Mongol."

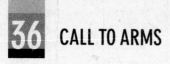

36   CALL TO ARMS

JUNE 2003

SLATS DIDN'T LIKE it. He didn't like it one bit. I didn't like his not liking it. He said it didn't make any sense. I said it made perfect sense. He told me that wasn't what he meant—it *did* make perfect sense to the Angels, but it didn't make sense to us. He reminded me, "We're *the good guys.*" He said it wasn't going to happen. He implied that he'd end everything before it came to pass.

I said, "Fuck you. It's happening, and it's happening soon."

He took a breath, spat another wad of chaw, and crushed his beer can between his hands. An eerie calmness overcame him. He said, "Jay, murder gets murder. *It's just too risky.* Maybe you die, maybe you don't—shit, maybe you don't care if you die—but showing these guys a murder? I don't know. You run the risk of igniting a biker war, a war you could be right in the middle of."

He was right, I didn't care. I said, "Dude, that's a risk I'm willing to take." I mashed out my cigarette and walked away.

I don't know why Slats didn't shut down the case right then—in the same way I didn't know why Gwen hadn't filed for divorce after I was such a jerk to Dale—but he didn't. The only thing I can think of now is that he wasn't ready. He needed more time to get his warrants together. Just a little more time. We both did.

The race was on.

I SPOKE TO my old partner Chris. I spoke to Timmy. I spoke to Shawn Wood, a task force agent who was very supportive of our attempting to get patched. I spoke to Chris some more.

We got a nice little conspiracy going.

The plan *was* simple, and the more I thought about it, the more I was convinced it was foolproof. We'd ask the Hells Angels for permission to kill a Mongol, and then we would. We'd do it down in Mexico, where the Angels could corroborate practically nothing. Chris wondered how I could get them to contribute. He asked if I could get a gun from them.

"Hell fucking yes," I said.

Here's why the plan was foolproof: They couldn't object. Since Laughlin, the guys were obsessed with killing Mongols. But though they were capable of it, they never went out and hunted them down. Like Dan Danza, the wired Angel whose toughness and aggressiveness I felt a kinship for, I thought this was ludicrous; Mongols weren't hard to find. They weren't like Osama bin Laden hiding in Tora Bora—these guys had clubhouses just like the Angels. So I decided I'd become their killer. If Steve Helland, the Angel Nomad, was willing to discuss hiring me to kill his son's murderer, then why couldn't I discuss killing a Mongol for the club? And how could they refuse? If they balked I could ask, "What part of 'If you see a Mongol, kill him' did I not understand?" If I did it, I'd fulfill their dreams and my potential.

We'd go through with our plan and either Slats would hastily end the case, or the Angels would kill me for overstepping, or I'd get fired, or I'd get patched. Having had the opportunity to take my best, most violent stab at becoming a Hells Angel, I'd have been happy to accept any of these outcomes, even death. At times, especially death. It was June in Arizona, and my willingness to die increased with the escalation of the mercury. There were even days when I woke up wanting to die. It was never something I was going to do to myself, but it *was* something I came to expect. It would've been so simple, and simplifying. I wouldn't be around to screw up my family anymore, they'd get a nice insurance check, and the nightmare that had become my life would be over. I knew I'd never quit on my own—this had to be decided for me—so what better way to do that than to die? Without knowing it, my old partner Koz's joking desire had become my own: I was now the guy who wanted to be duct-taped to a chair and shotgunned in the face. I wanted a good undercover death in the heat of my biggest battle. I wanted to die as the badass I'd become.

I thought, Fuck it. Maybe it would happen, maybe it wouldn't. I was a cop, but I was also a Hells Angel. All that was left to do was to take care of business.

LIFE IS PRETTY disrespectful of obsessions. As I spent all my time calculating and rehashing information and visualizing a crime scene, life went on. On June 6 we got called to guard duty in Dago for the funeral of another fallen Angel.

There'd been rumors that Timmy, Pops, and I would be guarding Sonny Barger at the World Run to Laconia, New Hampshire, in August—that weekend in Dago was a test run. The big heads were in the house—Sonny, Johnny Angel, and Chuck Zito, along with almost a dozen charter presidents from around the West Coast. I'd been assigned the back door. There was a high wall between the clubhouse and the street and I couldn't see anything beyond it. Mongols paranoia had rubbed off on me: The whole time I expected a pipe bomb to sail over the wall and blow me and the back of the building to kingdom come.

But nothing happened. Boredom was my main enemy. But after standing around for about eight hours I got a little surprise. Out of nowhere, standing on the back porch, appeared Sonny Barger. He carried a plate covered with food, and two bottles of beer. He put the food on a folding card table and pushed the cancer kazoo to his trach hole.

His voice buzzed, "Hot out here, huh?"

"Sure is, sir."

"You can call me Sonny, Bird."

"No offense, but until I get my stripes, I'll call you 'sir,' sir."

He smiled. He said, "I brought you some food if you want it. You can take a break, I'll cover for you while you eat."

No. There was no way in hell I was going to let Sonny Barger sub for me.

"I'm all right, sir, I just finished a candy bar."

"How about a beer, then?"

That was an easy one, one that convinced me he was playing a mud-check on me.

"I appreciate it, but I can't do that while I'm on duty. My sponsor would set me on fire if he found out."

"Suit yourself." He picked up a roasted chicken leg and bit into it. He drank half a bottle of beer, making a point of sounding refreshed. His electronic voice told me he'd continued to hear good things about me and that we were on the right track. He said he was pleased that we'd decided to come over, to leave that two-bit club behind. I told him I was happy about that too. Then he finished his food and beer in silence.

He left as suddenly as he'd appeared. He picked up the plates, put one under the other, and said, "Later, Bird," without the voice box. It was like a gale-force whisper. He was a strong old dude.

He left the full, ice-cold bottle of beer on the table. I didn't dare touch it. *Was* it a mud-check? I wasn't sure. I knew Sonny genuinely cared about his people. Maybe Sonny even cared for me.

ON JUNE 12, Joby called in a state of panic. He said we needed to meet ASAP in the Prescott Wal-Mart parking lot.

When we got there I asked him what was up.

"We got called in."

"Whaddaya mean?"

"I mean Teddy's sending us on a mission. We're going to Vegas tonight on a protection gig."

Pops said, "More guard duty, huh?"

"This ain't fucking guard duty, guys. It was, I wouldn't be going now, would I?" I shrugged. He said, "Listen, we're going up to support our brothers. Call Timmy, tell him to get all your guns in the Jeep and meet you at the clubhouse. Pops, you stay with me. Bird, go meet Bobby and Timmy and we'll meet for lunch. I'll tell you about it then."

I buzzed Timmy and told him to meet me at the clubhouse and that we were being invited to a party that was BYOG. He asked, "BYOG?"

I explained, "Bring your own gun."

He said enthusiastically, "It's about time. See ya there."

I rode to the clubhouse, breaking one of Teddy's rules: I was a Hells Angel riding alone. Timmy was there when I pulled up. I left him by the Jeep as I went to get Bobby. He was inside his apartment. I waited for him in the entryway. He emerged from the bedroom stuffing a Bersa .38 into his pocket. He yelled to Staci that he was leaving a .22 for her on the kitchen counter.

Over cheap Mexican food we learned what we were up against. From the minute they started to give details I thought of only one person: Slats.

There was a coalition meeting in Vegas that night that the Banditos, another rival gang, one much more powerful than the Mongols, had promised to bust up. The Vegas Angels couldn't allow this, so they'd called in the cavalry. Bobby and Joby both complained that there probably weren't enough guys willing to answer the call—but that wasn't us. Skull Valley, along with some guys from Mesa, would represent. Bobby had been ordered to hang back. Rudy wasn't even considered. It would be me, Pops, Timmy, and Joby, and we'd be armed to the teeth.

Bobby: "Teddy'll get you his sawed-off."

Joby: "Good. I want the shit that sprays a wide pattern."

Bobby: "I wish I were going with you. I've been on plenty of these things before—I'd be good."

Joby: "Teddy knows what he's doing. Can't send everyone. There'd be no one to protect the area. This happens, and they'll be looking for revenge. Before long we'll be seeing those motherfuckers in Arizona too. We gotta stay strong down here."

Bobby: "I know, but I still wish I was goin'."

Joby: "We'll probably all die."

Bobby: "Or go to jail."

Joby: "I'll take death. But he's right, you know." He addressed us. "Expect to kill tonight. Expect to shoot. Expect to die, go to jail, or skip country."

I thought sarcastically, This is great. We're going to have to kill for these guys before we get a chance to do it on our own terms.

We finished lunch and went back to the clubhouse. I needed to get away from them to call Slats, but they were jacked up and I couldn't get away for even a second.

Teddy and Bobby looked on as Joby loaded the Jeep with the shotgun, a box of shells, a sap, an ax handle, and three or four knives. Teddy looked distraught. He signaled to us to huddle around him.

He spoke, contemplating the ground. "I'm not happy about this, but this is what we do. I'm proud of ya and I'm proud of the Hells Angels. Ya be there for them, and they'll be there for ya. Do what ya gotta do, but I want y'all to come back alive." He gave each of us a big hug.

Bobby hugged us too. As he finished with me he grabbed my shoulders and said, "Remember, Bird—a Hells Angel may not always be right, but he is always your brother."

Teddy spoke again. "Half of what's mine is yours. Don't forget that either."

Their words made sense. Even though I'd sworn an oath to fight guys like these, I'd bought into some of their credo. I knew that any of these guys, and more than a few others across the state, would gladly take a bullet for me. In that instant I believed in some of what the Hells Angels stood for. I was genuinely touched.

We left. I drove. Timmy and Pops rode in the back of the Jeep while Joby made frantic calls to Mesa Angels Ghost and Trigger. He wanted to get a handle on the situation. It sounded like it was definitely happening. I smoked a relay of cigarettes, never pausing to breathe the fresh desert air we passed through. I watched the road, thinking only of Slats. I looked at the gas gauge. We had a quarter tank. Just before Kingman I pulled off to refill. We got out and stretched. Pops filled her up. I went to the can.

As soon as I was out of sight, I opened up my phone. The line rang. Slats answered.

"It's Bird. Listen, we're in deep. We're going to Vegas to knock down Banditos at some coalition meeting—*tonight*. We've got a fucking arsenal in the car and we've been told in no uncertain terms that we're expected to use it. You gotta call Gayland and fix us up."

He asked why I hadn't called sooner. I said I'd been with them all day, I had no airspace. I said I had to go, and told him to call back when he'd spoken to Gayland and tell me what's what. I said I'd make it sound like I was talking to Dale. He said OK.

Fifteen minutes later my phone rang. We were passing through Golden Valley in Kingman, headed to BHC and into Nevada via Laughlin, because Joby didn't want to risk a vehicle inspection if we crossed the Hoover Dam. It was Slats. He said he was on his way to Vegas, but that we had a good jump on him. He said Gayland was taking care of it—there wouldn't be a Bandito within twenty miles of the meeting. He said that Gayland knew where it was taking place and not to worry. Just go up and do what they expected us to do.

We got there. The lodge's parking lot was littered with bikes and Angels. Joby called a huddle with me, Timmy, Pops, Ghost, Trigger, Sockem, and a Vegas member named Phil Daskalos. Joby launched into a speech: "All right. If the Banditos show, we're gonna ambush 'em. Don't let any of them get off their bikes. Do whatever you have to, understand? Do not let them off their bikes." He paused and swiped his hand through his long gray mullet. He looked each of us in the eye. "Listen, if you don't have the stomach for this, then go home now. Come back and try again in a couple years when your balls drop. If you *can* do it, this is the shit that heroes and legends are made of. We will not fail each other. We are Hells Angels." I wouldn't have been shocked if he'd put his hand in the middle of our circle and we started to chant "Eight-One, Eight-One, Eight-One!"

We broke and were assigned positions. Joby sent Pops and Phil across the street, while he took Timmy and me to a street-side corner of the lot. Trigger, Ghost, and Sockem went to the opposite side of the lot.

We waited. I smoked like Philip Morris was going out of business. We waited some more. At eight fifteen the meeting broke, the guys got on their bikes, and a column of Hells Angels departed the location. It was over. There were no Banditos. Gayland had done us another favor.

The group of would-be defenders met at a 76 gas station around eight thirty. We shook hands, glad to have bucked up and even gladder to have not gotten in a shoot-out. Joby said these things happen, better to be prepared than to be shown up or worse. Pops introduced me to Phil. They'd gotten to talking guns while waiting. Phil was very eager to talk to me, said he was the "West Coast hook for HAMC iron." Said he had all kinds of shit—hand grenades, C4 plastic explosive, Mac-10s, remote-control bombs, silencers. I gave Phil a card and told him to give me a call.

We went back to Skull Valley.

In the Jeep, Joby told us over and over how proud of us he was. We dropped him off at his girlfriend's house in Kingman, giving each other big hugs, saying we'd see each other the next day.

I called Slats when we got back in the Jeep. He asked if I wanted to talk to Gayland. I did.

Gayland asked, "How was Vegas?"

"Awesome. Won on craps and got twelve free lap dances. What happened to our friends?"

"We knocked some down. Lockup's hosting a Bandito slumber party tonight. We'll let 'em go in the morning. Otherwise it's pretty quiet around here. I think Slats wants to take me out to dinner. He's been making eyes at me all night."

I laughed. I said thanks and told him to tell Slats thanks too. I said, "You saved our ass. Again."

SLATS COULD'VE SHUT everything down after that. Evidently the Angels weren't going to be shy about putting us in dangerous situations, and given enough opportunities, it was only a matter of time until something bad happened because we weren't in a position of control.

But Slats let us ride a little longer.

I took this as encouragement to go ahead with my plan. Letting us go to Vegas meant that Slats, no matter what he said, was prepared to take part in potentially nasty situations. In a way I felt vindicated.

The Skull Valley boys were also happy. When we pulled up to the clubhouse that night, we found Teddy and Bobby waiting up like nervous parents. They hugged us hard. Teddy tried to smile, but was out of practice. He repeated that he hadn't liked sending us, but that as Hells Angels we all had to chase ghosts. He told us to go home and get some rest.

After that night, the Skull Valley crew lightened up a little. They still ordered us around, but they made it more obvious that they were just busting our balls. Teddy would wax for five minutes about how he liked his fried chicken: old-style, not overcooked, original recipe, not that extra-crispy shit. He'd give us a little extra money for going out to get it. They started to really respect and like us.

At church one day, bored, I doodled on some paper plates. I drew stick figures of the guys, their names below their feet. Little bubbles above their heads said things like "I Love Bird" (Bobby) or "Go to McDonald's" (Teddy). I was engrossed and didn't notice that Teddy had walked up to me. When I finally noticed him staring at my bad drawings, hissing through his tubes, it was too late.

"What the *fuck* is that?"

I thought the "You think this is funny, like this is some fucking game?" lecture was coming. I exhaled like a guilty school kid and said, "Art?"

He made a desperate sound like a small cough, but not one of his emphysemic ones. It got a little louder. He was laughing. I'd never heard him laugh. I don't think anyone in that room had. He took the drawings out of my hands and held them up for everyone to see. They laughed too. We followed their lead. Rudy opened beers and handed them out. Timmy started telling stupid jokes and Teddy thumbtacked my art to the wall. We all felt good, we all felt like human beings. I realized that these guys weren't all bad—and was reminded that I wasn't all good.

The week after Vegas I was busy on all fronts. We went on two runs, did an intimidation of the Americans MC with Joby, set up a large guns-and-explosives deal with Phil from Vegas, and bought a scoped Browning rifle from Joby and some drugs and a pistol from Rudy. We ran up and down the state, from Mesa to Skull Valley to Bullhcad to Tucson and back. In Bullhead, Smitty was still worried about getting the Mohave Valley charter started up, but, on the plus side, he said he'd been keeping tabs on us and that we were going to be "rock stars."

Damn right.

As we ran around, my mind constantly spun with the specifics of setting up the Mongol murder. Shawn Wood, the task force agent most game with the plan, was in charge of arranging times and places, scouting locations, doing legwork. I told him I planned to plant the seed on the twenty-first, when we'd be doing prospecting duties at a run in Williams, Arizona.

He said, "Good, let's get this thing done."

THE WILLIAMS RUN was easy. We had prospecting duties, but they were low-stress. JJ and Pops sold T-shirts in the booth, and I wandered around with Bobby, acting as his bodyguard.

We came across a group of bikers who called themselves the Wild Pigs. One of their guys walked up to us, his hand extended to Bobby. He wore a big shit-eating smile. He said, "Hey, pleasure to meet you."

Bobby raised his sunglasses and looked at him intently. He did not offer his hand in return. "Get fucked."

"Hey, I—"

"You heard me, fuck off. Can you believe these cocksuckers, Bird?" I didn't lie—I said no, I couldn't. The Wild Pigs were cops, guys with badges who paraded around on weekends like a One Percenter club. In my mind, as in Bobby's, they were a fucking abomination.

The guy took his hand back and started to turn when Bobby said, "Wait. I gotta tell you something—you can't have it both ways, asshole. You can't pretend to look and act like us until the shit gets nasty and then pull a badge and gun and sit us down on the side of the road. Fuck you. Pick a side." He turned away in disgust and flipped the Wild Pig off. I followed him. Bobby couldn't have been more right. It was one thing to be undercover. It was another to be flying two flags at once.

We wandered back to our section—Skull Valley was there, along with a lot of Nomads—and hung around. Having returned to the safety of Hells Angels territory, I was able to leave Bobby to talk with Joby.

I'd decided Joby would be the point Angel for the murder. If I'd asked Teddy or Bobby, they would have wanted to think it over for weeks. I didn't have weeks. Joby, on the other hand, was like an old piece of leather, a tough guy who wouldn't think twice about sanctioning the death of a rival. I knew I could count on him.

He was talking with JJ and Pops as I came up to him. I pulled him aside and told him something had been eating at me. I'd heard things about a Mongol in Mexico who was talking shit and not paying a price. I told him I wanted to do something about it, but I wanted his advice. He asked for details—a name, a charter, a location. I told him I thought I could nail down his location, but I didn't know his name or even what he looked like, all I'd been told was that he was being a real dick, mocking us all over Laughlin, shitting on the Hells Angels in a place where no one could make him shut up. I said he was getting free shots at us. Joby looked from side to side and clenched his jaw. He said, "You did right coming to me. Find out more. We'll posse up and go smoke that motherfucker."

I said, "OK. Good. That's what I thought."

I LET JOBY simmer for a couple days. I went to Phoenix and hung out with Danza on the twenty-third. I told him I'd be going hunting soon.

He said, "Man, I wish so fucking bad I could come with you. Half these guys don't have the balls to do what you're doing—not even half. They want to be accountants and old men, like Sonny wants a warm glass of milk every night before he hits the sack at ten-thirty. Half the time I don't know why I signed up for this bullshit, Bird. We're the Hells Angels, we should be partying all the time, naked chicks everywhere, drugs everywhere, like no fucking bullshit, you know?"

I knew where he was coming from. We had a good case, but if the Angels hadn't been so cautious we would've had a hell of a lot better case. I told Danza I wished he could come to Mexico too, but that with Timmy and Pops I had my bases covered. "Still," he said, "I'd love to see that motherfucking bitch when you pop 'em. You should do it by stabbing him in the head." He paused, dreaming. "But don't forget to fuck him in the ass a little before you kill him. You know, let 'em know what you are." I told him he'd have no doubt who was doing it to him. He said good luck and when we parted he gave me a big hug. He called me his real fucking brother. Again, I was perversely touched. I knew Danza would probably be going back to jail because of me, and society would certainly benefit, but a small part of me wished he weren't. I knew that if circumstances had been different—if we'd been in a foxhole together or had to parachute out of an airplane over enemy territory—Danza was a guy I'd want at my side.

On the twenty-fourth I called Joby at Skull Valley to make sure Teddy or Bobby wasn't there. He said, "The boys are down at the Pines and I'm holding down the fort."

"If it's OK, I'd like to come over and talk about that guy I mentioned the other day."

He seethed, "Yeah. Let's do that. Come on over."

The place was dead. Joby lounged in a wooden office chair, his cowboy-booted heels kicked up on a stool. He played with a Buck knife, stabbing it into the arm of the chair. When he spoke, his voice was unusually eager and twangy, like he'd just spent a month in the desert and hadn't yet seen a naked woman. He said, "Bird."

"Joby. I got news."

"Tell me." He brought down his feet and sheathed the knife with a metallic whisper.

"Pops went down two days ago. He's trailing him until we get there."

"Good. Tell him to wait."

"I will. Can we do it?"

"Yeah."

"We can kill this motherfucker?"

"Yeah. Fuck yeah. The guys know, and they're down too."

"Good. Joby, I wanna be clear about something. We do this and prove we did it, we want our patches."

"Bird, you're my brother, I don't give a shit if you're a prospect, you're my brother to the fullest. Don't worry. I'll do whatever I can to make sure you get yours quick."

"Good. There's one more thing."

"What?"

"You got a scratched piece? Something without a record?"

He put his chin in his hand and rubbed it. This was a stretch. I'd just gotten him to approve a murder, and now I—a fucking gun dealer—was asking if he had a throwaway gun. Acrid, nasty stuff welled up in my throat. I lit a cigarette to choke it down.

Finally he said, "I don't know. I think so. Hold on."

He disappeared into a side room. I unsnapped one of my Glocks and pulled it out half an inch, just in case. As was the custom in those days, I had no backup. Slats wouldn't have supported me anyway, not with what I was up to. Joby could've come out and shotgunned me down and no one would've known for days.

Joby emerged from the room checking the action of a small, pigeon-gray pistol. He said, "This'll do it, but you gotta get close."

"Don't worry. That's the idea."

"It's still got a number, but it's got no papers. You do this thing, bring it back so we can get rid of it good."

He handed me the pistol, I checked the safety and stuck it in my back pocket. I said I had to go, that I'd be in touch, and that I'd be back in a few days.

He grabbed me by the shoulders and pulled me close, hugging me tight, slapping my back hard. He pushed me back, looked into my eyes, and said, "I want you to come home. All of you."

"Don't worry, bro, we will. We will."

37 ...

WE WENT INTO the desert, and we took care of business.

38 HATE AND MONEY

I SAT IN our trailer, chain-smoking. Timmy stood by the door breathing calmly. How he managed to stay calm throughout all our months of strife is still beyond me.

Pops was no longer with us. We'd gone and done the thing and called the boys to a meeting. JJ had spoken to Bobby several times, pretending to be distraught and clueless. We'd told them we'd taken care of business but that Pops was gone. He wasn't coming back. They weren't happy about that.

I kept repeating to myself, It'll work, it'll work, it'll work. In those tense, waiting moments I became convinced that I was overreaching, that I was diving out of bounds like I had so many years back in college to catch an uncatchable football, only to land in a patch of cacti. I was afraid of unfathomable outcomes while simultaneously certain I'd reach my goal—I'd become a Hells Angel. It had been a strange and terrible saga.

So we waited. Time became glacial: It moved for no living thing.

I fingered one of my Glocks. I thought, Yep, they're gonna kill me. I'm dead. I thought of the last time I'd felt that way, when Bad Bob had maneuvered me onto the corner of that restaurant's porch. This would be it for sure. It would all be over. I'd beaten Slats to the finish line, I'd sold the wares before he could close the shop, but maybe it didn't matter. I didn't know how the Skull Valley boys would react. Having seen what we'd done for them, would Joby and Teddy and Bobby suddenly realize they were accomplices to a murder they didn't want or need? Would they think they'd given us too much line and now we had to be pulled in? Or would they patch us on the spot, make us members from the word go? Those were the only two real options. They couldn't string us along anymore, I wouldn't let them.

My phone rang. I muted the ringer. Gwen had been leaving messages all day. I didn't want to call her back. I took a deep breath, mashed out a down-to-the-filter cigarette, and lit another. I decided to accept my fate. That night, Jay Dobyns would die—if not literally, then at least figuratively. If I became a Hells Angel, even an undercover version of a Hells Angel, then my life as Jay Dobyns would have to end. My marriage would be effectively over; my kids, whom I'd loved more than anything less than a year ago, would be further deprived of their father as I dove deeper and deeper into the bikers' world. As I sat in the trailer waiting for Teddy and the boys, my only measure of personal success was Black Biscuit. I was willing to lose everything else.

I released and engaged the slide on one of my pistols. Click, click. Repeat. Click, click. Repeat.

Timmy asked, "You remember that scene in *The Untouchables*, when they're waiting to ambush Capone's guys on that Canadian bridge, and Connery says to Garcia, 'You checked your weapon, now leave it be'?"

"Yeah."

"Well, you checked your weapon, Jay."

"All right." I put the gun down and reached into a pocket and drew out one of my Jackrocks. Timmy continued to watch me. He asked if I'd spoken to Jack lately.

"No."

Timmy said, "Hmmm. My kids are doing good."

"Good. Sorry I never ask."

"It's all right. We've been pretty busy."

"We have, haven't we?"

"Yeah."

I looked at the rock, turning it over in my hand. "It's funny. Months ago Jack told me something I never got until just now. This was like February or March, before we really started getting in with the guys." I paused to light another cigarette. "Anyway, I'm leaving the house, he runs out to give me another rock. I've got hundreds at that point, so I don't think about it too much. He wanted to talk, to keep me from leaving. I told him I didn't have time. So he gives me the rock and I say thanks and he asks if I know why he gives them to me. I say because he loves me, or he wants to show me how much he loves me, something like that. He shakes his head. Says, 'No, Dad, that's not why. I give them to you to help keep you safe.' I ask, 'So they're for good luck, then?' He shakes his head again, says, 'No. They're for whenever you get in trouble or are scared and you need help or something, you can touch one and know that I'm there with you.'"

"Wow."

"Yeah, no shit. I was too distracted to really get it then. In my mind I chalked it up to the rocks being for good luck, it was easier that way. But now, waiting for these guys, I finally get what he meant. He meant he could make me stronger, even save my life—not the rocks, but Jack himself."

"You miss him, huh?"

I thought about that for a second. I looked at Timmy and said, calling him by his real name, "Billy, I don't even know anymore." I should have cried, but I was all dried up. It was too much for me to think about.

I put the rock away; I put my eight-year-old son, mature enough to come up with such an idea, back into my pocket. I hated myself for making him think that way.

I was Bird, and hate was part of my MO.

I released the slide on my gun and racked a bullet into the chamber. I decided that if it came to it, I'd be ready. I'd flipped back. No more thinking.

I was Bird, and Bird was always ready.

Timmy said, "We're gonna be fine, you know."

"Maybe, but these guys don't owe us shit, dude. When they see what we're showing them, they might bug out."

Timmy walked to the desk and put his hands on it. He leaned in and said, "No way, Jay. I already said it—we're easy like Sunday morning."

"You said it. Please don't sing it again."

He chuckled. "Don't worry."

"Seriously, though. What if Teddy loses his shit?"

Timmy leaned back. "Forget Teddy. You and me are ten times the Hells Angel he is and he knows it. Pops too. Shit, I've never even seen Teddy ride a bike!"

He had a point. I took a deep drag off my cigarette and said, "OK. But still, keep tight tonight. Don't let anyone stand behind you."

He nodded, straightened up, and patted his chest, which was where he kept his gun.

We waited some more.

My cell vibrated, reminding me of my messages. I decided to listen to them.

It's Gwen. Your wife. Listen, the sprinkler system is broken and I need you to either come fix it or take care of it. I got my hands full with the kids. Give me a call soon. Um, that's it I guess. We miss you. Jack especially. Bye.

Beep.

It's Gwen again. Jack got in a fight at school yesterday and since you're his dad I thought you should know about it. Can you please call us?

Beep.

It's me. Are you alive? For most wives I know this is a rhetorical question, but in our case . . . Please call.

Beep.

You're being a real jerk, Jay. I called Joe so I know you're still breathing. Jack's fight was about him standing up for a mentally retarded girl with glasses. So in spite of the fact that his father is pretending to be a criminal, you must have done something right. The sprinkler is still busted. The lawn is going to die. It's on you. Don't bother calling.

Beep.

I deleted them all.

Suddenly Timmy turned and said, "They're coming."

I turned my phone off and stuffed it into a pocket. I stuck the gun under my leg and lit another cigarette.

Timmy coughed quietly into one of his fists. The calm bastard.

I heard two cars and a bike. The bike, coughing, fired down. The doors of the cars slammed shut. Footsteps in the gravel. Knock, knock, knock. Timmy opened the door and stepped aside.

I didn't get up.

Teddy waddled in first, his oxygen tank in tow. He had an awkward time moving up the trailer's narrow steps and getting through the small door. His eyes were serious-looking. He hugged Timmy and noisily kissed him on both cheeks.

Rudy came in second. His face was red and his eyes were swollen. He'd been crying—he'd really loved Pops. He hugged Timmy and held on to his sleeves a little too long. The guy was contradiction incarnate: an HA bruiser reduced to tears.

Bobby was next. Still wearing his shades. He hugged Timmy and kissed him on both cheeks. Next he stepped over to me and I got up, careful not to let the gun under my leg fall to the floor. My body obscured it. He gave me a big hug too.

Joby came in last. He hugged and kissed Timmy and then he hugged me. I sat back down.

We were six men—most of us quite large—in the living room of a single-wide trailer. The guys smelled of beer. I smelled of cigarettes. Teddy smelled of Devon, who smelled of cheap concealing powder and pussy. Put together, we smelled like the Pinion Pines strip club.

Teddy sat down and lit a long, thin, brown cigarette. Timmy closed the door and stood behind everyone. Rudy vigorously rubbed the top of his shaved head, while Bobby rocked back and forth on his heels. Joby was stock-still.

Teddy took a drag and exhaled through his nose. Smoke filled and surrounded the oxygen tubes that jutted from his nostrils. He said nothing, but he nodded curtly, signifying that he wanted to know what was up.

I couldn't believe it, but they were scared. I felt a flash of euphoria. Adrenaline and the threat of death concealed it.

I picked up the FedEx box from the floor and placed it on the table between Teddy and me. Joby leaned in and picked it up.

I told them Pops's story, of how he was eager to prove himself and desperate to erase all the ball-busting he'd endured. I told them how he'd tried to take care of the Mongol on his own before we got down there, of how he got shot in a Mexican cantina. I told them how we buried his body with a bottle of Jack and a handwritten note that read, *Pops, AFFA, Angels Forever, Forever Angels, we love you.* I told them how Timmy and I waited for the Mongol bitch to return to his crappy motel room the next night. I told them how we took care of business: how we whispered the old Solo motto, Jesus Hates a Pussy, and then knocked on the guy's door; how he opened it, fully dressed, Mongol cut and all, demanding, *"Qué* fucking *es?"*; how we beat him unconscious with my bat; how we broke his arms and knees like chicken wings; how we taped him up; how we gagged him with a pair of dirty underwear; how we wrapped him in the motel room rug and threw him in the trunk of the Cougar. I told how we drove and drove and drove and opened the trunk and dragged him to a dried wash in the desert. I said we told him the Hells Angels were killing him. I told them how Timmy leaned in and did the honors; how we stole the corpse's cut and drove home, full of rage, revenge, and redemption. I told them how we disposed of the gun, piece by piece, in the Mexican Sonoran desert.

I was Bird, and I could sing.

Everyone listened intently. When I was done I nodded at the package.

"We got proof. We knew we'd have to show something, but we weren't gonna drive over the border with evidence of a murder in the trunk, so we sent that box up from Mexican Nogales."

Everyone remained quiet. Teddy looked at me with a lazy, intense stare, his head cocked slightly to one side. He'd finished smoking. My cigarette was down to a hot nub. I mashed it out and lit another. Joby opened the box.

"Wow!"

The room was so small that no one could see around Joby's back. Bobby jockeyed to get a look. "Well, what is it?"

"It's a Mongol cut."

Joby turned. He held the vest by the shoulders. He huffed incredulously and shook his head. He turned the jacket around so everyone could get a better look. There it was: a Mongols top rocker, a California bottom rocker, the cartoonish center patch of the ponytailed Mongol rider on his chopper. The leather showed its wear—it was encrusted with sand and salt, grease and grit. And there was blood all over it, thickest around the neck and over the shoulders. Little streams of blood had dried all the way down to the hemline, front and back.

Teddy took three quick stabs off the tank. For a brief moment he was visibly nervous. There was no turning back. He knew that everyone in that small room was a murderer, an accomplice, or both. He stood and joined the group huddled around the jacket. I knew then that we were in control. I'd planted a seed of uncertainty, and it had blossomed into fear. Timmy and I looked at each other somberly, but I wanted to scream YES! and pump my fist at him.

Maybe I wouldn't die after all.

"There's pictures, too."

Joby reached into the box again. He pulled out an envelope, opened it, and removed a thin stack of photographs.

"They're digital. I downloaded them onto a flash card and printed them on a portable printer while we were down there. Those are the only copies. We burned the printer and the flash card."

The photos showed a graying white male laying facedown in a small ditch, his torso twisted in an uncomfortable position, his wrists taped behind his back and his ankles taped together. A hairy flap of skin opened at the back of his head. In the sand above his shoulder was a stain of blood and a pile of brains. Blood droplets had splattered into the sand and dirt, making small, dark constellations. His blue jeans were dotted with purple, quarter-sized splotches. His hands were limp.

Joby passed the Mongol cut to Bobby. Bobby inspected it and passed it to Teddy. Rudy watched the vest move around the room with contempt in his eyes.

When the pictures made their way into Rudy's hands, he pointed at the bloody pile and asked, "Those his brains?"

Timmy stepped in and said, "Don't know. I hit him point-blank. His head was all swollen like a balloon. He looked real stupid. When I shot him it made a popping sound like you dropped a bagful of water. Then it hissed."

Rudy chuckled and said, "Looks like grape jelly."

Joby said with an air of authority, "Those ain't his brains, Rudy. That's blood that coagulated when Bird hit him upside the head with his bat. Couldn't get out until he got popped."

"Oh," Rudy said.

Teddy turned around, breathing with effort. He sat down. I hadn't moved. I thought, They'll have to come to me now.

Teddy placed his terrifying hands palm-down on the table between us. They were fat and sun-baked, freckled with age. His fingers were covered with Death Head rings commemorating Hells Angels anniversaries. Some had been there for decades and were now simply a part of his hand.

He looked me dead in the eye and continued to say nothing. The room was silent. Everyone was staged up behind him, and Timmy was staged up behind them. If for some reason I'd misconstrued their cues and now they were going to try to pop us, my biggest worry was that Timmy and I would shoot each other from opposite ends of the trailer.

I put my hands on the table and laced my fingers together. My hands weren't fat like Teddy's. I kicked my feet out to the side, revealing that I was wearing flip-flops. Teddy didn't seem to notice. I'd worn them for him as a little fuck-you.

He reached up and pulled the tubes out of his nose. A thin bead of snot attached the tube to his nostril like a spider's web. He wiped it away with the back of his hand.

His voice was as steady as a rock. He said, "I don't like it when we lose one of our own."

I said, "Pops was one of my best friends. A true warrior."

"It's like when a parent loses a child." Teddy looked longingly at the surface of the table. We were silent for several moments.

He looked back into my eyes. "But ya did what it takes. Sometimes a Hells Angel has to fight and kill. We'll remember Pops as a hero, hang his cut on the wall. After we patch it, of course."

"That's great, but what about Timmy and me?"

"What about ya?"

"We took care of business, just like you always say. That Mongol was a bitch and he died like a bitch, courtesy of us. Courtesy of you, the Hells Angels."

"Bird, ya weren't listening. I said, 'Sometimes a Hells Angel has to fight and kill.' Congratulations, brothers. Ya Hells Angels now."

He smiled and reached across the table, grabbing the back of my neck with his meaty hands.

That was it.

We'd done the impossible. I felt like Lewis and Clark when they laid eyes on the Pacific, or Neil Armstrong when his boot hit moon dirt. I did what I had to do. I took care of business.

That's what a Hells Angel does.

WE WENT BACK to the Pinion Pines to celebrate, but since Pops was dead, it wasn't much of a celebration. Bobby cleared a corner of the club and ordered the bouncer, the bartender, and the manager not to let anyone near us. We got a round of shots. Even Joby and Bobby joined the toast. I said, "To Pops. At least he died in a bar." That drew a few smiles. We threw back and sat around. Teddy huddled us together and said we'd have to burn the evidence that night. He said with quiet terror, "No one fucking knows about this." He finished his drink and then he whispered, "We're gonna do what we can to get ya stitched up, but be patient."

I blurted, "Teddy—what do you mean, 'Be patient'?"

"Yeah, what the fuck do you mean?" asked Timmy.

"Look, ya full-up as far as me or any these guys is concerned. But we gotta run shit by the board, we can't act alone. Ya know how it is. We got rules."

Joby said, "Don't worry. I'll leave town tomorrow to lobby for you guys. I'll hit Vegas, Berdoo, Dago, San Fernando, Oakland, and call all the guys around here. I told Sonny what you were up to and he said he hoped you kill that motherfucker. So don't worry, you won't have any problems."

I said, "The fuck we won't. We did this because it had to be done, I don't give a shit about that Mongol, but I also did it to get in, and now that Pops is gone, I *really* want in." I was genuinely pissed. I could see everything drifting away as the guys hedged their promises. "I want my fucking patch."

Timmy growled, "I do too. We earned them."

Bobby put an arm around me and said, "Let's go outside." We did. He said, "Go put your phone in the truck," pointing at the pickup. I did. He led me to a secluded corner of the parking lot. "Calm down, Bird. You've had a rough couple days." He lit a cigarette and talked again about the murder he'd supposedly committed for his club. "When I did mine I was fucking jacked. He was a rat—I told you that—he'd put away some old-timers and I took it upon myself to even the score—but man, I was jacked." He chuckled. "Cruising down the road to where I was gonna meet the guy, pumping that Metallica song, 'Nothing Else Matters.'" He paused, lost in blood-thick memories. "Anyway, I did it and it took months for me to get my Filthy Few tab. Months. Even though it was in the paper the next day. Point is, you can't rush these things. Don't worry. You're gonna get your shit. We gotta see how it shakes down, is all."

"I'll be damned if I have to wait six months."

"We gotta see what happens. You know the feds, ATF, the Department of Public Safety, all those fucks are watching us. We give you a patch tonight, you roll out in it tomorrow, and they're gonna want to know what the fuck. We can't have that kind of attention." I didn't say anything. I lit another cigarette. "Look, even if the whole West Coast—even if the whole U.S.—wanted to vote you in, we might get overruled by the World Council. Those Euro fuckers been railing against us for years, and they don't always look lightly on fast patches. We gotta stay cool. *You* gotta stay cool."

"Fuck that, Bobby."

"Just be patient."

"Fuck that." I said the words with less conviction. Why was Bobby telling me this? To comfort me? To impress me? We'd been trying to pin this murder on him since he 'fessed up to it back in Vegas, but we'd never found an unsolved case that met the requirements. That didn't mean it wasn't true, but I couldn't help wondering—was Bobby Reinstra full of shit?

I decided that it didn't matter. Bobby put his hand on my shoulder and we went back inside. He guided me to the bar and I sat down and pounded a neat Jack Daniel's. I felt defeated. I'd gone from confidence to fear to euphoria to disappointment to nausea in less than two hours. These guys made me sick. I felt like yelling, "HYPOCRITE!" in Bobby's face. There I was, doing what I was supposed to do as a Hells Angel, and instead of getting patched—which, having all but signed off on my family and disobeyed Slats, was all that mattered to me—I was getting jacked up by politics. I felt like asking Bobby, "What are we, outlaws or lawyers, because I know a lot about both." I felt like screaming, "Fuck the cops, and fuck the World Council, and fuck the other charters!" I realized in that single moment that the brotherhood the Hells Angels claimed to be a part of was nothing more than a support group for misunderstood loners held together by hate and money. Everything revolved around money-hustling and protecting the club against those we hated. We hated all the other clubs, the public, the police. We hated work, our wives, our girlfriends, our kids. Occasionally we hated ourselves. We hated everyone that wasn't a Hells Angel, and even then we often hated each other. I say 'we,' because these were the people and things that I had come to hate too.

I'd been undercover for almost two years as Jay "Bird" Davis. That whole time I'd thought I was the one in control, I was the one making myself into a Hells Angel. I'd thought I was the one infiltrating them.

I had it backward. They were the ones who had infiltrated me.

We were all hypocrites.

Teddy lumbered up behind us and said, "C'mon. Let's get the fuck outta here."

WE RODE TO the clubhouse for another drink. As Rudy handed out beers, Joby put something over my shoulders. It was a cut—it was *his* cut. He draped it over me like I was a prince. I looked at him. He said apologetically, "Bird, you're in, man. You're a Hells Angel. Wear this one till you get yours." He looked at Timmy. "Teddy's got a spare that'll fit you."

I took the vest off, turned to Joby, and handed it to him. "Fuck that, Joby. I'm not wearing another man's cut." Timmy walked up to us. I said, "We came through the front door and I'll be damned if I go out the back to get my shit. I'll take my Death Head when it's mine. No offense, but I earned it and I don't intend to share." Joby stepped back, looking at me hard. He said OK. He knew I was right. They all did. HA cuts are not transferable.

As Joby put his cut back on, Teddy and Bobby started to grill us on how we'd handled the evidence. Joby went to fetch a fifty-gallon steel drum from behind the house. Bobby wanted to know what we'd done with the clothes we did it in. I said we'd burned them on-site. Bobby said good, you guys are thinking like us. My mood was in constant flux. I said, "Dude, we *are* like you," but I said it lightly. He laughed. Joby came up with the drum and two pairs of hedge clippers. Teddy told us to cut the Mongol cut into little strips and put them in the drum.

I was still pissed. I said, "Fuck this. I'll burn this shit, but I'm not waiting for my patch." No one said anything to that.

Timmy sheared the vest in half and we cut it up. Bobby and Teddy watched. Joby paced, went inside for a while, and then came out. He told us he'd called Bad Bob and Sonny. Bad Bob couldn't believe what had happened to Pops, but was glad Timmy and I were back in one piece.

When we were done with the cut, Joby covered the drum, hauled it into the bed of his truck, and strapped it into place. He got in his truck and started it up. Teddy pulled Timmy and me close to him. He looked back and forth at our faces. His smile was the biggest I'd seen, his eyes were sad. He said solemnly, "Welcome to the family, brothers." We each hugged him and climbed into Joby's pickup.

I sat in the back. Joby drove into the hills around Chino Valley. The cover team, who had been listening and following us around, lost us. I knew, as we went higher and higher on unpaved roads, that Timmy and I were alone with Joby Walters, himself a Filthy Few tab-wearer. The bumps of the road rocked me into an uneasy sleep. I was bone-tired. I thought, Maybe now I'll die. I thought, Maybe this is what Teddy had in mind, have Joby take us and the evidence out to the hills, out to where Jesus lost his sandals, and get rid of us, nice and quiet. After all, weren't we a kind of evidence too? It seemed fitting. I'd abandoned Jay Dobyns and I was tired of being Bird. I thought, Wouldn't it be nice never to wake up again?

But I did. The truck skidded to a dusty halt and my eyes popped open. Joby said, "We're here." We were in the clearing of an aspen grove. One of Joby's campsites. We got out. I rubbed my face while Timmy helped Joby with the drum. Joby told me to get the jug of gas out of the truck. I brought it over and handed it to him. He doused the contents of the barrel and told me to light it up. I clicked my Zippo, lit a twig, and threw it in. The fire went right up. Joby's long face turned orange. He clicked his tongue like the plains farmer he'd always reminded me of, his buckteeth sticking out. I smiled, thinking of the first time I'd seen him, at the Laughlin Harrah's, the night of the riot so many months ago. The Nestlé Quik Rabbit.

Nasty old rabbit.

I said, "Sorry we ditched that little pistol you gave us, Job."

"No worries."

"Guess you'll just have to look at it as your contribution to a dead Mongol."

"I'd do it again in a heartbeat. Best two hundred bucks I ever spent."

"Good."

I looked up. There was a hole in the stand of trees; there were plenty of stars in the sky. Little orange sparks rose up to meet them. The fire smelled like hamburgers and lamb chops. No one spoke for a long time.

Finally, as the last shred of the Mongol cut drifted into the night sky, Joby said, "Jesus Hates a Pussy—Pops."

Timmy and I repeated, "Jesus Hates a Pussy."

I meant it. Joby did too. He loved Pops, and he loved us. I knew only then that Joby wasn't going to kill me. But I also believed that Jay Dobyns was dead.

Only Bird was left standing.

39 THE BUST

BUT I WAS no Angel. The Mongol murder was not as simple as it appeared. I'd lied, and what a lie it was. I'd reached the pinnacle of my abilities: Deception had become my stock-in-trade. Like water that seeps into a crack and later freezes, expanding the crack into a fissure, deception had found the cracks in my character and exposed them. I felt like a soldier who'd become accustomed to killing—who even looked forward to it. Deceiving people had, at the beginning of my career, made me uneasy, but by the time I'd been accepted by the Hells Angels, my capacity to deceive defined who and what I was. I didn't think of myself as a liar—lying was simply what I did to do my job well. Nevertheless, I was a champion liar. I not only lied to my suspects, but I lied to everyone I knew, including myself. I'd been undercover for too long, and my experiences had altered me in some basic and dark ways.

One thing was true, however: As Joby drove us into the hills, I expected, even wanted, to die. But it was not true that I'd killed. In the end, getting a bullet would have been too easy, and delivering one much too problematic.

The fire at Joby's camp had smelled like lamb chops for good reason.

The blood, skin, and brains that spattered the Mongol's clothes had belonged to a lamb, not a man. While my loss of conscience had not been fun, the murder had been a game.

Our Mongol, who wore a genuine cut seized in another ATF case, had been played by Department of Public Safety detective Shawn Wood. He'd lain motionless in a ditch in the blazing sun while Jerry Laird, a Phoenix homicide dick, squirted blood and scattered brains over his head and torso. There he stayed while Timmy and I took pictures of each other pretending to kill him. Then he got up and we took trophy shots—me, Timmy, Woody, JJ—for posterity. Then we shot Pops's cut—Pops was alive, off the case for good, catching up with his little girls back home—and piled into the truck, heading to a bar for Miller Time. All this took place about twenty miles outside of Phoenix.

Following the presentation and destruction of the evidence, there were a lot of phone calls between me and Bad Bob and Teddy and Bobby and Joby and Smitty. On the thirtieth, Timmy, JJ, and I went to Skull Valley to talk things over. Teddy and the others weren't happy, but they weren't very upset, either. We were told that we weren't going to get patched, even though the local shot-callers had sided with us. The problem went back to Laughlin—it felt like all my problems went back to Laughlin—when some Angels had been fast-patched after the riot. This pissed off the European Angels. Those guys were over there fighting their rivals with RPGs, blowing up entire clubhouses, and none of them got patched early. We were told that Europe simply outnumbered the United States and none of our guys wanted to step on their European counterparts' toes. We were told that it looked good for getting made at the Laconia World Run, just two months out, but that there was no guarantee; otherwise, we had nine months to go. Teddy said it didn't matter to him—from then on Skull Valley and the rest of Arizona—Smitty, Bad Bob, Sonny, everyone—would consider us patches. He reiterated that, in his eyes, since we'd acted like Hells Angels, we *were* Hells Angels. He said, "Bird, we're a club of rules and bylaws. You're a Hells Angel and we'll make it official by everyone in Laconia."

I knew in that instant that the case was over. I'd managed to convince the ATF bosses of the value of running as a full patch, but without that status guaranteed, we wouldn't get the full go-ahead. Our bosses wouldn't wait for Laconia, let alone nine months. I thought, best case, that we had a month left.

But we didn't. In the weeks leading up to the murder ruse, Slats had told our bosses how much continuing the case would cost. They'd flipped out, told him to shut it down. Slats started the process of issuing warrants, which included testifying before a federal grand jury. He got his indictments. The counts included drug trafficking, trafficking in stolen property, RICO conspiracy, and innumerable felons in possession of a firearm. Slats knew the case had a hard-out since early June. He didn't tell me because he knew that as long as the case was still technically alive, there was nothing he could do to stop me from doing whatever I wanted. Like him, I was just too bullheaded.

But immediately after the murder ruse I was ignorant of all that. It was pointless, but we hung out at Skull Valley for a while on the thirtieth after we'd been told we'd have to wait for our Death Heads. I didn't want to give up. I knew that one of these days I'd be hanging out with the guys for the last time, and while I wouldn't miss the Hells Angels much, I'd miss Timmy and Pops and JJ and the weird life that we'd come to share. It was all I knew. I'd forgotten where I'd come from, and I wasn't sure I could go back even if I wanted to. I wouldn't let go of Bird so easily.

Bobby pulled me aside and told me more about his murder. Joby joined us and said he knew all about Bobby's work. He said that if Bobby ever went down, then Joby would make public the things that Bobby had done. Bobby said, "Yeah, can't let that shit out now or I'll go away for life, you know?"

After a while we got ready to leave. As I walked out, Bobby told me he had a couple of AK-47s he wanted me to move for him. I told him no problem, I was still Bird, wasn't I? He smiled, barely.

I'd never see any of the Skull Valley guys again.

We randomly hooked up with Duane "Crow" Williams, the old, senile Mesa Angel who used to call me Pruno, on that same day down in Phoenix. We went to his house and didn't stay for long. He was a nonsensical mess. When I got to the Carroll Street undercover house later that night, I wrote the notes that Slats would ultimately translate into the lines of the last Black Biscuit Report of Incident:

> At approximately 4:00 p.m., the Operatives arrived at the residence of Duane Williams, AKA "Crow," at ▮▮▮▮▮▮. Present at this location was a Dodge pickup truck bearing Arizona handicap license plate ▮▮▮▮▮▮.

During this contact Williams advised the Operatives of, but not limited to, the following:

- That we (HAMC) don't know who killed Hoover;
- That we think we know who killed Hoover;
- That we should just start killing the people who we think killed Hoover;
- That someone is going to have to die for the murder of Hoover.

This investigation is continuing.

THERE WAS A Fourth of July party at Skull Valley that we didn't show up for. We didn't bother telling them we wouldn't be there. We disappeared on July 1. I heard later, from suspect interviews, that our absence was a hot topic. Most thought we'd gotten called on a collection, or had gone to Mexico on business, but they couldn't be sure. It was very unlike us not to stay in touch.

Slats had ordered all of us home. He'd gotten us all four weeks off, paid, and he intended for us to use it. It was important that we did, he said. I told him we still had work to do. He said, "No, you don't. Your families need you much more than I do." He said it to all of us, but he was looking at me. "All right? We've had our differences, and you've done a hell of a job. But this phase is over." I followed his orders. On July 2, I headed home until after the Fourth, at which time I'd go back to Phoenix to help with the bust. Gwen was gone; she'd taken the kids on a driving tour back East. As I'd predicted, I was alone. No safe haven. No Hells Angels. No partners. No family. No peace. I had nothing and I deserved nothing.

Slats's closing of the case felt like a complete betrayal. But he knew what he was doing. It's now my belief that, from beginning to end, Slats served as Black Biscuit's moral compass—God knows I didn't—and acted as our collective conscience. It turns out that he really *was* dealing with the full 100 percent of the case, and I wasn't. Whatever he may have wanted for selfish reasons, he knew that the case had to end when it did. He was able to make the decision I couldn't.

By ending the case, Slats forced us all to return to ourselves before it was too late, before there'd be nothing to return to. He was, more than

I or anyone else, looking out for his friend Jay Dobyns, who'd gone missing.

Black Biscuit's search warrants were executed on July 8. Staci, Bobby's girlfriend, called after we started knocking the Angels down and left a frantic message, saying, "Bird, it's Staci. I don't know where you are, but wherever it is, stay there. They're coming for the guys. It looks like they're coming for *all* the guys. I don't know what the fuck's going on. Hopefully I'll see you soon . . ."

She wouldn't.

What was going on was predawn SRT and SWAT raids, conducted in Arizona, Nevada, California, Washington, and Colorado. The total haul was impressive. More than 1,600 pieces of evidence were collected; over 650 guns, eighty of which were machine guns, sawed-off shotguns, and other prohibited weapons; dozens of silencers; explosives, including pipe bombs, napalm, blasting caps, dynamite, and grenades; and over 30,000 rounds of live ammunition. The drug haul, mostly meth or meth-related, was not huge, but it was significant. We also seized over $50,000 in U.S. currency. We served search-and-arrest warrants on fifty defendants, two of whom were death-penalty candidates. Later we'd charge sixteen of them, including Joby, Smitty, Dennis, Bad Bob, Teddy, and Bobby, with RICO conspiracy violations. Paul Eischeid and Kevin Augustiniak would be charged with the murder of Cynthia Garcia. A few more faced parole violations and were looking at immediate time. One of these was Dan Danza, who decided he'd had enough. He couldn't be a member of a club that he felt no longer lived up to its reputation. He also wanted his teenage boys to have a shot at a better future. He agreed to work with the police. No one else cooperated. The rest awaited trial.

Owing to lack of evidence, Ralph "Sonny" Barger was left untouched.

EPILOGUE

LATE IN THE summer of 2004, JJ and I assisted Slats by listening to surveillance material. The work was tedious and mind-numbing, but I remember one recording from mid-May 2003. I recognized the voices of Bobby, Teddy, and Joby, who were having a general conversation about how great it was to be Hells Angels. But there was a fourth voice I couldn't place. He was a live wire, and his words hardly made sense. I hit Pause, passed my headphones to JJ, and played the conversation for her. After listening for a minute I hit Stop and asked, "Who the fuck is that asshole?"

She put her hands in her lap and said, "You don't know?"

"No."

She smiled slightly and said, "That's you, Jay."

It was a revelation.

That night I wrote an e-mail to everyone on the task force, apologizing for being Bird. I'd let our mission get the better of me, and I'd mistaken their duty for their support.

It was at that moment that I started to realize all that I'd wrought. My damage had gone far beyond my co-workers. I knew I'd accomplished what was perceived to be an impossible task—even Sonny Barger boasted that his club would never be infiltrated by law enforcement. But I was naïve. I knew I'd damaged my family, my peers, and my friends, but in the end I thought that, precisely because my task was perceived as impossible, I'd have their ultimate support. I was flat-out wrong. The night I reached the pinnacle—when Joby draped a cut over my shoulders and I refused it—should have been the night that everyone I knew to be on my side would be celebrating. But instead of being there to back me up they were distant and injured, pleading for me to return to the man I'd once been. I felt like I'd dropped a payload of napalm on them. The night I got what I'd wanted so badly was not a night of celebration. Instead, it was the loneliest night of my life.

By the summer of 2004 the Hells Angels had issued two death threats against my family and me. Over the following years they would issue three more. The things they claimed to want to do to us weren't pretty, and they put me on edge. The nightmare of Bobby and Teddy pulling out my tongue recurred often. When the boys came to visit me, there was nothing I could do but wake up, go to the bathroom, and splash water on my face.

I'd inherited the Hells Angels' deep paranoia. I perceived threats everywhere. A man sitting in a car that was parked too long on our corner became a biker spy. Animals in our backyard became a Hells Angels hit squad. More than once I jumped out of bed, grabbed my shotgun, and cleared the house and yard in my underwear.

ATF didn't take the threats seriously. Feeling unsafe and abandoned by my employer, I moved my family around the West Coast. Running was fruitless. My paranoia grew, and was only made worse by ATF's refusal to recognize what I knew was a mortal situation. They belittled my concerns and downplayed my accomplishments. I began to engage ATF in a drawn-out battle for compensations—to my bank account, my reputation, and my psyche. It was a dreary business, both heartbreaking and eye-opening. I'd expected to be betrayed by the Hells Angels, but not by the people I'd worked so incredibly hard for.

Another thing I didn't expect was for the Black Biscuit case ultimately to fail.

Sadly, disputes over evidence and tensions between ATF and the U.S. attorneys killed our case. Most of the serious charges were dismissed in early 2006, and as a result, hardly any of the guys who were charged with RICO violations saw the inside of a courtroom. A few, such as Smitty, Joby, and Pete, were still prosecutable for their actions at Laughlin, but aside from the guns and contraband we'd taken off the street, it felt as though most of our work had been for nothing. Sure, we'd sent several guys away for short sentences and forced many into probation, but these accomplishments were nothing compared to the backbreaking case we'd envisioned leveling against the Hells Angels.

Those were dark days. The press and the defense attorneys, not privy to the turf battles fought between the case agents and the prosecutors, hung the blame on the undercover operation. We were called rogue actors, reckless and impulsive, and the Hells Angels' legal representation publicly yoked us, confident the case would never go before a jury. Blaming undercovers is the easiest course in these situations. Sometimes it's the truth, but in our case it was a lie. The worst part for me was that, precisely because neither ATF nor the prosecutors revealed the full truth, I couldn't defend myself. My real name traveled through the papers as my unlikely story was told, and to some I became a pariah. Black Biscuit's failure became my own, and thus one of my greatest fears—failure—was realized.

It was ironic that some of my best undercover work had sealed my fate. My cover was blown and I'd never again be able to work the streets. I was so tired in those days—from fighting with Slats and Gwen, the Hells Angels and ATF—that I didn't really care about my blown cover, but it had some interesting consequences. My friends and extended family suddenly knew what I'd been doing my whole life, and they wanted to know everything about it. Principally, they wanted to know the answers to two questions: Was it worth it, and would I do it again?

I'm glad they asked me. I was forced to look in the mirror and assess who I was and what I'd done. Only recently have I been able to offer honest answers. Being an undercover agent had become more than what I did for living—it was what I'd become. This had to change.

In the beginning I thought of the Black Biscuit case as a classic Good-versus-Evil struggle. I knew the brutality and intimidation brought by the Hells Angels was real. Violence was their way of life. The pursuit of preventing violence was a way of life for some ATF agents like Joe Slatalla and me. Our team of elite investigators was an ideal adversary to the Hells Angels, and everyone on the task force was proud to throw themselves into taking down such an evil organization.

But as we've seen, things aren't always so cut-and-dried. I went in deep and realized that the Hells Angels weren't all bad—and I wasn't all good.

As I became Bird and abandoned Jay Dobyns, I dived headfirst into a sea of lies. The Angels will point out that all I did was lie to them, and although that is mostly true, I can say with a clear conscience that I didn't cheat them. I didn't put guns or drugs in their hands and I didn't force them to commit or confess crimes. The world had enough *real* bad guys—I didn't have to go around inventing them.

The Angels had a lot to say about me in the aftermath of the case, very little of it good. The odd Angel gave us respect, saying we'd gamed them fair and square, which I believe we had. According to his initial interviews, Joby refused to believe I was a cop unless I sat down with him and said the words myself. Bad Bob Johnston, after receiving a plea-bargained probation, told the press that he didn't agree with our tactics, but he grudgingly acknowledged that we were very good at what we did. Dan Danza, after turning informant, said he thought *we* were the real tough guys for doing what we did. He might not have agreed with the law, but he saw the adrenaline-fueled logic in being an undercover cop. I still regard Danza as one of the toughest guys I've ever met, and his compliments remain some of the highest I've ever received from anybody.

But mostly the Angels downplayed our successes. They raged that Timmy and I had never become actual Hells Angels. They circled the wagons, protecting the murderers and criminals we exposed. Bobby Reinstra now maintains that in the immediate aftermath of the Mongol murder ruse, he and Teddy became convinced we were cops. I don't believe him, but I guess hindsight's always 20/20. In the end, the Angels got it both ways. They claimed the high ground while never relinquishing the low, maintaining their coveted and hard-fought outlaw status while beating the law. They remained misunderstood American rebels while we, who stood and fought for order and decency, were cast as overzealous cops who'd thrown all of our cautions and ethics to the wind. In nearly every respect they won.

For two solid years the side of my personality known as Bird had developed into my rock and stone. He was the one I could always count on. But by belittling him, the Hells Angels took this accomplishment away from me too.

As I said, dark days. I turned to the only things I had left: God, friends, and family. I didn't deserve their allegiance, and why they hadn't abandoned me I'll never know. But there they were. I turned to them and saw with new eyes what was good in my life. I realized that only by the grace of God did I have these good things. I came to accept that whatever had been bad in my life was done by my own hand. It wasn't my job, it wasn't ATF, and it wasn't the Hells Angels that had transformed me into the worst version of myself. It was I alone who had done that.

I don't know when I realized these things, but when I did, everything changed.

I remember waking up one day no longer concerned with death or retaliation. If the Hells Angels wanted to do something bad to me, there was little I could do but be ready. If ATF wanted to treat me as an outcast, all I could do was stubbornly refuse. In my life I'd endured a bullet through the chest and countless beat-downs; I'd held ticking time bombs and had dozens of guns pointed at my head; I'd gone undercover with murderers and rapists and larcenists, spending a good portion of my life with society's most despicable elements. It had been an odd but full life. That day I realized that in spite of its bureaucracy, I loved ATF and its noble mission. I loved my fellow agents for their unacknowledged and selfless sacrifices. I realized that my long life of strange experiences had been genuinely wonderful and satisfying.

I woke up that day wanting to trade some of my righteousness for a patch of peace. This, too, was a revelation. My sense of determination—some might call it my arrogance—had allowed me to confront challenges that other people simply couldn't or wouldn't. I realized that I was proud of the chip I carried on my shoulder. I began to accept myself for who I was. Bird no longer defined me, but he lived inside me; he'll never again be the main player, but he remains a dear part of who I am.

I realized the thing that had been most dear to me: the honor and privilege of facing my challenges alongside the most courageous law enforcement officers and family members one could ever imagine or hope for.

With all my love and respect to those who've guided me, encouraged me, accepted me, and stood with me—to call you my friends or family is an understatement. You're much more.

You're my heroes.

Was it worth it? Would I do it again?

If I could have looked into the future and known the life I now enjoy . . .

ABSOLUTELY, YES.

Where Are They Now?

Law Enforcement

Carlos Canino joined ATF's management team and is running an investigative group for the bureau.

Greg "Sugarbear" Cowan followed in the footsteps of Joe Slatalla, and has become one of ATF's premier case agents.

Gayland Hammack retired with honors from LVMPD and currently owns and runs a law-enforcement training business.

Rudy Kramer is in the Federal Witness Protection Program, whereabouts unknown.

Billy "Timmy" Long returned to duty and proudly serves with the Phoenix Police Department.

Jenna "JJ" Maguire continues to work on all types of investigations and has developed into one of ATF's most highly regarded agents.

Pops filed a lawsuit against ATF alleging inadequate compensation and recognition for his work on Black Biscuit. He broke ties with the agency, and his whereabouts are unknown.

Joe "Slats" Slatalla has a mentorship role within ATF, guiding complex investigations and training new case agents. Slatalla is considered the country's premier expert on electronic and wiretap investigations.

Shawn Wood is considered one of the Southwest's top experts on gangs, with an emphasis on OMGs.

Hells Angels and Associates

Robert Abraham pled guilty to dealing firearms without a license and was sentenced to twenty-four months' incarceration with thirty-six months' supervised release.

Kevin Augustiniak was incarcerated on murder charges and is awaiting trial. He remains a member of the Hells Angels, Mesa charter.

Ralph Hubert "Sonny" Barger maintains active membership with the Cave Creek charter. He is heavily involved in promoting his books and various Hollywood film projects. Sonny is still considered the Godfather of the Hells Angels, and he remains the living icon of biker culture.

Doug Dam pled guilty to being a felon in possession of a firearm and was sentenced to eighty-four months' incarceration. He remains a member of the Hells Angels, charter unknown.

Dennis "Chef-Boy-Ar-Dee" Denbesten pled guilty to being a felon in possession of a firearm and was sentenced to seventy months' incarceration.

Paul Eischeid is a fugitive from murder charges. He has been featured on the *America's Most Wanted* television show and placed on the U.S. Marshals' "15 Most Wanted" list. He remains a member of the Hells Angels, charter unknown.

Tim Holt pled guilty to possession of prohibited weapons and was sentenced to twenty-seven months' incarceration with thirty-six months' supervised release.

Rudy Jaime pled guilty to armed narcotics trafficking and was sentenced to five years' incarceration. He remains a member of the Hells Angels, charter unknown.

Robert "Bad Bob" Johnston pled guilty to misprision of a felony and was sentenced to fourteen months' probation. After being one of the Hells Angels' most powerful and respected leaders, Johnston was conveniently blamed by his "brothers" as the lone scapegoat responsible for our infiltration. He was unceremoniously removed from the club.

Craig "Fang" Kelly's charges were dismissed with prejudice and cannot be refiled. He remains president of the Hells Angels, Tucson charter.

Michael "Mesa Mike" Kramer is in the Federal Witness Protection Program, whereabouts unknown.

Robert "Mac" McKay pled guilty to threats against a federal agent and was sentenced to time served (seventeen months). Now released, McKay is currently living in Tucson, operating his tattoo parlor, and remains a member of the Hells Angels, Tucson charter.

Sean McManama pled guilty to possession of prohibited weapons and was sentenced to twenty-four months' incarceration with thirty-six months' supervised release.

Robert "Chico" Mora was convicted of felon in possession of body armor and sentenced to eighteen months' incarceration. He remains a member of the Hells Angels, Phoenix charter.

Bobby Reinstra's charges were dismissed with prejudice and cannot be refiled. He is now a member of the Hells Angels Cave Creek charter, and a gang spokesman against the Operation Black Biscuit investigation.

Calvin "Casino Cal" Schaefer pled guilty to armed narcotics trafficking and was sentenced to sixty months' incarceration. He remains a member of the Hells Angels, Mesa charter.

Donald "Smitty" Smith's charges were dismissed with prejudice and cannot be refiled. He remains a member of the Hells Angels, Arizona Nomads charter.

Lydia Smith is still married to Smitty and running a beauty shop in Bullhead City.

Teddy Toth pled guilty to tampering with a witness and was sentenced to twelve months' probation. He is now a member of the Hells Angels, Cave Creek charter.

Scott Varvil pled guilty to possession of prohibited weapons and was sentenced to twenty-four months' incarceration with thirty-six months' supervised release.

George "Joby" Walters was a fugitive from justice for over four years. Walters turned himself in to authorities in February 2008, and was sentenced to six months' incarceration for absconding justice. His RICO and VCAR charges were dismissed. Walters remains a member of the Hells Angels, charter unknown.

Henry "Hank" Watkins's charges were dismissed with prejudice and cannot be refiled. He left the club in good standing before the conclusion of Operation Black Biscuit.

Family

Dale Dobyns displayed great bravery in the face of personal threats, and remains an inspiration to her father. Dale aspires to work in fashion, art, and design.

Gwen Dobyns is still the "patriarch" of her family. Still married to Jay, she is an active mother and a supportive wife.

Jack Dobyns is still Jay's "rock," following in his father's footsteps as a determined, overachieving, excellence-or-nothing student and athlete.

Jay Dobyns lives a contented and peaceful life devoted to God, family, friends, health, and hobbies. His motorcycle sits parked in a garage, covered with a dusty sheet, never ridden.

Author's Note

No Angel was never intended to be an investigative report, legal brief, or historical document. The best classification for this book would likely be "memoir," but after having read *No Angel*, you may wonder, "Is this really the way things went down? How did he recall such detail years later?"

This book was a team effort. I wouldn't have been able to produce the book you're holding without the dedication of my writer, Nils Johnson-Shelton. Nils was instrumental in focusing a chaotic and tangled storyline, and he helped grant my words a literary quality they wouldn't have had if I'd written this book on my own. Without him, my story wouldn't be the one you've just read.

My main concern in writing my story was that it be honest. The survival of an undercover operator often depends on one's ability to feel one thing yet bluff another while under the scrutiny of a societal element uniquely paranoid of police. The stories of undercover cops are the stuff of movies, and many of us are portrayed as superheroes. Most of us are; I, unfortunately, was not. As we wrote, I constantly reminded Nils, "I'm not interested in being the knight in shining armor. That wasn't me, and if we tell it that way it'll be a lie." If my book was to be believed as the truth, then my depiction of myself also had to be the truth.

The honest and shameful core that runs through this book details my devolution. As I hurtled from Jay Dobyns toward Bird, I became confused, tormented, and afraid. In writing this book, I wanted to admit my mistakes and atone for some of my sins. I wanted to make a book my children could someday read and maybe understand why I'd done the things I had.

As we wrote, our main obligation was to the story's accuracy, but in the interest of storytelling we did end up taking some liberties. What I consider to be incidental circumstances—things like food, clothing, a background character's physical description, or the weather—were captured to the best of my memory, but where my memory failed, Nils's creative and descriptive ability filled the void.

On rare occasions we took the practical liberty of combining events or conversations. The components of these events and conversations were real, but without the reader's permission to consolidate, this narrative would have filled several volumes.

Dialogue was also sometimes a collaboration of my memory and Nils's creative ability. We limited the number of epithets I used, and severely decreased the number of times I (sadly) said "Dude." I didn't make a habit of listening to taped conversations or reading transcripts as we wrote; instead, I made extensive use of reports that often quoted exact dialogue. I'd lived this story firsthand and then reaffirmed it during trial prep, repeatedly burning its most intimate details into my brain. I know what was said and who said it. This is an important point, because although *No Angel* attributes damning statements to real people, all of the conversations are true to their spirit if not to their letter—and many are true to their letter. All of the events, persons, and alleged crimes that occur in *No Angel* actually happened or existed. As I wrote in the epilogue, "The world had enough *real* bad guys—I didn't have to go around inventing them."

It needs to be stressed that in the absence of a trial by jury, all of the crimes detailed in *No Angel* must remain alleged. However, the evidence and testimony haven't changed since July 8, 2003. Black Biscuit is as prosecutable—and winnable—now as it was then. But while the crimes alleged in my book remain unproven in a court of law, for me they will always be hard, cold, and provable facts.

Jay Anthony Dobyns, February 2008

18 USC section 922(g)(1): This statute states: "It shall be unlawful for any person who has been convicted in any court of a crime punishable by imprisonment for a term exceeding one year to ship or transport in interstate or foreign commerce, or possess in or affecting commerce, any firearm or ammunition; or to receive any firearm or ammunition which has been shipped or transported in interstate or foreign commerce."

81: Euphemism for the Hells Angels, derived from the eighth letter of the alphabet (H) and the first (A).

AFFA: "Angels Forever, Forever Angels."

Altamont: The Altamont Raceway in Altamont, California. This was the site of the infamous 1969 Rolling Stones concert at which the Hells Angels got into a fight with and ultimately killed a concert-goer.

angel dust: Phencyclidine, aka "PCP." Made popular by the Hells Angels in the 1970s, it is sometimes called "Dust of the Angels."

ape hangers: Motorcycle handlebars with grips above the shoulder.

ASAC: Assistant Special Agent in Charge. See also *SAC*, below.

associate: Specific to motorcycle clubs, a person friendly to a club; more generally, a partner, usually in crime.

Berdoo: San Bernardino, California, the location of the first Hells Angels charter in 1948; the official "mother charter" of the Hells Angels.

BHC: Bullhead City, Arizona.

Big Four: The world's four major outlaw motorcycle clubs: Banditos, Hells Angels, Outlaws, and Pagans.

bottom rocker: See *rocker*.

C-4: Military-type plastic high explosives.

cage: A car, truck, or van; any vehicle that contains a person; so called because driving one is like being in a cage.

center patch: The large patch, stitched on the back of a vest between the top and bottom rockers, that depicts the club's insignia, which, in the case of the Hells Angels, is the Death Head. See also *Death Head*, *rocker*, *three-piece patch*.

charter: A local or regional division of a club; aka "chapter."

church: Regularly scheduled charter meetings.

CI: Confidential informant, someone who informs on his or her associates. Often CIs are facing charges of their own and choose to inform in exchange for legal leniency, though sometimes people approach law enforcement to inform of their own free will. See also *rat*, *snitch*.

colors: A biker's vest. See also *cut*, *patch*.

confidential informant: See *CI*.

cut: A biker's vest. See also *colors*, *patch*.

Dago: San Diego, California.

Death Head: The Hells Angels' winged-skull insignia.

dime bag: A $10 bag of marijuana, usually a little under a gram; aka "dime."

dime rock: A $10 rock of methamphetamine or cocaine, usually a little under a gram.

eight-ball: An eighth of an ounce of methamphetamine or cocaine; aka "ball."

Eighty-One: See *81*.

flash: The various small patches sewn onto the front and sometimes sides of a biker's vest. See also *tabs*.

FTW: "Fuck the world."

full patch: A member of a club who has received his rockers and center patch. See also *patch*.

girls, the: Hells Angels' disrespectful moniker for members of the Mongols motorcycle club.

HA: Hells Angels.

hangaround: A potential prospect who is "hanging around" a club to determine (a) if the club is interested in having the hangaround become a prospect; and (b) if the hangaround is ready to live the biker lifestyle.

hotwash: The act of taking all the information that is "hot" in one's memory concerning recent suspect interactions and "washing" it out into reports.

ink shop: Tattoo parlor.

MC: "Motorcycle club." A small "MC" patch is usually found on the back of a vest to the right of and below the center patch. See also *flash*, *tabs*.

Meth: Methamphetamine, a highly potent, extremely addictive stimulant. Most commonly snorted or smoked, occasionally injected; aka "crank," "crystal," "ice," "glass," "speed."

monkeys: Code name given to the Black Biscuit undercover operators to provide security from monitored police radio traffic, e.g., "Monkey One and Monkey Three are turning onto Main Street."

mother chapter: The "birthplace" or original location of a motorcycle club.

mud check: A test of fortitude to see if someone can "hold his mud."

nickel bag: A $5 bag of marijuana, usually a little under half a gram; aka "nick."

Oaktown: Oakland, California. Unofficial "base of operations" of the Hells Angels, which was presided over by Sonny Barger until he moved to Cave Creek. Referred to by some Hells Angels as "the center of the universe."

old lady: A female companion, usually a wife or steady girlfriend.

OMG: Outlaw motorcycle gang.

OMO: Outlaw motorcycle organization.

One Percenter: Moniker stemming from a 1947 Hollister biker riot, following which the American Motorcyclist Association stated that "ninety-nine percent of motorcycle riders are law-abiding citizens and only one percent are outlaws."

One Percenter Diamond: The diamond-shaped "1%" patch of the One Percenter symbol. See also *flash*, *tabs*.

open carry: Refers to a state's laws that allow the exposed and often unlicensed possession of a firearm.

OTB: "Over the bars"; euphemism for a bike crash; aka "digger," "eat asphalt," "nipple surf," "superman."

P: Abbreviation for "president" of a motorcycle club.

packing double: Two people on one bike—almost always a man driving and a woman riding. See also *riding bitch style*.

Panhead: A Harley-Davidson engine style in use from 1948 to 1965; so called because its cylinder head resembled a roasting pan. Other engine styles are Knucklehead (pre-1948), Shovelhead (1966–84), and V-Twin (1985 to present).

paid informant: An informant who is in the employ of law enforcement, but is not a law enforcement officer. This type of informant is a mercenary, and he or she is not working off any charges, as with a *CI*.

patch: Biker's vest (see also *colors*, *cut*); also a full member, i.e., a biker who has received his center patch and rockers, denoting full membership.

Patch, the: Nickname for the Black Biscuit task force headquarters in Phoenix, short for "Pumpkin Patch."

patch over: To give up one's club affiliation in order to become a member of another club; can refer to an individual member or to an entire club.

poker run: A run where riders stop at various locations to receive a playing card, and at the end of which the holder of the best poker hand wins a predetermined prize.

Pinks: The Mongols' disrespectful nickname for members of the Hells Angels (red and white make pink).

prospect: A prospective member; a member in training.

punked: To be embarrassed or humiliated; forced to show cowardice.

rat: A person who has turned informant; also the act of informing; see also *snitch*, *CI*.

rat pack: A fight in which several people severely beat a single victim; any fight in which one group vastly outnumbers another and whose aim is severe injury.

RICO: Racketeering Influenced and Corrupt Organizations Act. A federal statute that provides for extended penalties for criminal acts performed as part of an ongoing criminal organization.

rig: A holster used to carry firearms.

riding bitch style: Two patches riding one bike, as if the one on the back were a "bitch" (a rare occurrence). See also *packing double*.

rocker: A curved cloth patch that resembles the shape of a rocking chair's rocker. The *top rocker* contains the club's name and is stitched on the back of the vest across the shoulders; the *bottom rocker* contains the member's charter location and is stitched on the back of the vest across the waist. Together with the center patch, the rockers comprise the three-piece patch of a full member of an outlaw motorcycle club. See also *center patch*, *three-piece patch*.

Roofies: Slang for Rohypnol, a powerful hypnotic drug also known as the "date rape drug."

run: Biker rally.

SAC: Special Agent in Charge. See also *ASAC*.

scooter: Motorcycle.

secretary: A club officer responsible for a charter's paperwork, such as church "minutes" and financial accounts; aka "treasurer."

sergeant at arms: A club officer responsible for security, weaponry, and intra-charter discipline; aka "warlord," "enforcer."

snitch: A person who has turned informant; also the act of informing. See also *rat, CI*.

SoCal: Southern California.

soft tail: A Harley-Davidson frame style with a rear suspension.

SOS: "Sons of Silence," a Colorado Springs, Colorado, motorcycle club.

support club: A club designated to support another club; aka "duck club."

tabs: The various small patches sewn onto the front and sometimes sides of a biker's vest. See also *flash*.

TCB: "Take care of business"; i.e., to do whatever is necessary for the club.

teener: A sixteenth-ounce of narcotics, usually methamphetamine or cocaine.

three-piece patch: Collectively, the three patches found on the back of a vest worn by a member of an outlaw motorcycle club. See also *center patch, patch, rocker*.

tweaker: A methamphetamine user.

top rocker: See *rocker*.

UC: Undercover operator.

vice: Vice president of a motorcycle club; also short for vice squad, a law enforcement division dedicated to investigating vices like prostitution and gambling.

World Run: Usually an annual rally that all club members are required to attend.

Acknowledgments

OPERATION BLACK BISCUIT was conducted by numerous law enforcement officers, some not mentioned in the body of this story. Their personal sacrifices to our mission, both large and small, and the sacrifices made by their families, were no less than my own. Their omissions or limited descriptions are not intentional and are in no way meant to belittle their value. I greatly enjoyed their partnership and consider them valued friends. I'd like to thank them for their support, patience, and tolerance during our many months together. Without them I wouldn't have made it through.

These men and women are among law enforcement's best and brightest, and together they constituted an investigative Dream Team:

Alan "Foot" Futvoye; Andrew "Wallstreet" Worrell; Angelo "Calzone" Calderone; Bill Phillips; Billy Guinn; Blake "Bo" Boteler; Bob Swietzer; Brett Coombs; Carlos "Boxer" Baixuali; Carlos "Los" Canino; Chris "Chrisser" Bayless; Chris "Cricket" Livingstone; Chris "Elvis" Hoffman; Chuck "Big Cheese" Schoville; Craig "Triple C" Caridine; Dan "Mach One" Machonis; Dan "Rap" Raponi; Darrell "Cole" Edwards; Darrin "Koz" Kozlowski; David "Luke" Luther; Duane "Bubba" Williams; Dwayne Haddix; Eric "Big E" Harden; Eric "Otter" Rutland; Gayland Hammack; Greg "Sugarbear" Cowan; Hope MacAllister; Jenna "JJ" Maguire; Jerry Petrilli; Jessie "Breeze" Summers; Jim "Jimbo" Langley; Joe "Joey Lunchbucket" Slatalla; John "Babyface" Carr; John Ciccone; John Cooper; John "JDub" Williams; John "Johnny Mac" MacKenzie; J.P. "Sergeant" Wilson; Karen Evanoski; Kim Balog; Les Robinson; Lori Reynolds; Lou DeTiberiis; Marc "Grinder" Wood; Mark "Demon" Demas; Marty Dietz; Marvin Richardson; Michael Gillooly; Michael Kemp; Michelle White; Mike "Spike" Johnson; Mike Will; Nick "Buddha" Susuras; Nicole "Nikki" Strong; Pantano Christian Church; Paul "Pablo" Hagerty; Rachael Ehrlich; Ray Brotherson; Scott "Hydro" Hite; Sean "Spider-Man" Hoover; Shannon "Cook" Sheel; Shawn "Woody" Wood; Steve "Gundo" Gunderson; Steve "High Plains Drifter" Hauser; Steve Ott; Steve Trethewey; Tara Crubaugh; Tom Allen; Tom "Teabag" Mangan; Tracy Feminia; "Uncle" Don White; Vince "Vinnie D" Cefalu; Virginia O'Brien; William "Billy" Queen; William "Timmy" Long.

My special thanks to Nils Johnson-Shelton, who took the time to research and understand a complex story, possessed the talent to explain it accurately, and had the courage to write a truthful and honest book.

Thanks to Adam Lawrence for helping to take one thing off my plate by securing song lyric permissions.

And, last but not least, both Nils and I would like to thank our outstanding and dedicated editor, Rick Horgan at Crown, who believed in and fought hard for this telling of my story, and Richard Pine and Libby O'Neill, our faithful and indispensable agents at Inkwell Management.